Parish

'All things are done in some place; but if we consider place to be no more but the next hollow superficies of the air, alas!'

John Donne, *Devotions*

Parish

An Anglican Theology of Place

Andrew Rumsey

scm press

© Andrew Rumsey, 2017

First published in 2017 by SCM Press
Editorial office
3rd Floor, Invicta House,
108–114 Golden Lane,
London EC1Y 0TG

SCM Press is an imprint of Hymns Ancient & Modern Ltd
(a registered charity)

Hymns Ancient & Modern® is a registered trademark of
Hymns Ancient & Modern Ltd
13A Hellesdon Park Road, Norwich,
Norfolk, NR6 5DR, UK

www.scmpress.co.uk

British Library Cataloguing in Publication data

A catalogue record for this book is available
from the British Library

978 0 334 05484 9

Typeset by Regent Typesetting
Printed and bound in Great Britain by
CPI Group (UK) Ltd, Croydon

For my father,
the Revd Canon P. C. Rumsey (1921–97),
and grandfather, the Revd Canon H. H.
Rumsey (1876–1940), parish priests

Contents

Acknowledgements

'Consult the genius of place in all', the poet Alexander Pope once urged a correspondent. This book would not have been possible without consulting the genius of place in many different people, especially those of my parishes here in Oxted and Tandridge, who have been so supportive of my research.

'Parish' is the fruit of many years' study and thanks are particularly due to my doctoral supervisors, Luke Bretherton, Ben Quash and Sam Wells, for their wisdom, warmth and encouragement. Along the way, I have benefited greatly from the insight of numerous others, among them Andrew Davison, Jeremy Morris, Malcolm Guite, Paula Gooder, Jenny Taylor, David Perry, Johnny Sertin and Mark Brend. At each stage I have been affirmed in my conviction that there is a theological and cultural case for the English parish that has yet to be made. On completing the book, however, I am only too aware of all that is left unsaid, and how many questions my own position raises. Further work is required, most urgently into the parish's future form: this book looks forward to that developing conversation.

I'm grateful to Christine Smith and David Shervington at SCM Press and to Stuart Brett for his valued assistance in the final stages. Sincere thanks, finally, to my wife, Rebecca, and to our children, Grace, Jonah and Talitha, who make every place a home.

PART ONE

Christ in Our Place: The Anglican Parish in Theoretical Perspective

Introduction

At the dimming of Easter Day, a stranger draws alongside two companions, dragging their feet down the Emmaus Road. Followers of Christ, they seem entirely unaware that they are now walking next to their Lord. The outsider asks to hear the news from Jerusalem, so they respond: 'are you the only stranger who doesn't know the things that have happened here?' 'What things?' he persists – and the story unrolls.

Amid this familiar mystery from Luke's Gospel is hidden a radical vision for the local church. The risen Christ, it suggests, is not only found in the living word and broken bread, but also grounded in a definite kind of local encounter. The Greek term Luke uses here for 'stranger' – *paroikeis* – appears in several forms in the New Testament and from this stem grows our English word 'parish'. An alternative rendering of the conversation might then be, 'Are you a *parishioner* that you don't know what has happened here?' In Graeco-Roman society, *paroikia* described the community of people either living physically beyond the city boundaries (literally 'those beside the house') or as non-citizens within the walls. They were those who lived nearby, but didn't belong. That the early Church – much as it did with *ecclesia* – adopted this civil term for their organization abounds with contemporary significance. The Church was the fellowship of strangers, the community of non-belongers, who had found their place in Christ.[1]

This book is a description of that place as it took root in this country. The parish system was not the first or only form of ecclesiastical network in Britain, but, once established, it became the pre-eminent model of communal 'belonging' for close on a thousand years: 'the basic territorial unit in the organization of this country', as one historian has labelled it.[2] Nevertheless, it remains an enigmatic theme, especially in an era when 'parochial' is commonly used as a byword for blinkered insularity. With the parish system strained to breaking point and its relevance to society increasingly questioned, there is a pressing need to rediscover the principles that shaped it – not least because of an ever-growing political and environmental momentum to find resilient and fertile kinds of common life. The parish has always reinvented itself: no place could be so influential, for so long, without doing so. And while by no means the only description of English locality – parish has always vied and overlapped with towns, wards, 'vills' and various other forms – it has been an unrivalled building block of neighbourhood, uniquely combining religious meaning with local identity. As Oliver Rackham puts it in his *History of the Countryside*, parish is singular in being 'the smallest unit of spiritual and secular geography'.

This blend has always intrigued me. Raised in a rectory, I have instinctively viewed places in this way – as both spiritual and secular – and it has long been my vocation to live as though they were. For places are, I suggest, imagined first and then enacted: how we behave in a particular locale depends largely on what kind of place we believe it to be. Undergirding this book is faith in a spiritual tradition that exists as one among many currently practised in this country, each exerting a distinctive influence upon the social landscape. However, in both historical and geographical terms, the Church of England is not just another stakeholder, even as it rightly adjusts to a new and humbler role in national life. Any accurate realignment of its contemporary 'place' is not served by ignorance about the Church's remarkable formative influence, over many centuries.

As the source for much of that influence, the parish's standing is in a sense plain – one author going so far as to call it 'the bedrock of European civilization as a whole'.[3] But while the English, specifically Anglican, parish (varying types of parochial organization having spanned Christendom) is uniquely embedded in national culture, by virtue both of its antiquity and close allegiance with secular governance, its social and theological significance has hitherto been given remarkably scant consideration.[4] This is partly because, while ecclesiastical history has long formed a pillar of academic training for ordained ministry, ecclesiastical geography has not – even though parish ministry is, by definition, geographical. Unsurprising, then, that contemporary church debate about locality tends to be geographically denuded: a shortcoming, which in turn 'thins out' a theological appreciation of parochial ministry.[5] If geography is seen as theologically neutral, the parish system clearly risks being similarly undervalued. At a time when its viability is increasingly questioned within the Church of England and with plans progressing for the Church in Wales' dismantling of parochial (though not local) ministry, there is considerable and urgent need for redress.

This book has, therefore, a particular and pressing purpose, which is to explain the pastoral or theological geography of the Anglican parish – in effect, to begin answering the question *what kind of place is it?* In doing so, one is struck immediately by the diversity of the subject: each parish being as unique as its grid reference. Some are almost as large as dioceses, covering huge tracts of moorland; some have boundaries as arbitrary and baffling as in an imperial land grab; others are self-contained and perfectly circle their communities. This has always been the case – and, clearly, the parish 'took' in some places more than in others, because of the natural terrain, or the vitality of other communal forms.

Nevertheless, there is much common ground – indeed, this phrase recurs as a way of describing the effect of the parish system in general, even when its specific features vary greatly. It must be acknowledged from the outset that the English parish has by no means had only a benign impact: often compromised – cruel, even – as an arm of the nascent nation state; ponderous and resistant to change, a straitjacket for church growth in some places. Any assessment of its past and future value must face these failings evenly. It is by no means the only way for Christians to view social space: neither, given her global Communion, need it be Anglicanism's pre-eminent parochial mode. But it is one expression – and, I shall suggest, the local form that has had the most enduring effect upon this nation's self-understanding.

Just as the nineteenth-century radical William Cobbett confessed, I am committed to the Church of England partly because 'it bears the name of my country'. 'England' is of course a heavily freighted word and groans with a burden of associations, some of which are as troublesome as those evoked by 'parish'. This is unavoidable, but it is vital that the Church reckons with its English calling, not least so that the idea of England may be reclaimed for all who live there and that fruitful relations may be grown with neighbours who do not. The Churches of Scotland and Ireland maintain a parish system and, although it is hoped that the insights gained here are applicable in other provinces, nations and denominations, this book is intentionally English in its scope and concerns.

It must also be admitted that the Church – especially the worshipping congregation – can seem oddly absent in what follows. Little space is given to liturgy, the sacraments, evangelism or many other familiar ingredients of parish ministry. All this has consciously been avoided, partly because it is the common theme of pastoral studies, the theological (and, to a degree, spatial) dynamics of which have been ably considered elsewhere,[6] but mainly these are blurred because my focus is fixed on the geographical parish, which is somewhat harder to see. That said, the mission of the local church – especially its symbolic tokens of parish priest and parish church – is conspicuously, if implicitly, present in what follows. The book is an attempt to describe how 'place' looks when viewed from the parish church and not vice versa: if the Church is obscured from where I am standing, this is only because I have my back to its door.

Nor, it may be added, is this study a direct engagement in the importunate questions regarding the future of the parish system. These form its horizon and will be surveyed in outline in the concluding chapter, but the foreground to be covered here is the territory on which Anglican ministry has long been practised, but rarely delved into. To some extent, this marks a response to the question of 'what's in a word?' What are the distinctive connotations and associations of 'parish' – what does it *mean*? As such, this must be acknowledged to be a highly personal description. Coming from a long family line of parish priests, stretching back nearly 200 years, the parochial inheritance is of more than professional or academic interest: I am seeking defini- tion for a place that is, at heart, intuitively perceived. While my priestly forebears all practised from within the Anglo-Catholic tradition, my own formation has largely been within the evan- gelical wing of the Church. Recognizing that the greater part of contemporary theological scholarship about place follows a more sacramental path, it was also curiously apparent that many of the more interesting doctrinal considerations of space and time came, by contrast, from theologians in the reformed trad- ition. The doctrinal sections in Part One of the book reflect this, being an attempt to employ their thought as a lens through which to view the parish. In order to develop an Anglican theology of place, then, I shall be enlisting some distinctly non-Anglican thinkers.

The rector, currently, of four parishes in the south-eastern corner of the Anglican Diocese of Southwark, I have spent 20 years in parochial ministry, the majority of which has been in urban or suburban contexts – beginning in Harrow in north- west London, and then for ten years as vicar of Gipsy Hill in the London Borough of Lambeth. This research commenced during that time, when I began to appreciate the effect upon parish life of both natural ecology and built environment, and was further informed by moving to the more rural setting described at vari- ous points in what follows. With the M25 motorway cutting like a river through my parishes, London looms large in these reflec- tions; the tension between urban and rural has been profoundly felt and is expressed in the concluding sections on nostalgia and the 'pastoral'.

Viewing the land

Because the academic currents running into parochial theology draw on such diverse sources it may be useful to summarize these before sketching out the course of what follows. 'Parish', as a concept, finds its provenance in the integration of the Christian Church into the civic life of the Roman Empire. Academic studies of its adoption and adaptation by the early Church – when, in Hooker's words, 'the body of the people must needs be severed by divers precincts'[7] – and the subsequent spread of the parochial idea in early medieval Europe are, as might be expected, largely historical. John Godfrey (1962, 1969) provides two useful surveys that focus on the Gregorian mission to England under Augustine and the role of his successor at Canterbury, Theodore of Tarsus (often credited with 'introducing' the parish to England),[8] in implementing regional organization upon the hybrid of Roman and Celtic influences that formed the Anglo-Saxon Church before 'England' had any unified national identity.[9] For Godfrey, the parochial idea as a 'local gathering' was so fundamental to the early Church that he can describe it as 'native to the Christian religion as such'.[10]

Nevertheless, many scholars of the English parish express reservation as to its origins[11] and examination of its gradual establishment – a process that, by common recognition, did not form any coherent 'system' until the twelfth century[12] – is made imprecise by the relative invisibility of the parish in historiography. As the revered medieval historian F. M. Stenton remarked 50 years ago: 'The development of the parochial system is the central thread of ecclesiastical history following Theodore [of Tarsus], but it is virtually ignored by contemporary writers.'[13]

In the late 1980s, this began to change, with the gradual emergence of 'parish studies' from social historians for whom the parochial became a key to opening and understanding the dynamics of late medieval and early modern community life. Susan Wright's 1988 collection *Parish, Church and People: Local Studies in Lay Religion 1350–1750* and Katherine French's *The Parish in English Life, 1400–1640* (1997) have been particularly influential in this respect, as have Professor Keith Snell's major works *Parish and Belonging* (2009) and its recent companion *Spirits of Community* (2016), both of which explore the symbolic and actual function of the parish in framing local identity.

Aside from the three classic works on its secular function: Toulmin Smith's *The Parish* (1854), Sidney and Beatrice Webb's *The Parish and The County* (1906) and W. E. Tate's *The Parish Chest* (1946), all of which examined its legal responsibilities and civil administration, there have been few works of substance that have considered the parish system's underlying ethos and purpose.[14] The important collection of interdisciplinary essays edited by Giles Ecclestone, *Parish Church?* (1988), and an earlier study, P. D. Thompson's *Parish and Parish Church* (1948), are exceptions, the latter proving especially useful in analysing how the parish emerged as a curious hybrid of church life and civil government. This communal role has been thoroughly appraised – in terms of local history, if not theology – in N. J. G. Pounds's magisterial *A History of the English Parish* (2000), which to some extent filled a long-vacant place for a single-volume parochial history, together with Anthea Jones's more popular-level, but none the less useful, *A Thousand Years of the English Parish*, published in the same year. The principal shortcoming of Pounds's survey is its conclusion at the end of the nineteenth century, leaving the parish's place in contemporary social history relatively unexamined, although several important local studies focusing on Greater London have appeared in the last 30 years – notable among them being Jeffrey Cox's *English Churches in a Secular Society: Lambeth 1870–1930* (1982); *Religion and Urban Change: Croydon, 1840–1914* by Jeremy Morris (1993), and Rex Walford's pioneering work, *The Growth of 'New London' in Suburban Middlesex and the Response of the Church of England* (2007).

Historical accounts aside, the postwar period saw a flurry of books (Joost de Blank's *The Parish in Action*, for example) that sought to address the parish in missionary terms at a time when, some commentators suggest, the British Church was beginning to slide into terminal decline.[15] Central to the ideal they defend is the unique historical place of the established Church in its 'cure of souls' for all parishioners, which remains a vitally important strand of parochial theology, with deep historical roots in the origins of English nationhood. In the same period began what Harbison (1992) calls a 'vast avalanche' of books about England's parish churches.[16] Essentially gazetteers for church-spotters, of which John Betjeman's *English Parish Churches* remains the standard, these often contain introductory reflections of interest to the broader place of the parish church in the English natural and social landscape.

The inherent bond – appraised in Chapter 4 – between parochial ministry and the Church of England's status as established in law is a relatively unmined seam in parochial theology – an exception being Sarah Coakley and Sam Wells's *Praying for England* (2008), which persuasively affirms the continuing value to the nation of parish priest and parish church as the celebrants of, in Rowan Williams's phrase, 'what will not fit anywhere else'.[17] In reaction to perceived threats to the viability of the parish system[18] the last decade has seen a growing harvest of literature that – like Coakley and Wells's work – has begun to plough more deeply into its theological and social significance. Significant works in this respect have been *The Parish*, edited by Malcolm Torry (2004), a volume of essays by ministerial practitioners working in south London; *The Future of the Parish System* (2006), edited by Steven Croft – another collection, consciously engaging with the sometimes anti-parochial 'Fresh Expressions' movement – and Andrew Davison and Alison Milbank's *For the Parish* (2010), an eloquent apologetic for the enduring value of parochial ministry. Echoing these in more personal and narrative form are books – Roger Scruton's *Our Church* (2013) and Roy Strong's *A Little History of the English Country Church* (2008) being two prominent examples – that appear as elegies for a particular kind of secular Anglicanism.

Nevertheless, few of these works attempt any thoroughgoing engagement with what Edward W. Soja (1989) called the 'reassertion of space' in social theory in recent decades,[19] a development that has only lately begun to send ripples through practical theology, as evinced by John Reader and Chris Baker's study *Encountering the New Theological Space* (2009).[20] While the 'geographical turn' in social theory is bringing in its wake a renewed appreciation of locality and 'place' within Christian theology, this has, as yet, found only limited application to the study of the parish. A seminal work for the emerging discipline of place-theology has been Walter Brueggemann's *The Land* (1977): his study of place as a motif in the Old and New Testaments. Drawing upon W. D. Davies's earlier study (1974), *The Gospel and The Land*, this provides a fascinating theological reflection on place as a governing motif in Scripture. According to Brueggemann, land in Scripture is always 'storied place'[21] – personalized locale, dependent on the experience of God's presence, promise and call.

This narrative understanding of place in relation to God is taken up in John Inge's pioneering study *A Christian Theology of Place* (2003). For Inge, a Christian understanding of place has a sacramental quality that stems from his doctrinal conviction that, in Jesus Christ, created space-time becomes imbued with the presence of God. Inge is particularly helpful in examining the classical metaphysics of *topos* in Greek thought, which contributes to his theological description of place as 'the seat of relations ... between God and the world'.[22] This is a pivotal insight amid the definitions of place abounding in the extensive library of geographical and social studies about locality, in which the work of Doreen Massey has proved to be of particular significance for this research. Her recognition that not only is space socially constructed, but that society is *spatially constructed*, is, Massey explains, one of the leading social scientific developments in recent times.[23] This post-historicist outlook has been greatly influenced by French writers such as Pierre Bourdieu and Henri Lefebvre – the latter's *Le Production de L'Espace* (1991) presenting space not as a static concept, but something 'produced' by human agency. Lefebvre's case found echoes in Michel de Certeau's seminal volume *The Practice of Everyday Life* (1984), in which he describes how social 'place' is formed by ordinary activities such as walking to work and eating meals, all of which shape the social context. As such, spatial practices have huge ethical and political import: a significant theme in this research.

Alongside John Inge's monograph on the explicitly theological dynamics of place must be included a number of other studies – by Philip Sheldrake (2001), David Brown (2004) and Mark Wynn (2009) – each of which follows a similar (that is, broadly sacramental) approach, while providing a welcome and necessary redirection of focus away from church buildings or, more generally, ecclesial notions of sacred space.[24] As such, they have a certain amount in common with doctrinal works that, while only tacitly addressing the theme of place, offer valuable theological scaffolding for its development. Karl Barth's *Dogmatics* (especially volume three), Dietrich Bonhoeffer (his *Ethics* and *Christology* in particular), and various works by Colin Gunton and T. F. Torrance have all been influential in defining the theology of the parish presented here. For Bonhoeffer, the incarnation binds the Church to space and time in its thinking about God: a point powerfully advanced by Torrance (employing insights from physics) and, more recently, by Timothy Gorringe in his important study *A Theology of the Built Environment* (2002).[25] Finally, mention must be made of a hitherto untapped vein of nature writing that has landed on 'parish' as an essential motif for local ecology. Notable among these are works by Richard Mabey (1980) and Sue Clifford and Angela King (1996, 2006) and, most recently, Robert Macfarlane (2012, 2015), which represent a fascinating recovery of parish as a symbol of local belonging.

Surveying the salient literature on the theme, two related convictions have emerged, underpinning all that follows here. The first is that the Church's vision for parish ministry would be greatly clarified by the insights of contemporary social and spatial theory and also the consideration of 'place' as a theme in Christian doctrine. The second is the corresponding belief that place-theory (whether Christian or secular) would, in return, be enriched by comprehending the inheritance of local praxis contained in the parish system, which offers a unique tradition of

'Christian place'. In short, there is a need for theory to illuminate practice and vice versa.

The relation of theory to practice inevitably raises the question of methodology, especially given that the theology of place is increasingly viewed as a branch of practical theology, which has an acknowledged tendency to prioritize the analysis of local contexts over engagement with theological or other theoretical traditions.[26] This book aims to redress such an imbalance insofar as it relates to the parish, by engaging first with theoretical traditions and then with practical ones, with the intention that each may be enriched by the other. The methodological priority given to engagement with theory (in this case, the integration of Christian doctrine and spatial theory) is due both to theological conviction – which, in Barthian terms, interprets human culture 'in the light of the word of God'[27] – and the consonant claim of social theory that local practice is shaped by and contingent upon the particular questions and traditions with which communities approach their context.[28]

Part One of this book, then, considers how place may be 'seen as' parish in theological terms, beginning with a methodology that grounds place-formation in a dynamic cycle of ontology, revelation, tradition and vocation – which also serves, albeit loosely, as a pattern for the structure of the book. Chapter 2 explores the basis for viewing the parish in terms of 'Christ in our place', a significant theme in Protestant Christology, but not often applied geographically. Building on this doctrinal foundation, I will consider how recent developments in human geography enable the perception of parish as a spatial, ethical practice of 'neighbourhood'. Part Two of the book sees parochial description move into the foreground, weighing the parish's theoretical form against its enduring historical role in English society. This 'vocation', it is argued, comprises a threefold call to nation, neighbour and nature: each expressing a different aspect of 'common ground'. The Conclusion, having assessed these findings, will address certain challenges facing the Anglican parish, proposing its renewal as a radical form of local belonging.

In doing so, the intention is to avoid those signifiers of Christian practice commonly employed by sociologists of religion, who – since the first census statistics for religious practice were gathered in 1851 – are apt to assess the health of Christianity *centripetally*: that is, by concentrating on allegiance to the Church as an institution, rather than the kind of wider society it helps to create.[29] While effective in portraying Christian practice from one angle, this arguably misunderstands the nature of the Church of England, which tends by contrast to operate *radially*: directed beyond itself towards wider society. To make the ecclesiological point, the Church is primarily concerned not with 'the world' becoming 'the Church' but with the world finding its true place by virtue of the Church's action and presence. The Church has no need to extend its own territory into the world: rather, as yeast working through a batch of dough, it seeks to effect the transformation of the whole – not, plainly, that the batch should all become yeast. In this parochial ecclesiology, where the local congregation is a transforming agent – a means not an end – the nature and condition of society is of the greatest interest.

As the sociologist David Martin deftly acknowledged, however, 'parish' easily becomes just a code word for 'mere communitarian nostalgia'. Because parochial life is vulnerable to this familiar criticism, both Parts One and Two of the book take care to balance theoretical or idealistic conceptions of the parish with evidence of its historic place in English life and are interspersed with more reflective pieces, grounded in personal experience of the places in which I minister. These are intended to complement the more in-depth analysis that accompanies them – and may be read separately, or as part of the whole.

Notes

1 Martyn Percy makes this etymological connection, describing the ideal parish as 'an inclusive place for the local stranger', in Steven Croft (ed.), *The Future of the Parish System*, London: CHP, 2006, p. 4.

2 N. J. G. Pounds, *A History of the English Parish*, Cambridge: CUP, 2000, p. 3. Bishop Stillingfleet, writing in 1702, grants 'that at first there

were no such parochial divisions or cures here in England', noting the 'itinerant and occasional' church life that accompanied the Church's early missionary form (in *Ecclesiastical Cases Relating to the Duties and Rights of Parochial Clergy etc.*, 2nd edn, London: Henry Mortlock, 1702, p. 88). According to the Church's 2015 Statistics for Mission report, there are currently 12,510 ecclesiastical parishes in England (including the Isle of Man and the Channel Islands).

3 Anthea Jones, *A Thousand Years of the English Parish*, Moreton-in-Marsh: Windrush Press, 2000, p. 27.

4 For a historic overview of parish in the European context, see Katherine French, *The Parish in English Life, 1400–1640*, Manchester: MUP, 1997, ch. 2; also John Godfrey in *The Church in Anglo-Saxon England*, Cambridge: CUP, 1962, ch. 9. Authors generally concur both on the universality of the parochial idea in the Western Church and also its unique penetration in England.

5 The report *Mission-Shaped Church* states, for example, 'a geographical approach (that is, to the organization of churches) alone is not sufficient', without recognizing the essentially geographical nature of the alternative forms it espouses (London: CHP, 2004, p. 12).

6 Of particular value in analysing the psycho-spatial dimensions of liturgical life are Bruce Reed's *The Dynamics of Religion*, London: DLT, 1978, and James Hopewell's groundbreaking study *Congregation*, Philadelphia: Fortress Press, 1987.

7 Richard Hooker, *Of the Laws of Ecclesiastical Polity*, London: J. M. Dent, 1954, Book 5.80.2. Hooker, with nice precision, dates the organization of pastoral cures to 'about the year 112'.

8 See, for example, Godfrey, *Anglo-Saxon England*, p. 310; P. D. Thompson, *Parish and Parish Church*, London: Thomas Nelson, 1948, p. 54.

9 Such is Adrian Hastings's assertion in *The Construction of Nationhood: Ethnicity, Religion and Nationalism*, Cambridge: CUP, 1997, ch. 2.

10 John Godfrey, *The English Parish, 600–1300*, London: SPCK, 1969.

11 Graham Hutton's disclaimer 'we do not really know how the English parish originated' is typical (in E. Smith, O. Cook and G. Hutton (eds), *English Parish Churches*, London: Book Club Associates, 1977, p. 14).

12 See Jones, *English Parish*, p. 15.

13 F. M. Stenton, *Anglo-Saxon England*, Oxford: OUP, 1947, p. 157.

14 Katherine French's reflection that 'the complex matrix of religious, secular and cultural factors contributing to the idiosyncratic character of some 9000 local communities is a most promising area for future research' is common in the historical literature (in French, *The Parish in English Life*, p. 13).

15 See Callum Brown, *The Death of Christian Britain*, London: Routledge, 2001, ch. 8.

16 In *England's Parish Churches*, London: Aurum Press, 2006, p. 15.

17 Samuel Wells and Sarah Coakley, *Praying for England*, London: Continuum, 2008, p. 181.

18 Either as a model for mission (following the influential Church of England report *Mission-Shaped Church*) or as a financially sustainable pattern for the deployment of ministry.

19 The subtitle of Soja's *Postmodern Geographies*, London: Verso, 1989.

20 Aldershot: Ashgate, 2009, pp. 7–8. Local or 'vernacular' theologies are recognized as a significant strand of modern theological method, in Elaine Graham, Heather Walton and Frances Ward, *Theological Reflection: Methods*, London: SCM Press, 2005, ch. 7.

21 Walter Brueggemann, *The Land*, London: SPCK, 1978, p. 185.

22 John Inge, *A Christian Theology of Place*, Aldershot: Ashgate, 2003, p. 68.

23 See Derek Gregory and John Urry, *Social Relations and Spatial Structures*, London: Macmillan, 1985, pp. 2–12, and Doreen Massey, *For Space*, London: Sage, 2005, ch. 1.

24 In addition to these works, a new volume from the United States, Leonard Hjalmarsson's *No Home Like Place: A Christian Theology of Place*, Portland: Urban Loft, 2015, usefully relates the New Testament perspective to, in particular, urban and public space.

25 See T. F. Torrance, *Space, Time and Incarnation*, Oxford: OUP, 1969, ch. 3; and T. F. Torrance, *Space, Time and Resurrection*, Edinburgh: Handsel Press, 1976, pp. 133ff.

26 As Graham, Walton and Ward acknowledge, 'the analysis of local context [in Practical Theology] ... is often more accomplished than engagement with church history, doctrine and Bible' (in Graham, Walton and Ward, *Theological Reflection: Methods*, p. 7).

27 Karl Barth, *The Doctrine of Creation, Part 2, Church Dogmatics III.ii*, trans. by G. W. Bromiley and T. F. Torrance, Edinburgh: T&T Clark, 1960, p. 20.

28 What Gadamer, drawing on Plato's dialogical schema, calls 'the hermeneutic priority of the question' (in Hans-Georg Gadamer, *Truth and Method*, London: Continuum, 1989, pp. 362ff).

29 See Bryan Wilson, *Religion in Secular Society*, Harmondsworth: Penguin, 1969. While Wilson defined secularization in terms of declining *social* influence, his statistical evidence (of, for example, infant baptisms, numbers of children in Sunday Schools, and Easter Day communicants) is overwhelmingly congregational. See also Steve Bruce, *God is Dead: Secularization in the West*, Oxford: Blackwell, 2002.

Steadying Jacob's Ladder:
A Place-Formation Cycle

'The highway ran through the parish', writes priest-poet R. S. Thomas, in *The Echoes Return Slow*. 'The main line ran through the parish. Yet there were green turnings, uncclesiastical aisles up which he could walk to the celebration of the marriage of mind and nature.'

Sweating up the North Downs for Ascension Day: the perfect vantage point for these parishes, and for courting Thomas's nuptial vision. Here, beneath the ridge of the Surrey Hills, the land unrolls in an awesome sweep: the familiar, folded fields and, threading between, the grey-green turnings of the M25 motorway. Oxted has hosted major east–west routes since prehistoric times, with the Pilgrim's Way that shadows the carriageway marking an ancient and fabled footpath running from Winchester to Canterbury. Directly below me, trains from East Croydon arrow out of the earth, ducking the M25 in a hallowing crosshatch. Arterial roads also intersect its path, pumping out of London, while the motorway circulates cautiously, a slate-coloured halo for the capital.

Each day, close on 200,000 extra parishioners throttle, stall and swear their way through the two-mile meander cutting through my patch. Opened in 1976, this stretch was one of the first to be completed, and now has its own deposit of folklore, including the elderly lady found by police cycling the wrong way up the slow lane near Godstone – either battily unaware or, as I like to think, engaged in her own perilous psycho-geographic experiment.

The Outer London Defence Ring also clings to these hills – not the grim name of a far-right association, but a chain of pillboxes and tank traps still awaiting the call to fend off invaders sweeping up from the south coast. The M25 would now perform the same task admirably, forming as it does an uncrossable contra-flow torrent that even St Christopher would hesitate before stepping into. Certainly the North Downs feel defensive: south London's earthwork, moated by the motorway. To gaze at its current is oddly akin to river watching: sometimes a slim, silver charge, by eight o'clock this morning its serpentine course had already slowed to become an exhausted, horseless canal. Yet despite its preoccupation with time, the road-river has no memory: Monday's multi-vehicle collision was rapidly cleared, its crippling ripples untraceable now. When the motorway is abandoned and brambly, what scores of traumatized ghosts will return to process all that happened at such speed?

Today, though, all is at rest but for a hot air balloon, hung in the sky like a question mark. Ascensiontide is the right time to weigh things above and things below. Like most Christian festivals, it plays with concepts of locale, calling us to picture our life uplifted to heavenly places in Christ – with God, subsequently, settling down in the world by the Holy Spirit. Despite the critique that their preoccupation with heaven is a damaging distraction from earth, Christians have usually insisted they are citizens of both – to the extent that, in Britain, even the most flag-rattling patriotism carries a note of caution. Consider how the second verse of the hymn 'I Vow To Thee My Country' comes in like a pricked conscience: having pledged to our land 'all earthly things above', and sacrificed our best to the bloody soil, we are reminded – almost in apology – of 'another country', dearer still to them that know.

So, in one sense, the Christian really is of no earthly use unless they resolutely keep their head in the clouds. After all, the collect for Ascension Day prays that, as we believe Christ to have ascended, 'so may we also *in heart and mind* thither ascend'. Dwelling in heaven is something dreamed or imagined, in order that this world may be seen aright: Jacob's ladder alighting at Charing Cross, as Francis Thompson's poem envisages.

In St Luke's portrayal of Christ's ascension, he has the angels appear like marshals after a spectacle: 'men of Galilee', they challenge the disciples (who are left, gaping aloft), 'why do you stand looking up towards heaven?' This hard-to-picture scene diverts the Church's gaze to the ground. Like Christmas in reverse, the ascension illuminates the place where God, we believe, met humanity in Christ. As T. F. Torrance writes: 'we cannot know God by leaping beyond the limits of our place on earth, but only by encountering God and his saving work within space and time, within our actual physical existence'. So we look up, therefore, only to look down with greater clarity.

Taking the angels' advice, it is time to move along, like the easing traffic below: piloted home by the balloon's low bulb and faint rasp of flame.

Then Jacob awoke from his sleep and said, 'Surely the LORD is in this place – and I did not know it!' (Genesis 28.16–17)

Jacob's bleary epiphany at Bethel is a useful location at which to begin. His outburst not only identifies the principal relations under consideration here – those of God, place and people – but also orders them in ways that are methodologically suggestive. As so often in the Old Testament narrative, this episode from the Book of Genesis finds the reality of God and the reality of 'place' simultaneously affirmed – recognition of the former leading immediately to the latter. Understood this way, in the context of divine–human encounter, place is perceived not merely as having an influence upon humanity's relation to God, but as being entirely contingent upon God for existence. Place, in other words, has no ontology – or 'being' – unless the prior 'being' of God is first affirmed: a presupposition of belief in a divinely created order. To affirm the earth as created infers its dependence upon God, while simultaneously its distinction *from* God. To name a living thing as a 'creature' bestows upon it this basic procession and status.

Karl Barth considered that the nature of divine–human relationship was, in part at least, a question about how heavenly and earthly 'places' relate: the answer to which lay in the trinitarian nature of God – for Barth, the means whereby God's 'movement' towards humanity 'really takes place where we really are'.[1] In order to determine what 'really takes place' in the particular context under investigation here – the Anglican parochial system – there is a dynamic to Jacob's encounter with God at Bethel (repeated in other, similar episodes, such as Moses at the

burning bush) that, while fragmentary and figurative, may usefully be employed here. The first point to observe is that, for
Jacob, God's 'being' precedes his own 'knowing' – 'God is' in
this place and 'I knew it not'. The existence of God 'in place' is
thus independent of Jacob's knowing it, but, second, is nevertheless *revealed* to him, imaginatively -- and in that revelation comes
the awareness and symbolic construction of 'place'. Third, this
recognition of what might be termed God-in-place is not, to put
it crudely, 'any god', but quite specifically 'The LORD' – in other
words, the God of his ancestors, as understood within his own
inheritance of belief. There is, then, a hermeneutic at work in
Jacob's processing of this encounter, the meaning of which is
interpreted according to communal tradition. Fourth, the recognition of God-in-place is perceived as, and results in, a call to
personal action – as evidenced by the symbolic construction of
place in the bestowal of a meaningful name and, crucially, in the
impact of the revelation upon Jacob's subsequent practice. There
is a *vocational* tenor to the encounter, which thereafter invests
the place with narrative significance.

To a certain extent this dynamic may be seen at work in the
whole scriptural understanding of place. In the Old Testament
narrative, certainly, it can be argued that the primal experience
of Israel was of God's *prevenience* in the territories they entered.
Typically, in the Pentateuch, encounters with God are characterized by a sense of epiphany and of call ('Go from your country
... to the land that I will show you', to take a primary example).[2]
These encounters result in a renewed appreciation of vocation
and of place *as* place: that is, as *personalized space* – signified by
the act of naming the sites where God has made himself known.
In *The Land*, Walter Brueggemann explains how the Old Testament presents land as 'gift' – somewhere promised and prepared
by God for his people, the essential context for their covenant
relationship. In Israel's theological reflection, Brueggemann
writes: '[The land] is not just an object to be taken and occupied.
It is rather a party to a relation. Because the land is the means
of Yahweh's word becoming full and powerful for Israel, it is
presented as a life-giving embodiment of his word.'[3]

While the New Testament may be seen as bringing a radical *dis*placing of Israel's faith, it also *re*-locates it in the person and practice of Christ. Encounters with God-in-place henceforth become encounters with God-in-Christ: he becomes, in effect, the hermeneutic of place for those who obey his call to 'follow me'. Although reconfigured both in terms of space (via the agency of the Holy Spirit, Christ may be encountered in all places) and time (the earthly locale becoming relative to the eschatological, heavenly 'home'), the early Christian 'spiritualized'[4] understanding of place retains the vocational sense identified above: of being addressed by God in particular – often surprising – locations, in ways that serve to transform the call and practice of the Christian community.[5] This four-stage cycle then – of ontology or 'being', revelation, tradition and vocation – forms the frame for the methodological considerations that follow.

While these include little direct reference to, or description of, the Anglican parish as such, the aim is to build a deeper foundation for parochial theology than that which assumes 'place' as given, without fully considering either the gift or the giver. For the parish system to be viewed by the Church as more than a blank canvas on which to depict its diverse pastoral scenes requires some initial philosophical groundwork.

Being

The question as to 'what kind of place' the Anglican parish is may, at heart, be one of perception: how local contexts are viewed and how this is both informed by, and also informs, traditions of practice. Such an enquiry thus concerns the relationship between subjective appearance and objective reality: between what we see and what is actually there – and how our perception is then reflected and mapped on to the space-time locale. In the Western philosophical tradition, this relationship has been closely allied to the question of God's existence, whereby the reality of an external world independent of human consciousness is, in some sense, guaranteed by divine presence and physics, as Descartes believed, firmly founded upon metaphysics.

That in effect there is 'no place without God' was the assumption, in one form or other, of all classical metaphysical thought – whether in the Platonic sense of the world being 'a likeness of something else'[6] originating in God, or in the Aristotelian theory of its underlying substances, which reached its zenith in Liebniz's 'monadology', where God is himself affirmed as the 'supreme substance' from which all others proceed. While trading on a kind of divine collateral that underwrote the mind's ability to perceive truth, the essentially deistic, 'distanced' view of God characteristic of such rationalist thought allowed for his effective detachment from the act of knowing.[7] In the face of the empiricist reaction of the eighteenth century, the assumed basic coherence of God, the rational mind and the external world could, therefore, not be sustained – so that, for Scottish philosopher David Hume, all *a priori* foundations to knowledge, divine or otherwise, were 'building entirely in the air'.[8]

It was the achievement of Immanuel Kant to synthesize these antithetical strands in European thought. Neither sense experience nor *a priori* understanding could alone provide a satisfactory basis for knowledge of the world: rather the two worked in conjunction, the former being filtered by the latter and the prior concepts and categories it employs to interpret sense data. For this priest to look from his study window and 'see' parish, for example, requires the application of prior judgements to sense experience, which arrange and condition what is seen into recognizable forms of thought. An estate agent, looking through the same window, might perceive things rather differently.

In this way, the act of knowing applies 'internal' concepts to the 'external' world. Crucially, however, Kant saw this reunion of subject and object, sensibility and understanding as being possible only in so far as objects of our perception appear to the individual. While affirming that 'the world is as we think it',[9] this was only true with respect to the *phenomenal* world: the one presented to human senses. As Kant writes:

When therefore we say, the senses represent objects *as they appear*, the understanding *as they are*, the latter statement must not be understood in a transcendental, but only in an empirical signification, that is, they must be represented in the complete connection of phenomena, and not according to what they may be ... as objects of the pure understanding. For this must ever remain unknown to us.[10]

The 'unknownness' of things-in-themselves – including, crucially, God – has proved to be an enduring, if often contested, aspect of Kant's legacy. Returning to Bethel under this scheme, Jacob's perception that 'God is in this place' has little objective validity, both God and place being essentially incognito.[11]

While Kantian ideas (especially as refined by later German idealists, notably Schelling) were profoundly influential on his thought, such a conclusion was unsupportable for romantic poet and Anglican visionary Samuel Taylor Coleridge – this chapter's principal partner in dialogue – whose writings sought to restore, within a Christian theological frame, the threefold relationship between God, human perception and the objective world or 'place'. Critical to this restoration was Coleridge's insistence on the priority of ontology over epistemology – that is, *being* over *knowing*. Far from being unknowable, the external, objective world presents itself to the rational mind by virtue of its own existence: truth, as he puts it, 'is correlative to being ... if we know, there must be somewhat known by us'.[12] Indeed, Coleridge draws subject and object into such correlation that the act of knowing is entirely dependent on the 'being' of what is known. Thus, when seeking the 'substantiating principle of all true wisdom', Coleridge affirms: 'Let it not be supposed that it is a sort of knowledge: no! It is a form of BEING, or indeed it is the only sort of knowledge that truly *is* ...'[13] Coleridge developed this analysis, so crucial to the poetic sensibility, in the tangled chapters of his *Biographia Literaria*. Reworking the familiar Cartesian dictum, Coleridge asserted, 'I think *because* I am'.[14] Furthermore, he grounds this ontological assurance in *ultimate* being: the God who Christians hold to be 'the maker of *all that is*, seen and unseen'.[15] Thus Coleridge concludes: *sum quia in deo sum* ('I am because I am in God'). Unlike the detached and anonymous God of rationalism, however, divine presence in Coleridge's scheme was intimately involved in human conscious-ness: 'We begin with the I KNOW MYSELF, in order to end with the absolute I AM. We proceed from the self in order to lose and find all self in GOD.'[16] His assurance that (citing Malebranche) 'we see all things in God'[17] likewise grounded Coleridge's faith in the basic 'knowability' of the external world and the 'co-inherence' of subject and object. The beholder is, therefore, inherently connected to that which they behold, and the relation-ship between them is animated only by the application of *faith* – faith that, in the words of Scottish theologian T. F. Torrance, '"sees", not with any special faculty of vision on the part of the observer, but with the powers of the reality seen'.[18] The reson-ance with Jacob at Bethel is clear: knowledge of the world, of place, springs from conviction that it really 'is' – and that this ontological reality finds its source and head in the being of God.

Revelation

Crucial to this connection is the 'givenness' of what we behold: not just in the mere presentation of phenomena to the senses, but what Torrance calls the 'self-evidencing reality and reveal-ing power' of the objective world.[19] Although he is writing with regard to scientific knowledge, Torrance's remarks are highly pertinent for the consideration of place. As he continues: 'our fundamental beliefs are ... basic acts of acknowledgement in response to some intelligibility inherent in the nature of things ... but as such they pivot on the *objective* pole of the knowing rela-tionship'.[20] Understood thus, perception is very closely linked to *revelation* and has everything to do with how we receive and respond to objective reality – an experience, Torrance continues, which requires what he calls 'an ontology of commitment': 'for two poles of knowing are involved; the being of the knowing mind and the being of what is known'.[21] For Coleridge, the relation between subjective and objective 'being' is always both *personal* and *particular*: personal in that it is contingent upon the source of all being in God (for which he coins the term 'personeity') and particular in the sense that knowledge is grounded in the concrete specifics of time and place. All knowledge is thus local knowledge, to some degree. Reflecting at length on 'the mere act of existing' in *The Friend*, he seeks for its 'birth-place', concluding, with typical lyricism: 'By what name canst thou call a truth so manifested? Is it not revelation? And the manifesting power, the source and the correlative of the idea thus manifested – is it not God?'[22]

This emphasis on the priority of divine revelation prefigures the work of much later theologians, for whom epistemology would begin with the initiative of God, not in human endeavour.[23] Karl Barth, particularly, finds man to be the object, not the subject, of theological knowledge, whose being depends utterly upon God's creative and redemptive action. From this standpoint as 'known' and not 'knower', Barthian epistemology proceeds towards a relational understanding of truth: 'At the root of my being and from the very first I am in encounter with the being of the Thou, under his claim. "Being" means "encounter".'[24] But to what extent is the experience of place to be equated with the revelation of God in Christ? The two are linked in important ways – for, as Colin Gunton writes, 'If we cannot know the spatiality of things in themselves, then we cannot begin – except as a mythical projection – to conceive of a spatial and historical human life which is also the locus of something transcendent, i.e. beyond space.'[25]

In a recent study, *Faith and Place*, Mark Wynn takes up John Inge's Christian conception of place as 'the seat of relations' between God and the world, to consider how the classical concept of the *genius loci* might provide a key into human experience of God. For Wynn, knowledge of place 'epitomizes in miniature' knowledge of the world in general,[26] and he writes persuasively of the way in which the 'spirit of place' – the collective frameworks of meaning and memory attached to 'indwelt' locations – provides the pathway into meaningful experience of God. Viewing God as the *genius mundi*, Wynn argues that place is the way in which knowledge of God is mediated *ostensively* –

in that it 'points towards' God. In other words, the way in which place is known is not only analogous to the way in which God is known, but the former gives real access to the latter.

The idea that God is reached and revealed 'through' place is similar to the way in which artists and poets often express the mediation of divine presence, as we have seen with Coleridge. Aldous Huxley, for example, writing of Rembrandt's interiors, describes how they illustrate 'the impossible paradox and supreme truth that perception is (or at least ought to be) the same as Revelation, that Reality shines out of every appearance, that the One is totally, infinitely present in all particulars'.[27] The challenge of both, however, is to avoid this apprehension lapsing into a kind of pantheistic equation of God with the spirit of place. For the Christian, this can only be achieved through an appreciation of God as Trinity – which, as Barth emphasized, is the key to grasping how the creator 'enters space-time and all structures distinct from himself'.[28] In particular, there can be no attempt to consider the question of *how* knowledge of God is locally mediated without giving clear Christological definition to the answer, for it is in Christology that the theologian comes to terms with what is real – not just in time but also in space.

Tradition

Tradition – 'that which is handed down' – represents the given frameworks of meaning by which individuals and societies make sense of their world: indeed, tradition is the principal means by which it becomes *their* world. While the objective reality of place must faithfully be affirmed within a Christian theory of knowledge, the personal *apperception* or 'grasping' of it will always be subjectively conditioned. In other words, what an individual or community 'sees' will vary according to the customs and concepts that have shaped their mindset. In this respect, Einstein's approach to scientific observation bears a far broader application: 'Whether you observe a thing or not depends on the theory which you use. It is theory that decides what can be observed.'[29]

This filtering process not only retains a subjective impression of the reality beheld, but also *reproduces* the place seen and lives within it in correspondent fashion, so that local reality is always being constructed according to the worldview of the beholder. Crucial to this intuitive process – which 'makes the external internal, the internal external'[30] – is the role of the creative imagination, which, in a much-discussed passage in the *Biographia*, Coleridge divides into both primary and secondary categories. While the former is the more 'everyday' function, akin to what he elsewhere calls the 'understanding', the secondary imagination is the creative re-processing of what is perceived – a reflection upon reflection, so to speak. So significant is this faculty that the poet mints a new word to describe it – the *esemplastic* power – literally, the 're-shaping' of reality.[31] Through this work of imagination, he writes: 'Every day we are creating or half-creating the world around us.'[32]

While for Coleridge this is an essentially poetic endeavour, the *esemplastic* faculty he identifies has great significance for a consideration of place-formation, echoing Shakespeare's view that imagination 'gives to airy nothing a local habitation and a name'.[33] It is here that place truly begins to be formed and transformed; here that we interpret and personalize our locale according to our particular traditions. As John Berger explained, in his influential essay *Ways of Seeing*, there is a reciprocity to this process, whereby place is formed in the negotiation of different points of view: 'It is seeing that establishes our place in the surrounding world ... Soon after we can see, we are aware that we can be seen. The eye of the other combines with our own eye to make it fully credible that we are part of the visible world.'[34] The way we perceive things, Berger affirms, is 'affected by what we know or what we believe'[35] – which itself is moulded by the cultural traditions we indwell. Certainly, the fact that knowledge is culturally conditioned is one of the principal insights of twentieth-century thought, powerfully expressed in, for example, Hans-Georg Gadamer's *Truth and Method*, his major philosophical work, published in 1960. Gadamer merits mention here because of his assertion that knowledge involves *situation* – 'a standpoint that limits the possibility of vision'.[36] The situated nature of perception leads to his concept of *horizon* – 'the range of vision' that can be obtained from our particular standpoint. According to Gadamer, the horizon of the present is always being formed and 'tested' by that of the past, as carried to us by tradition. 'Understanding', he writes, 'is always the fusion of these horizons which we imagine to exist by themselves.'[37]

Gadamer's special concern here is engagement with the historical horizon, but explicitly *geographical* traditions (in art and architecture, forms of government, transport, or demographic patterns) also determine the way in which places are perceived and, in Coleridge's terms, 'half-created'. No sooner have we seen a certain place than we tell ourselves a story about it, before enacting that story and mapping it on to the place we behold. A complex web of assumptions, associations and aspirations is instantly employed, informing our view as to what kind of place this may be – and, therefore, how we might act in relation to it. An industrial estate, hospital ward or parish church: each elicits a particular traditioned response – as, equally, do unfamiliar situations, where this instinct for local meaning intensifies, helping us decide what the new setting is *like*, and whether in some sense we belong there.

Vocation

Place, it is suggested, begins to be formed in the imaginative, traditioned processing of what 'is', locally, as revealed to human agency in space-time. Thus, the 'knowing' of place is a response to the 'being' of place, which, in Christian belief, is grounded in the creative action of God, issuing from his own prior existence. Furthermore, because it is *situated*, knowledge of place is, in the Aristotelian sense, a 'practical wisdom' or *phronesis*, only gained 'through' local experience and action.[38] There is much resonance here with Michael Polanyi's groundbreaking work on scientific epistemology, which argues that the intuitive, *fiduciary* dimension is foremost in all genuine enquiry, as evoked by his maxim, 'we know more than we can tell'.[39] Thus understood, knowing is an act of faith that reaches beyond the boundaries of self towards a reality that, as it were, draws forward to meet us. Critical here is Polanyi's contention that, because all knowledge is *personal*, universal truth only 'finds us' via our particular situation. This is not to say that personal knowledge is hopelessly subjective and self-referential, because it is always an encounter with that which lies 'beyond' us – calling us forward. Against the prevailing inductive methodology in science, Polanyi writes: 'Critical philosophy would reduce all our convictions to the mere products of a particular location and interest. But I do not accept this conclusion ... I accept these accidents of personal existence as the concrete opportunities for exercising our personal responsibility. The acceptance is the sense of my calling.'[40] This sense of being 'called' by reality, or truth, allows a person to transcend the limitations of circumstance; he concludes: 'because we hope to be visited by powers for which we cannot account in terms of our specific capabilities. This hope is a clue to God ...'[41]

The knowledge of place has a similarly vocational character to that which Polanyi ascribes to scientific endeavour – namely, one that evokes and elicits from us a definite kind of social response or 'traditioned action'. This relationship between 'act' and 'being' is at the heart of all theology and philosophy and, in the Christian worldview, is embodied in the person of Jesus Christ, whose explicit call to follow him along a distinctive way of life is given social and spatial form by the Church. An encounter with Christ in the Gospels invariably means a challenge both to see the world differently (that is, as he sees it), and to act differently within it (as he acts), so that God's new place, the kingdom of heaven, draws near.

While Christianity has this overtly vocational tenor, all human actions and lifestyles are, in effect, 'called forth' in response to local conditions – indeed, the way in which place is formed by such 'enacted narratives' has been a signal theme in social theory in the last 50 years.[42] Different social practices have been recognized as having different spatial consequences, such that cultures continually make and remake – and are themselves remade by – the places they inhabit. One never, to adapt Heraclitus, stands in the same place twice. Place-formation proceeds, then, from an imaginative interplay between the concrete reality of an area and its perception and recreation by local society (see the diagram below). If we discern the presence of God in that reality (by which we often mean a sense of being personally addressed in – almost 'by' – a particular spot), we cannot but act on this belief, so that our behaviour becomes, to some degree, a response to God in that place. Hence, there is an evident coincidence of *vocation* and *location* in the biblical story.

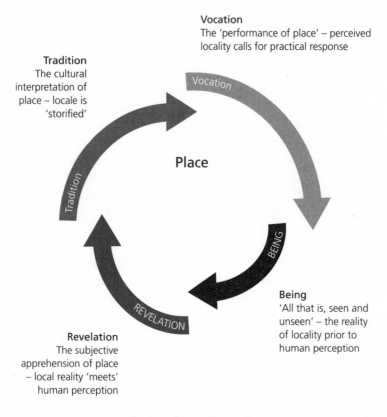

Vocation
The 'performance of place' – perceived locality calls for practical response

Tradition
The cultural interpretation of place – locale is 'storified'

Vocation

Place

Tradition

BEING

REVELATION

Being
'All that is, seen and unseen' – the reality of locality prior to human perception

Revelation
The subjective apprehension of place – local reality 'meets' human perception

A place-formation cycle

Our relationship to a particular place naturally deepens over time. When, for example, we first move home to a new location, our knowledge of it is often quite 'shallow' – based on, perhaps, certain practical factors such as transport links, local shops, schools and so on. As we live there, connections are gradually made, relationships established, memories accrued, and the place becomes enriched and 'deepened' in our imagination. While in one sense it is the 'same place' as when we arrived, in another it is entirely altered: invested now with personal meaning and association. In truth, the place is not only altered 'to us', but also for everyone who lives there, because of our presence and practice within it. Our presence there in time and space has remade that place for all, in myriad ways. This is, of course, true of our fleeting presence in places that we may not feel any special personal connection to – 'non-places' such as motorways and railway carriages, where our brief encounters also define a particular local culture, complete with its own ethical norms, such as the unspoken protocols of a tube journey. The longer we abide in a place, however, the deeper (and thus more 'traditional') it becomes: growing a texture of meaning and personal association.

Where this happens, both perception and practice are enriched – we 'see more' and 'do more' as our spatial, social behaviour becomes complex and, inevitably, more meaningful. In other words, the place is not 'just anywhere' but has become a 'somewhere'. This process – the natural result of human settlement – has very clear benefits and pitfalls. Positively, the more committed or faithful we are to places, the more we tend to care about them; conversely, the more we care about a place, the more likely we are to defend our own perception of it – the place, as it were, that we have made it. Unless this can be set within a larger narrative, one unavoidable consequence of 'deep place' is, therefore, an idolatrous sense of 'possessing the land' that can be resistant to change or challenge.

An old country like Great Britain is, as we shall see, chronically prone to this paradox, not least because the parish has been so successful in fostering deep and productive local attachments.

When place is interpreted theologically (when England becomes Jerusalem, and Jerusalem, God's dwelling place) the stakes become even higher. Considering the land to be God's gift wonderfully deepens a sense of local attachment and the likelihood of committed vocational practice, but this quickly turns very sour indeed if our earthly home is not also located eschatologically – unless, in other words, we recognize that the present place is emphatically not the end of the world.

The idea of an ultimate place introduces hope and perspective into local practice. Consciously or unconsciously, we enact our understanding not only of the places we presently live in but also the places to which we aspire. It is therefore in place that we receive the call beyond our existing situation to possible future locations, meaning that hopeful action in any locale requires a degree of faithfulness to a vision of how our place might one day be: such faith being the motor of all political and moral change in society, utopian or otherwise. In this way we emulate Abraham who, by faith, obeyed when he was called at Haran to leave for a place that he was to receive as an inheritance; and set out, not knowing where he was going.

Notes

1 Karl Barth, *The Doctrine of Creation, Part 2, Church Dogmatics III. iii*, Edinburgh: T&T Clark, 1960, pp. 430ff.

2 Genesis 12.1.

3 Walter Brueggemann, *The Land*, London: SPCK, 1978, p. 48.

4 John Inge recognizes this quality in the early Church (in *A Christian Theology of Place*, Aldershot: Ashgate, 2003, p. 57), as does W. D. Davies (in *The Gospel and the Land: Early Christianity and Jewish Territorial Doctrine*, Berkeley: University of California Press, 1974, pp. 366ff).

5 Peter's vision in Acts 10 being a key example.

6 Plato, *Timaeus and Critias*, Harmondsworth: Penguin, 1977, p. 41.

7 While revolutionary for the modern understanding of physics, Liebniz's 'perspectiveless' depiction of divine involvement in the world arguably allowed the empiricists to dispense with a divine being who is, in essence, *unrelated* to the world. See Gottfried Wilhelm Liebniz, *Philosophical Writings*, London: J. M. Dent, 1961, pp. 10ff.

8 Hume, *Dialogues Concerning Natural Religion*, Indianapolis: Hackett, 1998, p. 64.

9 Roger Scruton, in *Kant*, Oxford: OUP, 1982, p. 23.

10 Immanuel Kant, *Critique of Pure Reason*, London: J. M. Dent, 1934, p. 190.

11 See D. W. Hamlyn, *The Theory of Knowledge*, London: Macmillan, 1971, p. 176: 'there is no way in which belief in an independent world can be justified once we are committed to the idea that what primarily exist are sense data'.

12 Samuel Taylor Coleridge, *Biographia Literaria, or Biographical Sketches of my Literary Life and Opinions*, London: J. M. Dent, 1960, p. 149.

13 From 'On Method' cited in I. A. Richards (ed.), *The Portable Coleridge*, Harmondsworth: Penguin, 1977, p. 386. See also Coleridge, *Biographia*, pp. 154–5.

14 Coleridge, *Biographia*, p. 152.

15 In whom, according to Coleridge, 'knowing and being are identical and co-inherent'. Quoted in Catherine M. Wallace, 'Coleridge's Biographia Literaria and the Evidence for Christianity', in *Interspace and the Inward Sphere: Essays on the Romantic and Victorian Self*, ed. Norman Anderson and Margene Weiss, Illinois: Western Illinois University Press, 1978, p. 24. See also Basil Willey, *Samuel Taylor Coleridge*, London: Chatto & Windus, 1972, p. 197.

16 Coleridge, *Biographia*, p. 154.

17 Coleridge, *Biographia*, p. 155.

18 T. F. Torrance (ed.), *Belief in Science and in Christian Life*, Edinburgh: Handsel Press, 1980, p. 10. Similarly, Blaise Pascal: 'no one can be sure, apart from faith, whether he is waking or sleeping' (in *Pensees*, Harmondsworth: Penguin, 1966, p. 62).

19 Torrance (ed.), *Belief in Science and in Christian Life*, p. 10.

20 Torrance (ed.), *Belief in Science and in Christian Life*, p. 12.

21 T. F. Torrance, *Transformation and Convergence in the Frame of Knowledge*, Belfast: Christian Journals Limited, 1984, p. 159.

22 Richards, *Portable Coleridge*, pp. 377–8.

23 See John Thompson, 'Was Forsyth Really a Barthian Before Barth?', in Trevor Hart (ed.), *Justice the True and Only Mercy*, Edinburgh: T&T Clark, 1995, p. 239: 'Knowledge of God begins not with human discovery, but God's own action in revelation.'

24 Karl Barth, *The Doctrine of Creation, Part 2, Church Dogmatics III.ii*, Edinburgh: T&T Clark, 1960, p. 247. Similarly, 'Man without God *is not*; he has neither being nor existence' (in *Dogmatics III.ii*, p. 345).

25 Colin Gunton, *Christ and Creation*, Carlisle: Paternoster Press, 1992, p. 114.

26 Mark Wynn, *Faith and Place: An Essay in Embodied Epistemology*, Oxford: OUP, 2009, p. 36.

27 In *Heaven and Hell*, Harmondsworth: Penguin, 1959, p. 97.

28 Barth, *Dogmatics III.iii*, p. 430. Colin Gunton emphasizes how trinitarian relations are essential in order to demonstrate how 'God is able to come into relation with the world while remaining distinct from it' (in Gunton, *Christ and Creation*, p. 77).

29 Quoted in Torrance, *Transformation and Convergence*, p. 115. In similar vein, Willey explains Coleridge's 'secondary imagination' thus: 'we see what we deserve to see, what our eye brings means of seeing' (in *Coleridge*, p. 198).

30 Coleridge's *Lecture on Poesy or Art*, in H. N. Coleridge (ed.), *The Literary Remains of Samuel Taylor Coleridge*, London: William Pickering, 1836, pp. 223f.

31 Coleridge, *Biographia*, XIII; cf. Willey, *Coleridge*, pp. 196ff.

32 Quoted in Willey, *Coleridge*, p. 89.

33 In *A Midsummer Night's Dream*, Act V, scene I.

34 John Berger, *Ways of Seeing*, Harmondsworth: Penguin, 1972, pp. 7–8.

35 Berger, *Ways of Seeing*, p. 7. Similarly, Lakoff and Johnson aver that 'we experience our world in such a way that our culture is already present within the experience itself' (in *Metaphors We Live By*, London and Chicago: University of Chicago Press, 1980, p. 57).

36 Hans-Georg Gadamer, *Truth and Method*, New York: Crossroad, 1975, p. 269.

37 Gadamer, *Truth and Method*, p. 273.

38 See Aristotle, *The Nichomachean Ethics*, Oxford: OUP, 1980, p. 146. As Aristotle writes: 'practice is concerned with particulars'.

39 Michael Polanyi, *The Tacit Dimension*, London: University of Chicago Press, 1966, p. 4.

40 Michael Polanyi, *Personal Knowledge*, New York: Harper & Row, 1962, p. 324.

41 Polanyi, *Personal Knowledge*, p. 324. In this spirit, see John MacMurray, *The Self as Agent*, London: Faber, 1991, p. 31.

42 Thomas Eriksen writes: 'the person is a social product but society is created by acting persons' (in *Small Places, Large Issues: An Introduction to Social and Cultural Anthropology*, New York: Pluto Press, 2010, p. 79).

2

The Lord is Here: Towards a Christology of Place

It was an especially soggy Good Friday, the sky grey as a pavement. Nevertheless, the small band of believers went ahead with their customary walk around the parish. This year, the mood was dampened not merely by the weather, but by the fatal shooting, five days previously, of a young man named Ezra Mills, on the Central Hill Estate, the huge (and now doomed) housing project that spreads in brutal beauty around the slopes of Gipsy Hill, south-east London.

With sopping songsheets behind a rough cross, we formed our familiar, quiet crocodile, halting here and there to read a scripture and arriving, finally, at the alley where the lad had been gunned down by six youths, on the day after his birthday. The significance of being on the precise spot, the wooden cross, the impossible command to love our neighbour – all converged in that one bedraggled moment, as we began to sing 'When I Survey'. A couple of windows opened as the hymn continued, guttering the mood; a pause as all stood still, then mingled down and away.

This experience touched and tagged everyone present: and though we left SE19, a splinter of the scene still snags. Poignant as the brown flowers of a wayside shrine, such 'acts of witness' tap deeply into England's Christian past. The high or standing cross was our original sign of hallowed ground and represents a unique tradition in British and Irish vernacular art. In the seventh century, as English kingdoms were converted, stone or wooden crosses became the local focus of spiritual meaning in most parts of the country, often pre-empting the building of a parish church. At their foot, prayers would be offered, the Eucharist celebrated, gatherings held. Unhoused – a spiritual commons predating later acts of enclosure – the standing cross mapped our places of worship, staking the claim that God was here, known or not.

The cross is the Church's point of orientation in time and space: we return there to gain our bearing, our heading. Attractive or repulsive, it has always been magnetic: the Christian's true north, setting their course for 'a better place', raising inevitably parochial sights towards an eternal home. When they survey, the authors of the New Testament find in the cross not only a key and compass, but also their sense of scale, linking locality to the broad, blurring cosmos. They portray Jesus as one pulled apart in a turf war, yet simultaneously drawing together a torn universe – such a stretching claim, far-reaching more than far-fetched.

Viewed through this theodolite lens, human locale becomes both more and less important than we are usually given to think, at once demoted and promoted to glory. And where no memorial, mossy cross stands, there we affirm Christ in our place: under the sky's slab, propped up like an impromptu signpost for the lost.

The great missionary bishop Lesslie Newbigin made the observation that, in the New Testament, the Church is always and only designated by reference to two realities: first, God in Christ, and second, the place wherein it is set.[1] The relationship between these two realities is our primary concern in this chapter and requires consideration of how belief in Christ gives distinctive focus and frame to the resulting topography of the Church.

We have previously considered how, in Christian theology, the existence or 'being' of God is prior to, and intertwined with, the reality of place. Furthermore, that God's being is, as it were, *in revelation*, which is to say that, in the biblical tradition, God is perceived as giving himself to be known by those he has created – and that this self-revelation occurs within created space-time. God, Christians affirm, is only ever encountered locally: not because *he* is local, but because we are, and God elects to be known *by us*. Knowledge of God, then, is always in a sense *local knowledge* – knowledge from a particular standpoint. The fact that people encounter God from their own cultural 'place' does not, however, prevent them from knowing him 'verily': indeed, it is basic to the Church's confession that Christ embodies 'very God' precisely within these local constraints.

It follows that such distinctive beliefs about God will inevitably have distinctive local implications and, furthermore, that the kinds of places we make will bear witness to those beliefs. This much may be inferred by faith in the God of Jacob, 'who is in this place'. In order to explore the theological import of local – especially, parochial – practice, the next task is to ask, like Paul on the Damascus Road, '*who* is the God who is in this place?'

The affirmation of the Nicene Creed that the 'one Lord, Jesus Christ' is 'of one substance' with God the Father indicates the Church's belief in God's incarnate presence within the human existence of Christ. Given that this same Lord is also confessed as the 'eternal Word' through whom all things were made, forms a bond in Christian teaching between Christ and the cosmos – however outlandish this idea may appear to a secularized worldview.[2] Christology thus becomes the focus of the Church's quest to understand *how* the reality of God and the reality of the world exist in relation to each other and the inevitable questions of their distinction or unity.[3]

Crucial to this relationship is the Church's equivalent affirmation of Christ's *humanity,* which requires us to home in on the particular 'place' of the man Jesus.[4] In the specific history and culture of Jesus' earthly life, death and resurrection, God, who is 'one' in the universal sense, becomes 'one' in the little, local sense: creator as creature. Thus, for Christians, Jesus Christ becomes the *locus* of God's loving identification with his world: not a general cosmic principle, but the definitive mediating point between divine and earthly life. This conviction underwrites the Church's commitment to locality and its validity in God's purposes. It also means that, in the Christian tradition, the local or particular is always dynamically related to the catholic or universal, to which extent their Lord, Jesus, is also deemed to be the saviour of the *world*: of Knebworth as much as Nazareth. We become so domesticated to this confession – the mild assumption of so many sermons – that we forget its audacity.

Clearly, the Church has a great deal riding on the bridge

between particular and universal – one of the most well-trodden paths of Western philosophy. Engaging with Karl Barth's approach to this crossing in the essay collection *Christ in Our Place*, John Thompson encapsulates the Christian position thus: 'Since God has taken man and his history into union with himself in this particular form and place, it has special significance for all times, places and people, whether they know it or not.'[5]

Thompson presents this position in narrative terms: the story of God's 'mission' to reconcile and save the world is 'primal history', but 'with a particular historical manifestation'.[6] This manifestation – the incarnate life of Jesus Christ – happened 'once upon a time', yet extends to all times and places.[7] Despite this rooting, it is common to find the incarnation presented, as it were, under laboratory conditions – the sterile combination of two unlike properties.[8] Vital, then, to remember that the doctrine proceeds from a *life,* uniquely and divinely real: lived amid the taint and untidiness of the human situation.[9] As such, through belonging to a particular cultural tradition, Christ was immersed in the Jewish understanding of place, which viewed the destiny of God's people as being inseparable from that of the land. Relation to Yahweh involved relation to territory and the former was worked through in thoroughly geographical terms, meaning that place emerges in Scripture as both *promise* and *problem*, as Walter Brueggemann observed in *The Land*, his classic study of the theme. Surveying the biblical record, he writes:

> In the Old Testament there is no timeless space but there is also no spaceless time. There is rather storied place, that is a place which has meaning because of the history lodged there ... This means that biblical faith cannot be presented simply as an historical movement indifferent to place ... And for all its apparent 'spiritualizing', the New Testament does not escape this rootage ... He [God] is Lord of places as well as times.[10]

The Garden of Eden marks the essence of 'Godly place' and yet the Lord's very first response to human sin is also expressed in locational terms – immediately after the fall, God asks of Adam and Eve, '*where* are you?' Thereafter the testimony is both of a lost place with God that was Eden, and yet – via the covenant – the promise of a new homeland and the hope that, as the psalmist sings, 'I will see the goodness of the Lord in the land of the living'. Thus, the land both exemplifies God's gift and yet also encapsulates the idolatry of Israel's faith, at which point in the scriptural narrative divine judgement intervenes.

In the New Testament, human encounter with the divine is still in particular locations – the Mount of Olives, the Damascus Road and so forth. In Jesus' teaching, however, Israel's faith had become 'over-localized' around temple territory, so must be re-imagined in terms of the kingdom of God: not a territorial domain, but a spiritual reality. This radical *displacing* of belief does not divorce people from the land: rather, it transforms the way they are to live in it. The need for a home in the world – a rooted and just society for all – is embraced by Jesus, but in paradox. The way home is through death and loss, giving up one's place for God's sake in order to find it again, in a form of eschatological belonging revealed as the New Jerusalem. Here, 'Land's End', as it were, is reached as the Holy City descends from heaven to earth.

'Place' is thus by no means incidental to the scriptural narrative: indeed, it may confidently be seen as one of its principal motifs. According to W. D. Davies, whose 1974 work *The Gospel and the Land* pioneered this kind of theological geography, the processing of the Jewish attachment to territory was one of the most complex theological tasks faced by the early Church,[11] which needed to balance the tension between, on the one hand, the need for faith in Christ to *transcend* the land and, on the other, to also *attend* to it, as the location of God's revelation. As Davies writes: 'The need to remember the Jesus of History entailed the need to remember the Jesus of a particular land. Jesus belonged not only to time, but to space; and the space and spaces which he occupied took on significance, so that the *realia* of Judaism continued as *realia* in Christianity. *History in the tradition demanded geography*.'[12] The effective 'downgrading' of place in the early Church was, Davies argues, the inevitable result of the need for Christianity's existence as a local sect to express

Christian faith in universal terms – with the consequence that this could not fail to place the 'local' in shadow: 'Any local or geographic particularistic elements in Judaism could not but be regarded as insignificant, or at best secondary, and could safely be overlooked.'[13] Nevertheless, the geographical particularity of Christ meant the resulting tendency to a placeless, disembodied spirituality – despite, it may be added, the best efforts of Neo-Platonism – had to remain firmly tethered to space and time, such that: 'To do justice to the personalism of the New Testament, that is, its Christo-centricity, is to find the clue to the various strata of tradition that ... reveal their freedom from space and their attachment to spaces.'[14]

The point to emphasize here is that the early Church's ambivalence towards place was, in part at least, a consequence of its Christology. Its faith could not be over-localized because Christ's divinity transcended human culture; at the same time, his full humanity meant it could not be anything but embedded in place. Entire worldviews have thus rested (as Colin Gunton observed) on the way in which the two natures of Christ are understood to relate to each other.[15]

The positive and lasting gain of the early Church's pivotal council at Chalcedon in AD 451, through a negative process of ruling out either their confusion or separation (Christ, they concluded, was both truly God and truly man), was to define the creative centre of orthodox debate, and thus effectively to preserve the mystery of 'how' divinity and humanity might be so conjoined.

The process that led to this 'both/and' resolution in the creeds involved re-thinking and even abandoning certain existing philosophical categories – especially those relating to place and space. Not only did the incarnation invalidate the traditional Platonic separation between the visible world of time and space and the 'intelligible' world of unchanging forms; it also stretched to breaking point the prevailing, Aristotelian, concept of *topos* or 'place', as that which 'contains' each object or body – for how could the finite 'contain' the infinite?

The incarnation thus required the Church to pioneer a new and more dynamic kind of spatial language, whereby God was neither closed off from, nor contained within, his world. Instead, space and time were understood in terms of the relationship between creator and creation in Jesus Christ who, in T. F. Torrance's words, became '*the place* in all space and time where God meets with man in the actualities of his human existence'.[16] Torrance examines this unique capacity for God in Christ in his seminal 1969 work *Space, Time and Incarnation* and concludes that, while we are thus bound to space and time in all relations with God, earthly place becomes 'infinitely open' to the divine in Christ.

The person of Jesus Christ – in all his historical and geographical particularity – may thus be seen as the response to King Solomon's question at the dedication of the first Temple: 'But will God indeed reside with mortals on earth? Even heaven and the highest heaven cannot contain you ...' As such, Christology offers an alternative to what the geographer Lily Kong has described as the two 'general spatial orientations' evident in the study of world religions: the 'locative' (fixing religious experience into a particular culture) and the 'Utopian' (unbounded and transcendent of any specific place or society).[17]

Despite this bursting of the bounds within patristic theology, Aristotelian cosmology came to dominate the medieval worldview, which ensured that the Church in the West continued to wrestle with how an infinite God might be accommodated within finite reality. A significant case in point arose at the Reformation when Lutheran and Reformed Christologies diverged on this very issue. Lutherans emphasized the inherent 'haveability' of God: drawing on the early Church's doctrine of the *communicatio idiomatum*[18] they insisted that, in the historic man Jesus, the eternal God is made wholly present for humanity. Thus, when Calvinist theologians, who placed greater emphasis on the separation of Christ's divine and human natures, insisted that Christ became incarnate without abandoning his 'place' in heaven, Lutherans could parody this as the '*extra Calvinisticum*' – inferring that some part of Christ was thought by Calvinists to be, in effect, 'left outside'.

At stake in these abstruse disputes over the location of Christ (which became acute when considering his 'real presence' at the Eucharist) was the way in which God avails himself *for* his creation. This was a matter that could not avoid also contesting the very nature of space-time boundaries: do they 'seal God in', seal him out, or are they in some measure permeable to divine presence? When, in Part Two, we come to examine in detail the historic record of the parish, a not dissimilar question will pertain to human relations: namely, do spatial boundaries deny or permit full relationship with God and neighbour? Then, as now, there were clear pitfalls on either side. T. F. Torrance argues that the Lutheran principle of *finitum capax infiniti* – the idea that the finite can hold the infinite – resulted from the 'containerized' notion of space and time mentioned above. While firmly placing God's saving presence in the 'here and now', this risked sliding into a natural theology that deified human nature in general – thus implying humanity's inherent capacity for eternal truth and effectively preparing a home for Enlightenment rationalism.[19] If the Christian belief in 'God with us' neglects an equal trust in divine transcendence, then it is not too great a stretch for 'us' to do without him. Even with its focus firmly on the atonement, one logical end of Lutheran Christology – with its attendant stress on the 'self-emptying' of God in Christ – is that God 'lets himself be pushed out of the world onto the cross', in Bonhoeffer's memorable phrase.[20]

If the conflation of human and divine places is the danger of Lutheranism (and, in a slightly different sense, Catholicism), the contrasting risk of Reformed Christology, as Torrance admits,[21] is their separation, such that the 'being' of God with us is reduced to isolated saving 'acts', in which an essentially remote God becomes knowable only in existential moments of encounter. The resolution of this ancient Christological problem is not found, however, by first affirming the capacity or non-capacity of the finite for the infinite; it must be sought in the nature of the God who, in the luminous words of P. T. Forsyth, 'is not hampered by space, but can enter spatial relations without being tied to them, can exist in limits without being unfree, or ceasing to be God ... *Finitum non capax infiniti* is the principle of Deism; the principle of Christian theism is *infinitum capax finiti*'.[22] This view, which posits the basic freedom and 'spaciousness' of God, underlines the dependence of earthly places on their creator, as well as, in Christ, their participation in the divine nature. Not so much 'God was in this place' as 'this place was in God'. In order to avoid the charge of pantheism, however, such a theology of place must hold the balance between the distinction and union of Christ's divine and human natures, our approach to which tends to determine how the similar boundary between creation and God is viewed. Unsurprisingly, perhaps, this balance has not been easy for the Church to achieve. In his early, insightful work *Yesterday and Today*, Colin Gunton lucidly explained how Christologies both modern and classical have usually been either 'from below' or 'from above' – they have sought, in other words, either a 'this-worldly' or 'other-worldly' starting point for understanding Jesus Christ. Summarizing the tendencies, he writes: 'Whereas ancient thought tended to abstract Jesus from history by eternalizing him ... modern thought tends to abstract him from eternity by making his temporality absolute.'[23]

For present purposes, 'history' might equally read 'geography', and 'temporality' read 'locality', in order to express how place is prone to being abstracted at both sides of the Christological pendulum. The only way to avoid this, Gunton concludes, is to reckon with the confession of the New Testament that 'in the same piece of space' God and humanity are equally present – 'without loss of the deity of the one, or the humanity of the other'.[24] Emphasizing that there is no 'Christ' available from Scripture other than this – no theology-free presentation of the Son of Man – Gunton presses that Christology must be done simultaneously from 'above' and 'below', which inevitably means coming to terms with questions of space and time, and how God may be present within them. Thus, he concludes that 'Christology must take its centre from that place where the eternal God takes a place alongside us in time.'[25]

For Gunton, the key to this 'placing' of God in space-time is found in the doctrine of the Trinity – in particular, the central role of the Holy Spirit in enabling both distinction and unity within Christ and among the persons of the Godhead. In this assertion he echoes Karl Barth who, especially in the later volumes of *Church Dogmatics*, makes many tantalizing allusions to 'place' without entirely pressing them home. For Barth, the Trinity is 'the way He [God] enters space and time and all structures distinct from himself',[26] and becomes the means whereby the 'movement' of God towards humanity 'really takes place where we really are', as mentioned previously.[27] In turn, Barth's dynamic understanding of Christ's humanity and divinity owes much to the Edwardian Congregational theologian P. T. Forsyth, quoted earlier. Forsyth's seminal work *The Person and Place of Jesus Christ* (1909) portrays the humanity and divinity of Christ as 'two personal movements'[28] of God to man and vice versa, in whose conjunction human place is saved and redeemed. The salvific effect of this dual movement in Christ, so central to Protestant Christology, is crucial to a robust view of parochialism, resisting as it does any tendency to consider the incarnation as mere consolation – the unqualified hallowing of our turf.

For Forsyth, Christ represents the *crisis* of human place, not just its consummation: a theme that Karl Barth carried forward in his doctrine of reconciliation.[29] In one of the most lyrical and persuasive sections in his *Dogmatics*, 'The Judge Judged in Our Place', Barth pursues God's total immersion into human locale, the baptism by which he chose, 'to share with it its place and status, its situation, by making it His own situation'.[30] For Barth, it is critical that this identification with fallen humanity is not just static 'presence', but an *act*: an *event* in which Christ takes 'our' place.[31] In the baptism of the man Jesus into our situation, each stage of the place-formation cycle essayed in the previous chapter – ontology, revelation, tradition and vocation – is assumed and saved, a new 'place' is made possible through his redeeming work.

Central to this advocacy, Barth presses, is that Christ acts thus for a fallen humanity that has effectively 'lost its place'. In Christ, God's stance towards the world (from 'above' in Gunton's terms) is revealed in a new stance of humanity towards God ('from below'), whereby the perilous consequences of our situation are borne by the creator himself.[32] Barth's conclusion is worth quoting in full: 'He acted justly in the place of all and for the sake of all. In their place and for their sake ... he returned to the place from which they had fallen into sin, the place which belongs to the creature in relation to God. In so doing, in His own person, He reversed the fall in their place and for their sake.'[33]

The crucial contribution of reformed Christology to the theology of place is perhaps a conviction that 'our' place is not as it should be – and that Christ, at the cross, has taken that place in reconciling action. This is an important theme to emphasize, not least because theologies of place more commonly take an incarnational route that lacks a precisely soteriological focus. However, while Barth expresses Christ's recapitulation of the human condition in local terms – 'He does in our place the opposite of what we usually do'[34] – and insists that 'everything depends on its concrete expression',[35] the overriding impression is that place is conceived by him existentially rather than *geographically*. Although, with great force, he presses the utter immersion of Jesus into the human situation, the spatial implications are left as just that – hinting at far more than they describe.

Ironically (and Barth is by no means alone in this), history is rarely abstracted in the same way as geography – a shortcoming of much theology and social theory in the twentieth century. Topological language is often used doctrinally, especially by evangelical scholars, but invariably abstracted from any physical or social definition, in a manner that simply does not pertain when using the language of 'time'. By way of redress, it must be stressed that Christology binds the Church (and theological discourse) to locality, planting it in the reality of place. Salvation-history is, in equal measure, salvation-geography.

If Christ is 'really' rather than merely metaphorically 'in our place', then – one is bound to enquire – *how*? For Richard Hooker, the founding theological genius of the Church of England, answering this question tested the bounds of normal spatial terminology. In the fifth book of his *Laws of Ecclesiastical Polity*, he affirms that 'the substance of the body of Christ hath no presence, neither can have, but only *local*'.[36] This ongoing humanity of Christ means, continues Hooker (lyrically quoting Augustine), that 'he spreadeth not out himself into all places', but must 'be restrained and tied to a certain place'. [37] Nevertheless, he exhibits the inevitable tension of holding this essential locality together with its equally essential universality – and one senses the bonds straining as Hooker writes: 'The manhood of Christ may *after a sort* be everywhere said to be present, because that Person is everywhere present, from whose divine substance manhood nowhere is severed.'[38]

But the challenge remains, after what 'sort' is Christ everywhere? In this next section, three twentieth-century responses will briefly be sketched, each of which holds valuable implications for the Church's role as a place-maker.

Christ the sacramental place

With the emergence of 'place' as a coherent strand within academic theology, sacramental approaches have, to date, provided the main route into the theme – naturally enough, given the high value they ascribe to the divine significance of material things. In his *A Christian Theology of Place*, John Inge observes how twentieth-century sacramental theology focused on the idea of Christ himself as sacrament: *the* visible and outward sign of God's presence. At Jesus' instigation, this presence is then extended and transmitted by the sacraments of the Church, so that all created things might reveal him.[39] One can see this position maturing in the works of Jesuit priest and philosopher Teilhard de Chardin who, writing in 1917, considered how: 'The effect of the priestly act extends beyond the consecrated host to the consecrated host to the cosmos itself ... the entire realm of matter is slowly but irresistibly affected by this great consecration.'[40] By the time of his later work *Hymn of the Universe*, de Teilhard had developed this early conviction, to the extent that he could describe the universe as 'an immense host' consecrated by the Word of God in Christ. By virtue of the incarnation, 'all matter', he concludes, 'is henceforth incarnate'.[41]

Drawing this sacramental principle into a more recognizably Anglican frame of reference, William Temple's substantial 1934 work *Nature, Man and God* affirmed this basic materialism inherent in Christianity: 'By the very nature of its central doctrine Christianity is committed to a belief in the ... reality of matter and its place in the divine scheme.'[42] In Christ, Temple continues, earthly locale becomes 'the condition' of the possibility of 'special' (i.e. particular) revelation,[43] and thus the medium of God's presence 'with us'.[44] This radial movement from the particular *locus* of God's presence in Christ to his presence – via the Church – across the world chimes with Bonhoeffer's view that God's existence is never, as it were, 'self-contained', but always extending beyond itself for the sake of the world.

The 'worldliness' of theology is precisely the concern of David Brown in *God and Enchantment of Place*, a major study in which he addresses the theme of sacramentality as a window on to the world. For Brown, its extension 'reclaims' vast areas of human experience largely lost to theology since the Enlightenment – especially the spirituality of place. The increasing marginalization of religion, he argues, has gone hand-in-hand with the withdrawal of academic theology into an ever-tighter frame of engagement. Barth's insistence on the inadmissable nature of religious experience beyond a strict trinitarian matrix is, he argues, emblematic of this gradual 'disenchantment' of the theologian's world. To counteract what he sees as this erroneous tendency, Brown proposes a much broader conception of the sacramental: 'So far from the sacramental being seen as essentially ecclesiastical or narrowly Christian, it should instead be viewed as a major, perhaps even the primary, way of exploring God's relationship to our world.'[45]

By calling attention to the theological potency of the material world, and away from an abstracted, evaporated Christianity, this reassertion of sacramental method makes a vital contribution to the theology of place. The danger, however, of making a general principle of sacramentality is that it easily ends in an indiscriminate hallowing of the natural world that disregards the reality of radical evil (the 'dislocation', as it were, of man and

God) and risks making the incarnation merely a confirmation of God's latent presence in all creation.[46] William Blake's elegant call to 'arise and drink your bliss, for all that lives is holy', is certainly seductive – and sound up to a point – but can only be ignorance if blind to all that is *un*holy.

John Inge responds to this susceptibility by stressing that encounter with God (in both church and wider world) is always an 'event': it involves, in other words, the revelation of God to particular people at particular times and places. Far from being a general rule, sacramentality – Christ's life signified within his creation – is, he urges, 'historical, temporal and singular', much as was the earthly ministry of Jesus himself.[47] Such encounters are, by virtue of our situation, fleeting and fragmentary, always suggesting infinitely more than they can contain. They are, we might say, *eventual* in both senses: 'happenings' that are partially realized in the 'here and now', yet directed towards a future consummation in the kingdom of heaven. Employing his Christian definition of place as 'the seat of relations ... between God and the world', Inge concludes that sacramental encounters: 'lead to a transformation of the place as well as the individuals and communities associated with them. The role of such places is to root believers in their faith and point towards the redemption of all places in Christ.'[48]

In thus seeking to reconcile 'act' with 'being' in a sacramental theology of place, Inge preserves an Antiochene accent on distinction in Christology (between the natures of Christ and, by extension, between God and creation) and its attendant concern to uphold the particular humanity of Jesus Christ. It is only by acknowledging human place to be *created* – that is, distinct from, but dependent upon, God – that the freedom of God *for creation* and, in Christ, creation's corresponding freedom *for God*, can be realized.

If earthly place is perceived sacramentally as the 'gate of heaven', in Jacob's phrase, the question is raised as to whether the Church may be viewed in some sense as the 'continuance' of the incarnate presence of Christ in the world – which, broadly speaking, is the position of the Roman Church.[49] How one assesses the Church's 'place' in this respect depends rather upon how one interprets its credal keynotes of catholicity (pertaining here to its *geographical* arrangement, globally and locally) and apostolicity (the *historical* transmission of the gospel) – and the work of the Holy Spirit in constituting both. Central to this interpretation is the function of *tradition* within the life of the Church – the acknowledged or unacknowledged 'passing down' of Christian practice and belief, so that it may be realized afresh in each situation. In his significant 1964 study *The Meaning of Tradition*, the Roman Catholic theologian Yves Congar described Christianity as 'essentially an inheritance' whose possession tradition makes possible:[50]

> Tradition is an offering by which the Father's gift is communicated to a great number of people throughout the world, and down the successive generations, so that a multitude of people physically separated from it by space and time, are incorporated in the same unique, identical reality, which is ... the divine revelation made in Jesus Christ.[51]

While Congar concludes that church tradition thus represents a 'victory *over* space and time', it may more helpfully be seen as the necessary means of transport or communication *in* and *through* space and time – the gospel's carriage, the apostolic broadcast. And although he is concerned primarily with tradition 'within' the Church (its doctrine and liturgy, primarily), Congar affirms that it concerns the whole life of the Church, likening it to a river that 'carries a little of everything'.[52] A 'high' view of ecclesiastical tradition as a sacrament of Christ's local presence must necessarily include its external praxis – in mission, certainly, but also the Church's more implicit secular activity, which is less commonly consecrated.

Christ the 'concrete' place

The second approach to 'Christ in our place' to highlight is explored in the writings of German theologian Dietrich Bonhoeffer. Although rarely cited in relation to this theme, Bonhoeffer is immensely helpful in establishing a method for theological geography, by his insistence that the Church's thinking about all reality must flow from an explicitly Christological source. In his early works, Bonhoeffer developed a concern for God's existence in the midst of the world, which presents divine and earthly 'places' in the closest possible relationship, with the Church as the 'hidden centre' of reality. The connection between the Church (the 'place' where Christ is acknowledged and confessed as Lord) and the world (the 'place' of his dominion) is thus of crucial significance in his writings, and highly relevant for our theme. The grounded nature of his theology often finds Bonhoeffer returning to the word translated into English as 'concreteness', used by him to describe the manner in which Christ takes form in the world today. It is not only that the message of Christ needs to be *made* concrete by the Church, but, as Bonhoeffer's biographer Eberhard Bethge points out, that Christ's revelation is *itself* concrete – tangible and this-worldly.[53]

The desire that God in Christ should not be 'invisible' was a recurrent motif for Bonhoeffer – and perhaps is his main point of contention with Karl Barth, to whose theological method he otherwise owed so much.[54] The fact that scholars appear divided as to whether Luther or Barth was his primary theological influence is itself notable, highlighting the middle path he sought between the two, as explored in his major work *Act and Being*. Bonhoeffer's Lutheranism, with its emphasis on the fullness of God being present – *placed*, so to speak – in Jesus, also reckoned with Barth's more Calvinist concern to safeguard God's freedom and distinction from the world. Thus, he can assert in *Creation and Fall*: 'God is not bound to the work [i.e. creation], but he binds the work to himself ... God is never in the world in any way except in his absolute transcendence of it.'[55] God's transcendence is here the precondition for his salvation, and Bonhoeffer's synthesis lay in declaring that, in Christ, 'God is not free *from* man, but free *for* man',[56] foreshadowing his later ascription of Jesus as 'the man for others' – the *pro me*, who 'stands there in my place, where I should stand, but cannot'.[57]

In seeking the focus of his theology, commentators often settle upon Bonhoeffer's desire to know 'who Christ really is for us today'. In his lectures on the theme, written up into the slim volume *Christology*, Bonhoeffer recognizes, however, that this 'who' question begs another: namely, that of 'where' Christ really is. His simple answer, to which he makes a frequent return in subsequent writings, is *in the centre*. 'It is the nature of Christ to be in the centre both spatially and temporally', he asserts.[58] But what does he mean by this? Accepting that it is a perennial pitfall when reading Bonhoeffer to infer too much from ideas that, because of his early demise, were never fully developed, there are perhaps three aspects to this 'centrality' that may be identified.

The new reality

In one of the most potent sections in his *Ethics*, Bonhoeffer writes: 'Sharing in Christ we stand at once in the reality of God and the reality of the world. The reality of Christ comprises the reality of the world within itself.'[59] One might add 'whether the world recognizes it or not', for, as Bonhoeffer observed ten years earlier, the presence of Christ in the midst of life has a hiddenness to it: he stands at once in the centre *and* at the boundary of existence; the boundary lying between the old creation and the new. As he writes: 'In the fallen world the centre is also the boundary ... So [Christ] is in turn the boundary and judgement of man, but also the beginning of his new existence, its centre.'[60]

'At the centre of human existence' is the first of three short answers Bonhoeffer gives in these lectures to his own question about 'where' Christ is, each of which is characterized by this tension between Christ as the centre of the new world but the boundary of the old. The second location is at (or 'as') 'the centre of history'. History, he states, 'lives between promise and fulfilment' and, in the life of Jesus Christ, the key to history is concealed within its own narrative. Because the Church is the place where this centre is, as it were, an 'open secret', the Church becomes for Bonhoeffer 'the hidden centre of the state', a new ordering of humanity within history. With regards to the third location, and significantly, Christ is 'the centre between God and nature' – the 'new creature'. Nature, like human existence and history, lies in bondage to decay; with a muteness (following Psalm 19) that cannot proclaim the word of God. Nature's re-creation flows outwards from the central presence of Christ: God's 'new place' in the midst of the old.

The centre of the Church

Much attention is given in Bonhoeffer studies to the development of his thought towards the 'religionless' Christianity outlined in *Letters and Papers from Prison*. While there is a broad continuity in his Christology from the early work through to 1945, what changes, perhaps, is that Bonhoeffer pushes ever further the implications and applications of holding Christ to be the centre of reality. In earlier works, he is quite clear that the place where Christ takes visible form is the Church, defined by the phrase 'Christ existing as community'.[61] Christ is not merely represented by, but really present *in*, that body, which is the essential bond between his past and present revelation.[62] While the Church is thus described as 'the place where being is comprehended',[63] Christian ontology is never static, but always a 'being-for', such that the church community becomes the place where a new relation between God and neighbour takes shape. Although simply 'a bit of the world', in Bonhoeffer's words, the Church is also, like Christ, the 'new place', which bears witness to the destiny of all places in him.[64] Importantly, the space that the Church occupied within the world did not need to be extended; did not (unlike Hitler's Reich) need ever more *lebensraum*; it needed only the space sufficient to proclaim *to* the world that all space and time had been re-created in Christ.

The centre of the world

The Church, for Bonhoeffer, is the 'hidden centre of world history',[65] and is thus in the midst of the world, yet, like Christ, is also at its boundary. A clear distinction between the two is necessary precisely in order for the Church to be the world's new centre. Yet in Bonhoeffer's prison writings this dialectic, so starkly defined in his Bible studies, *The Cost of Discipleship*, appears to find a new synthesis – the boundary expanding to affirm the real presence of Christ outside the Church. Some of the clearest passages about this occur in his *Ethics*, where he tackles the Lutheran (and Augustinian) concept that divides reality into two 'spheres' or 'kingdoms' – one divine and Christian, the other worldly and profane. Bonhoeffer argues instead that there are not two such realities, but only one: the reality of a world suffused with the presence of God in Christ. In so far as he is transcendent or 'beyond', 'God is beyond in the midst of our life. The church stands, not at the boundaries where human powers give out, but in the middle of the village.'[66]

Such secular Christocentrism displays a certain kinship with the broad sacramental theology outlined earlier, but is distinctive in sustaining a sharper focus on the cross as the point of dislocation, of disjuncture between 'old' and 'new' places.[67] It thus offers an alternative, rarely explored, route into an Anglican conception of locality – one that stresses the Church's role in relocating what has become dislocated from its central place in Christ. The Church's *cognition* – that 'God is in this place' – is therefore the heart of its *vocation*, as it is carried into the cascading movement of God's love for the world. As Karl Barth writes:

In this history [i.e. of Jesus Christ] all history has its meaning and centre ... All existence has its root there, hastening towards and proceeding from it. The history of the Christian community ... lives – in virtue of the Holy Spirit poured out thence – in and with what took place there. *But all creation unwittingly does the same in a wider circle around the Christian community.*[68]

This last – strikingly Bonhoefferian – sentence is key: places are 'unwittingly' disorientated from their centre in Christ, so that the Church's role is essentially one of reorientation. The boundary between 'witting' and 'unwitting' places is precisely the territory of the ecclesiastical parish – and, while the English pastoral context may not at first seem to offer the most fertile soil for Barth and Bonhoeffer, their Christology is a surprisingly good 'fit' for a parochial theology. Either of them could, for example, have written the following – by the Anglican theologian F. D. Maurice, a century earlier:

> The church is, therefore, human society in its normal state; the World, that same society irregular and abnormal. The world is the church without God; the church is the world restored to its relation with God, taken back by him into the state for which he created it. Deprive the church of its centre and you make it into a world.[69]

Yet, although this may make theoretical sense – and affirms the interrelation of 'church' and 'world' in Christ – the danger is that such an exalted depiction fails to ring true in the light of ecclesiastical history and practice. The Church, we know, is often far worldlier, and the world far godlier, than this model would suggest. How, then, can Christ's 'central place' in human culture take a more recognizable form?

Christ the particular place

Despite its undoubted potency, Dietrich Bonhoeffer's overriding concern to express God's being 'for' the world – and Christ's embodiment of that stance – runs the risk of obscuring the reciprocal movement, by which the world recovers its own existence 'for' God. In the humanity of Christ, earthly 'place' is reoriented towards its creator – not so that it merges with divinity, but so that it will be created anew. Colin Gunton, whose writings (along with those of T. F. Torrance) exemplify the third approach considered here, sees the renewal of God's image in humanity as central to Christ's earthly purpose, for it is this that restores our original 'priestly' vocation to the earth as a whole. In *Christ and Creation*, he writes, 'The human calling, as made concrete in the incarnation of the mediator is, simply put, to enable the creation to praise its maker.'[70]

There is also the danger that, in stressing Christ's *existential* location (that is, his existence 'for us' in all situations), Bonhoeffer downplays his *historical* location: an emphasis that threatens to dissipate Christ's presence in the world until he becomes more principle than person. The writings of Torrance and Gunton are sensitive to any Christology that might undermine Christ's particular humanity, especially as it relates to the distinctive role of the Holy Spirit. For Torrance, Christological precision demands careful thinking about the spatial and theological boundaries marked out by the events recorded in the Gospels. In *Space, Time and Resurrection*, he highlights the importance of the ascension in marking the 'withdrawal' of Christ from human place, an episode which, in his words, 'sends us back to the historical Jesus Christ as the *covenanted place* on earth and in time which God has appointed for meeting between man and himself'.[71] The historical Jesus thus becomes 'the *one locus*' where creaturely existence is reconciled to God. Far from leaving the world without the presence of God in Christ, such an affirmation directs the Church's attention – as the angels did the disciples' – to the coming of the Holy Spirit, through whom we can think of Christ as, in Torrance's words, 'historically absent and actually present'.[72] The ascension thus imagines a divine exchange between (so to speak) 'down here' and 'up there', whereby God's 'place' indwells humanity, and human 'place' is carried to heaven. Crucially, the New Testament describes the Church becoming the 'dwelling place' of the Holy Spirit, so that, Torrance claims:

The church on earth, in the continuing space-time of this world, is the 'place' where God and man are appointed to meet. In the incarnation we have the meeting of man and God in man's place, but in the ascension we have the meeting of man and God in God's place, but *through the Spirit* these are not separated from one another.[73]

It is thus *through the Spirit* that the vital connection is made between the universality and particularity of Christ. For, as Torrance continues, 'It is through the Spirit that things infinitely disconnected by the distance of the ascension – are nevertheless infinitely closely related.'[74]

In Colin Gunton's trinitarian theology of creation, pneumatology is the essential clue to resolving the tension between God's union with, and distinction from, created reality, the Holy Spirit being the agent of 'their continuing free relatedness'.[75] Importantly, Gunton sees this agency as extending beyond the Church to include the whole creation, highlighting the work of the Spirit in establishing the unique 'place' of each created thing. If, as is suggested, the reality of God and the reality of earthly place become one in Christ, the Spirit enables this union, not by a conflation of one into the other, but – in John V. Taylor's phrase – by 'going between' them so that each recognizes their distinct being *in relation to* the other. By so doing, the Spirit affords local participation in the very life of the Godhead. In his influential work on this theme, *The One, the Three and the Many*, Gunton puts it in this way: 'The Spirit's peculiar office is to realize the true being of each created thing by bringing it, through Christ, into saving relation with the Father.'[76]

'Through Christ' is essential: not as mere code, meaning creation's general capacity for God, but rather the historical, geographical Christ in all his singularity. The work of the Holy Spirit is thus to bring into simultaneous focus both Jesus and the myriad places wherein he is encountered. As the Church of England Doctrine Commission report *We Believe in the Holy Spirit* put it some years ago: 'We may legitimately infer [from scripture] that it is the Spirit who makes possible our perceiving of Jesus as the clue to the world's intelligibility.'[77] For Gunton, the Trinity is an *idea* in the fullest sense of the word, enabling us to conceptualize the way in which all things hold together, universal and particular. With Coleridge, therefore, he sees trinitarian theology as a poetic, imaginative endeavour – transcending our limitation, our locality, without denying it. This, he argues, was what modernity signally failed to do, with Western thought since the eighteenth century tending to abstract universal ideas from their concrete situation. The ethicist Sabina Lovibond characterizes this return to a more 'grounded' philosophical approach, exemplified by Gunton, as 'transcendental parochialism', which nicely captures the local implications.[78]

For Christians, this receptiveness to universal presence or meaning – 'man with his mind ajar' in Elizabeth Jennings's felicitous phrase – is always anticipatory, eschatological. As such, the Holy Spirit may be seen as giving teleology to spacetime: an orientation towards its end in Christ. Importantly, this constitutes the Church as a *provisional* community that has not reached the 'place yet to come': vital to affirm in order to avoid an overly idealistic distinction between church and world that does few favours to either. Only when Christology is explicitly connected to the work of the Holy Spirit – understood by St Paul to be a kind of tantalizing foretaste of the new creation – do we gain an eternal perspective and purpose that, by locating it here and hereafter, puts the Church in its proper place.

Conclusion

In a Christian worldview, there can be no place without God, because space-time existence is seen first of all as relative to, and contingent upon, its creator. Christology forms the centre of place-theology because the Church finds Christ to be the nexus of that relationship, in which a new kind of space-time – a new place – is established. Christians thus tend to answer universal questions in a very particular way: beginning with Jesus of Nazareth and working outwards, inferring the global from the local.

The existing Anglican pathway into this subject has been a broadly sacramental approach to locality, whereby occasional experiences of God (for example, in 'holy places' or acts of pilgrimage) are instances or expressions of the truth that, in John Inge's words, 'all time and place belong to God in Christ'.[79] What sacramentalism gains by bonding credal affirmations with actual spiritual experience, however, it tends to forfeit in Christological precision. Protestant theology has, by a different route, made a similar mistake – stopping short of grounding its Christological conclusions so that they are left suspended in the abstract, untethered to particular situations. This becomes acute when weighing the local church's relationship to topography. In Bonhoeffer's *Christology*, for example, the scant conclusions reached about Christ as the 'centre between God and nature' are suggestive at best; given the 'blood and soil' connotations of Nazism, he would no doubt have been cautious about drawing too close a tie between Church, community and territory. These very concerns (no less pressing in contemporary politics) mean, however, that a relationship must be sought between human society and the land which neither idolizes or divinizes the latter, nor detaches the former from it.

None the less, it is contended that Protestant Christology has great riches to offer a theology of the Anglican parish, not least in clarifying the Church's response to three fundamental 'where' questions, namely: where creation is in relation to God (and vice versa); where the Church is in relation to wider society; and where both Church and society stand in relation to the land they inhabit. Perhaps its most potent contribution, though, lies in presenting the cross as a central point: a universal joint, where earth, heaven and hell effectively intersect and 'our place' is taken by Christ, who bears the fatal, dislocating effects of the Fall. The 'triumph' of the cross is thus to win for all a new place before God, where humanity's original calling can be recovered. Despite its tendency to abstraction in doctrinal terms, the cross operates, I would suggest, as a *felt* place as much as anything – an emotional location or orientation. *You are here*, the cross seems to indicate, redirecting the believer along particular moral and personal paths.

Implicitly or explicitly, there is a Christology playing out in the local practice of every church, a more or less coherent sense of who the Lord is and where he is abiding. Whatever these shades of emphasis, belief in the incarnation charges the Church with the task of 'place-forming': fostering in each locality the conditions that enable loving encounter with God and neighbour. This new place in Christ is always in the midst of the old, the tension between them primarily being eschatological. Nevertheless, Christian theology since the Enlightenment has arguably lacked a truly spatial eschatology, one that redeems place as well as time and takes seriously the geographical implications of being 'in Christ'. Of the theologians considered above, Forsyth, Barth and Bonhoeffer all employ place-language liberally, but never press it home: Torrance and Gunton refine these basic dimensions with trinitarian perspective, but their insights have not hitherto been translated into the Anglican situation.

How, then, to employ the broad idea of 'Christ in our place' as a useful means of interpreting the English parish, a very specific kind of Christian geography?

Perhaps the first step is to link metaphor with agency and action: to appreciate that metaphorical language – as all theological language must be, to a degree – is never 'merely' such, but realized by being lived and felt. Which is to say that a person's perceived 'place' in relation to God relates directly to their physical, 'actual' place in the world. Moreover, in Christian teaching, our local actions (in charity, love of neighbour and so on) are the very test of that theological 'place': my 'standing' before God is proved by my standing in relation to my world – my posture towards the particular places I inhabit.

Local behaviour, it was contended in the previous chapter, is a direct outworking of our symbolic world. As Lakoff and Johnson demonstrated in their groundbreaking study *Metaphors We Live By*, human actions are fundamentally metaphorical, because our conceptual system is largely so. We make sense of the world in metaphorical terms because metaphor imbues our actions with meaning, and very few human actions are meaningless. Lakoff and Johnson provide a welter of linguistic examples, such as the personification of non-human entities (for example, terms like 'life has cheated me') that help make sense of our environment and experience – arguably a human trait since the naming of animals in the first chapter of Genesis and closely related to the place-making instinct. The Christian worldview is likewise composed of countless metaphorical ideas: often stray phrases like 'Good Samaritan' that have structured the actions of church and society down the ages. *Tradition* is the combination of this metaphorical 'world' and the everyday practices that issue from it. Tradition translates existence into metaphor, metaphor into action, and action into vocation, by giving our individual story a meaningful narrative 'place'.

In this vein, Anglican priest-poet R. S. Thomas describes the incarnation (the Christian Church's great 'tradition') as a bridge between metaphor and action. Describing the function of imagination in George Herbert's poetry, he writes: 'If poetry is concerned with the concrete and the particular, then Christianity aims at their redemption and consecration. The poet invents the metaphor and the Christian lives it.'[80]

Wittingly or not, the incarnation has shaped the local form of the Church from its earliest times: a persistent counterbalance to other-worldliness. This enacted tradition of belief, as we have seen, grounded the Church in ordinary communities, insisted it proclaimed 'the Lord is *here*'. Without such a theological legacy, there would arguably be no parish system, however tacitly the Church's polity has been linked with its Christology. So, then, if asserting the spatiality of theology is the first task in strengthening this connection, the next must be to draw out the theological implications of space, by considering how geography, as a way of 'reading' our situation, can enable parochial life to be viewed more clearly. Turning to Christ, after all, implies a radical change of position.

Notes

1 Lesslie Newbigin, in Giles Ecclestone (ed.), *The Parish Church?*, Oxford: Mowbray, 1988, p. 28.

2 'For the first fact you must grasp is this: the renewal of creation has

been wrought by the self-same Word who made it in the beginning' (St Athanasius, *On the Incarnation*, London: Mowbray, 1982, p. 26).

3 As Colin Gunton puts it: '"God creates" means there is reality other than God. The next question is how the two relate' (in *Trinity, Time and Church*, Grand Rapids: Eerdmans, 2000, p. 80).

4 The doctrine of the incarnation means, Rowan Williams and Richard Bauckham attest, not that God became 'man', but 'God became *this* man' (in Christina Baxter (ed.), *Stepping Stones*, London: Hodder & Stoughton, 1987, p. 28).

5 Trevor Hart and Daniel Thimell (eds), *Christ in Our Place*, Exeter: Paternoster Press, 1989, p. 218.

6 Hart and Thimell (eds), *Christ in Our Place*, p. 218.

7 Hart and Thimell (eds), *Christ in Our Place*, p. 219.

8 I have expanded on this theme in *Beholding the Glory*, ed. Jeremy Begbie, London: DLT, 2000, ch. 3.

9 Wolfhart Pannenberg highlights the problem of developing Christology 'from the concept of the Incarnation instead of culminating in the assertion of the Incarnation as its concluding statement' (in *Jesus, God and Man*, London: SCM Press, 1968, p. 291).

10 Walter Brueggemann, *The Land*, London: SPCK, 1978, p. 185.

11 W. D. Davies, *The Gospel and the Land*, Berkeley: University of California Press, 1974, p. 5.

12 Davies, *The Gospel and the Land*, p. 366 (my italics).

13 Davies, *The Gospel and the Land*, p. 4. Thus of the early believers it could be written: 'Every foreign land is their native place, every native place is foreign' ('The Epistle to Diognetus' in H. Bettenson (ed.), *The Early Christian Fathers*, Oxford: OUP, 1956, p. 74).

14 Davies, *The Gospel and the Land*, p. 367.

15 Gunton, *Trinity, Time*, pp. 47–8. As evinced by, for example, the twentieth-century 'Christ and Culture' debate in the United States, following the classic typology of H. Richard Niebuhr.

16 T. F. Torrance, *Space, Time and Incarnation*, Oxford: OUP, p. 75 (my italics).

17 Lily Kong, 'Mapping "New" Geographies of Religion: Politics and Poetics in Modernity', *Progress in Human Geography*, 25, 211 (2001), p. 10.

18 The 'communication of properties' – a concept referring to the integration of Christ's human and divine natures.

19 Torrance, *Space, Time and Incarnation*, pp. 30, 41.

20 Dietrich Bonhoeffer, *Letters and Papers from Prison*, London: SCM Press, 1967, p. 196. On the significance of place in Luther's theology, see Jon MacKenzie, 'Luther's Topology: *Creation Ex Nihilo* and the Cultivation of the Concept of Place in Martin Luther's Theology', *Modern Theology*, 29, 2 (2013), pp. 83–103.

21 T. F. Torrance, *Transformation and Convergence*, Belfast: Christian Journals Limited, 1984, pp. 279ff. Cf. also Robert Jenson on the 'Excessive Separation of God and World in Reformed Christology' (in Gunton (ed.), *Trinity, Time*, p. 91).

22 P. T. Forsyth, *The Person and Place of Jesus Christ*, London: Hodder & Stoughton, 1909, p. 309. Resonating with Irenaus' assertion from the second century AD, that God 'must needs include all things in his infinite being' (in H. Bettenson (ed.), *The Early Christian Fathers*, Oxford: OUP, 1956, p. 90).

23 Colin Gunton, *Yesterday and Today: A Study of Continuities in Christology*, London: DLT, 1983, p. 54.

24 Gunton, *Yesterday and Today*, p. 114.

25 Gunton, *Yesterday and Today*, p. 202.

26 Karl Barth, *Church Dogmatics III.iii*, Edinburgh: T&T Clark, 1960, p. 430.

27 Barth, *Dogmatics III.iii*, p. 430.

28 Forsyth, *Person and Place*, p. 333.

29 As John Thompson writes of Barth's soteriology: 'Ontological and dynamic or functional are ... not just complementary terms, but embody twin aspects of the whole reality of the person and work of Christ' (in Hart and Thimell (eds), *Christ in Our Place*, Edinburgh: T&T Clark, 1960, p. 216).

30 Karl Barth, *The Doctrine of Reconciliation, Church Dogmatics IV.i*, Edinburgh: T&T Clark, 1960, p. 215.

31 Barth, *Dogmatics IV.i*, pp. 18ff.

32 John Thompson notes that Barth overcomes the above/below dichotomy in modern theology (in Hart and Thimell (eds), *Christ in Our Place*, p. 216).

33 Barth, *Dogmatics IV.i*, p. 259.

34 Barth, *Dogmatics IV.i*, p. 236.

35 Barth, *Dogmatics IV.i*, p. 16.

36 Richard Hooker, *Of the Laws of Ecclesiastical Polity*, 5.15.6, London: J. M. Dent, 1954, p. 221 (my italics).

37 Hooker, *Laws*, p. 222.

38 Hooker, *Laws*, p. 223 (my italics).

39 John Inge, *A Christian Theology of Place*, Aldershot: Ashgate, 2003, pp. 59–67. Cf. also John Macquarrie on 'Incarnation as the Root of the Sacramental Principle' (in David Brown and Ann Loades (eds), *Christ: The Sacramental Word*, London: SPCK, 1996, ch. 1).

40 Recalled by Teilhard de Chardin in *Hymn of the Universe*, New York: Harper & Row, 1961, p. 7.

41 de Chardin, *Hymn*, p. 17.

42 William Temple, *Nature, Man and God*, London: Macmillan, 1949, p. 478.

43 Temple, *Nature, Man and God*, p. 493.

44 Taking up the theme, John Habgood puts it thus: 'Once given, the sacramental principle can be extended to the whole of nature. Natural things can be clothed with new meaning by relating them to Christ' (in *Making Sense*, London: SPCK, 1993, p. 22). This is also affirmed in David Brown and Ann Loades (eds), *The Sense of the Sacramental*, London: SPCK, 1995, p. 21. David Brown, in *God and Enchantment of Place*, Oxford: OUP, 2004, sees this sacramental approach as a means of re-enchanting the whole of life.

45 Brown, *Enchantment*, p. 6. From a literary perspective, C. S. Lewis was concerned with a similar re-enchantment of the world in *The Discarded Image*. He remarks: 'The old (pre-modern) language continually suggests a sort of continuity between merely physical events and our most spiritual aspiration' (Cambridge: CUP, 1964, p. 94).

46 See Inge, *Place*, p. 67. Many theologians have shared this reservation, as Inge indicates (pp. 66ff).

47 Inge, *Place*, p. 81.

48 Inge, *Place*, p. 86. See also David Brown on the sacraments as the 'Place of Encounter' in *Enchantment*, ch. 2.

49 As Karl Rahner avers. See Gerald A. McCool (ed.), *A Rahner Reader*, London: DLT, 1975, p. 28. The Parish Communion movement is of particular significance in this respect and will be considered in the next chapter. For a good introduction and history, see Donald Gray, *Earth and Altar*, Norwich: Canterbury Press, 1986.

50 Jaroslav Pelikan concurs in *The Vindication of Tradition*, New Haven: Yale University Press, 1984, ch. 4.

51 Yves Congar, *The Meaning of Tradition*, New York: Hawthorn Books, 1964, p. 17.

52 Congar, *Meaning of Tradition*, p. 64.

53 Summarizing Bonhoeffer's theology, Bethge asserts that 'concreteness is the attribute of revelation' (in R. Gregor Smith (ed.), *World Come of Age*, London: Collins, 1967, pp. 33ff).

54 In a 1931 letter to Bethge, he writes of 'this absurd, perpetual being thrown back on the invisible God' (in Eberhard Bethge, *Dietrich Bonhoeffer*, London: Collins, 1977, p. 129).

55 Dietrich Bonhoeffer, *Creation and Fall*, New York: Macmillan, 1959, p. 23.

56 Dietrich Bonhoeffer, *Act and Being*, London: Collins, 1962, p. 90.

57 Dietrich Bonhoeffer, *Christology*, London: Fontana, 1971, p. 61.

58 Bonhoeffer, *Christology*, p. 61.

59 Dietrich Bonhoeffer, *Ethics*, London: SCM Press, 1964, p. 197.

60 Bonhoeffer, *Christology*, p. 63.

61 Dietrich Bonhoeffer, *Sanctorum Communio*, London: Collins, 1963, p. 197. See Dietrich Bonhoeffer, *Life Together*, London: SCM Press,

1954, p. 13: 'Christianity means community through and in Jesus Christ'.

62 Thus 'the being of revelation "is" the being of the community of persons, constituted and embraced by the person of Christ, wherein the individual finds himself to be already in his new existence' (Bonhoeffer, *Act and Being*, p. 123).

63 Bonhoeffer, *Act and Being*, p. 6.

64 Bonhoeffer, *Ethics*, p. 202.

65 Bonhoeffer, *Sanctorum Communio*, p. 146.

66 Bonhoeffer, *Ethics*, p. 155.

67 Indeed, as the Church all but disappears into shadow in Bonhoeffer's final musings on 'religionless Christianity', it is this that saves his Christology from syncretism – a point made by Regin Prentor in Gregor Smith (ed.), *World Come of Age*, pp. 178ff.

68 Barth, *Dogmatics III.iii*, p. 515 (my italics).

69 F. D. Maurice, *Theological Essays*, London: James Clarke & Co., 1956, pp. 276–7.

70 Colin Gunton, *Christ and Creation*, Carlisle: Paternoster Press, 1992, p. 102.

71 T. F. Torrance, *Space, Time and Resurrection*, Edinburgh: Handsel Press, 1976, p. 133.

72 Torrance, *Resurrection*, p. 135. Cf. also Gunton, *Christ and Creation*, pp. 94ff.

73 Torrance, *Resurrection*, p. 129 (my italics).

74 Torrance, *Resurrection*, p. 135.

75 Colin Gunton, *The Promise of Trinitarian Theology*, Edinburgh: T&T Clark, 1997, p. 203.

76 Colin Gunton, *The One, the Three and the Many*, Cambridge: CUP, 1993, p. 189.

77 *We Believe in the Holy Spirit*, London: CHP, 1991, p. 148.

78 Sabina Lovibond, *Realism and Imagination in Ethics*, Minneapolis: University of Minnesota Press, 1983, pp. 210–19. Gunton refers to her work in *The One, the Three and the Many*.

79 Inge, *Place*, p. 90.

80 R. S. Thomas, Introduction to *A Choice of George Herbert's Verse*, London: Faber, 1967, p. 15.

3

Sheer Geography: Spatial Theory and Parochial Practice

We arose to snow: a great creaking carpet laid over yesterday's green and grey streetscape. So, unknown neighbours are out, working to the bark and spark of spade on driveway, rallying like a curling team to assist the antic, skimming motorists. A man I have never met before (or since) grins over the gate: 'Hilarious, isn't it? The snow gives us that sense of belonging together', he said, '… which we crave', he adds, before trudging up the hill. It's the 'which we crave' that stays with me – he probably knows I'm the vicar, but it was quite far to go, for a momentary exchange. Extreme conditions build neighbourhood, little doubt about that. We behave differently when deluged: familiar territory is transfigured, new routes are taken: the myth of independence thawing instantly. Different place: different rules.

According to American sociologist Erving Goffman, prevailing norms of local behaviour tend to be suspended at times of 'crisis' and 'festival'. Parish priests, it strikes me, spend a fair proportion of their time inhabiting these contrasting states – explaining, perhaps, the curious permission we retain to act in public as if it was always snowing. That, in one sense, is the vocation of the local church: to live as if, in Christ, normal service has been permanently suspended. The old has gone: the new has come.

It being Advent, this symbolic blizzard – unifying crisis and festival – will be in the air whether or not the real stuff melts by morning. December deals in belonging, after all: shovels it on in deep, muffling drifts. We become attuned to our displacement with every keening carol, each cultural sign directing us homeward. Snow on snow. And though a cold coming for so many, the path to Christmas is the right one for rearranging our ideas of society. Here along the Surrey Hills – 'the place where London ends and England can begin' in G. K. Chesterton's somewhat miscarried phrase – we have, for several years, engaged in a kind of festive psycho-geography called the Oxted Adventure. Every night in Advent, for an hour in the evening, one small space (a garage, perhaps, or porch) opens its doors like a calendar to a gathering of locals. On some nights there is live music, or a seasonal story; on most, there is the familiar, indigestive blend of warm wine and mincemeat. The Adventure aims to be a journey home by another route, a parish map in the making. This year the North Downs are appealingly portrayed in Tolkienesque style: Middle England as Middle Earth.

It's the opening night, but I'm delayed in another small space: a recess in the wall of the boiler house behind Morrisons supermarket. Here abides Simon – a man become, in the psalmist's words, a monster unto many. A kind of local portent or parable, Simon made and lost a fortune developing the sizeable homes that decorate the A25, just yards away. Beside an acrid barbecue, attended by Magi firefighters, he now raves in the car park, *para oikos*.

'You do not believe, because you do not belong to my flock', Jesus chides the Pharisees, inverting the usual criteria for religious community. Believing in belonging is an attractive idea, perpetually frustrated by our desire that the world should belong to us (for 'belongings'), rather than to the Lord, thereby finding our place as the people of his pasture. However, if creation is defined not by an almighty accumulation, but a kind of divine allowance, stepping back to make space for another, then let it snow, let it snow.

Some years ago, Simon Jenkins in the London *Evening Standard* paid tribute to parish priest and theologian Kenneth Leech on spending 40 years in ministry in the East End of the city. His column included the following observation: 'The doctors, teachers, social workers and police who work here commute from more salubrious parts. But the priests stay. They stay even when their flock is 70 per cent Muslim. *They seem wedded to sheer geography.*'[1] It was an arresting comment, and one that proved to be an inspiration for this research. But are parish priests wedded to 'sheer geography' – and, if so, to what end? The Anglican covenant with place is so instinctive, so *given*, that an answer is surprisingly hard to articulate. My Edwardian grandfather settled in one parish at the commencement of his ministry and simply stayed put: without, one suspects, dwelling for too long on why or how his ministry was thus rooted. Partly, of course, it had to be: life for the majority of people was by necessity settled – often intolerably so. Partly, too, because secular Christianity was still so tightly stitched into the social fabric that pulling apart the threads would have been fruitless and counterintuitive. If pressed, his response would doubtless have been pastoral: that closeness to his flock was his calling, after the pattern of the good shepherd.

The fact that the parish system underwrites this commitment to all English places and people, whatever their beliefs, commonly remains the first reason given by those supporting its continuing value. Quite often, however, the case for the parish's defence rests there, leaving it vulnerable to the counter-argument that if some other, more contemporary, version of local arrangement could be found, then that might serve rather better. Successive attempts to do just this over the last 50 or so years – Paul (1963) and Tiller (1983) Reports in particular – have, despite their achievements, faltered at the point of delivering alternate descriptions of locality. This, I suggest, is not due simply to a lack of resource or enterprise on the part of the Church, or the inevitable tendency of written reports to remain shelf-bound, but to the soulless task of attempting to introduce new forms of place that are devoid of any cultural meaning. Each attempt to transcend or replace the parish (and the legacy this word carries) faces this Sisyphean challenge.

Parish is tenacious, partly because – like the mythical bobby on the beat – it is people-scaled, and thereby a popular ideal, especially so in communities that are (or aspire to be) rooted. Yet here the Church struggles with the paradox of a society that longs for roots while simultaneously denying them: an inevitable consequence of rapid and unsettling cultural change. In this climate, the norms of even the very recent past appear anachronistic and impossibly remote, so that social institutions tend to be assessed on the basis of their current utility or popularity alone. The Church's trailing tail of tradition is especially prone to being cut short as this door to the past is closed, prompting the kind of painful spiritual disconnection to be analysed in the final chapter. In this climate, an innate, inherited localism is insufficient to secure a viable future for the parish system, which will swiftly unravel if defended by mere custom or muscle memory. To understand, and contend for, parish ministry requires a grasp not only of the Church's genius for place, but also of place's genius for absorbing and embodying belief.

For better and for worse, English place is steeped in Christianity – almost every other street signs a saint. However offensive to the contemporary mind, it is vital to recognize that, to his followers, Jesus Christ is the aperture through which the world is entered afresh: the gateway to everywhere. This was, for centuries, the given basis of Western culture and art: in particular, our developing understanding of the physical landscape, which grew from the sense of wonder that, in Kenneth Clark's words, 'we are surrounded by things which we have not made'.[2] This general sense or 'spirit' of place in art – the idea of a visionary, God-haunted landscape, was directly (though not exclusively) refined by a Christian vision of divine ground. No tree in a woodland scene, for example, could be viewed other than, to some degree, a cross (or, indeed, *through* the cross), so powerful was the metaphor of dead into living wood.[3]

Notwithstanding the fact that most today would find such a conclusion incredible, in a Christian society Jesus Christ is not only the clue to history (as the philosopher John Macmurray described him): he is also the clue to geography. If the leap from his particularity – merely one man, at one place and one time – to this universal role as the very genius of place feels unsupportable, inconceivable even, the first step is encouraged by recognizing that Christ *has* been so, demonstrably, for the majority of our civilization's history. England was, until quite recently, considered to be a kind of Jerusalem.

The Church tends to be better at speaking about this in the abstract than in the concrete setting – in other words, quite ready to confess Christ as the one 'in whom all things hold together' – but less ready, perhaps, to explain how he may be the one in whom Crewe or Crowhurst hold together. While the Christological links have rarely been made explicit, the Anglican parish is clearly a fundamental way of seeing not just place, but 'Christ in our place'. In him – so the New Testament suggests – place becomes open to God in a new way, released from its 'bondage to decay', as St Paul writes to the Romans. By the agency of the Holy Spirit, the possibility of this 'new place' is extended to all people and situations, in order that they may be signs of Christ's coming and heavenly kingdom. But to 'see' this place theologically, we also have to 'see' it geographically: parish, as a geographical concept, can never be properly valued in Christological terms until spatial terms are also recognized and employed. This chapter will, accordingly, proceed to identify several insights of contemporary human geography that can aid this perception, before presenting the parish as a specific type of spatial praxis: that of 'common ground'.

The spatial construction of reality

The last 50 years have seen a transformation in the relationship between social and spatial theory. Perhaps the principal development has been an increasing measure of collaboration between the formerly estranged disciplines of geography and sociology: a tendency that reached its zenith in the 1960s, when geography became viewed as (in Doreen Massey's words) the 'science of the spatial', operating by virtue of its own fixed laws and causalities.[4] In part, the isolation of geography may be seen as a reaction against the historicism that was such a dominant feature of the modern era. Time, as Foucault observed, was modernity's 'great obsession': the era when, in myriad ways – steam travel; imperial expansion; a fixation with the myth of progress – the clock conquered the map. Space, perceived as a static commodity, was something to contain and overcome; time, by contrast, was dynamic, the engine of social development and advance.

By the second half of the twentieth century this general tendency, which affected all academic disciplines (including, as we saw in the previous chapter, systematic theology), was hard to sustain. The idea that, as Karl Popper put it in *The Poverty of Historicism*, 'social science is nothing but history' itself became consigned to the past, and space, not time, emerged as the grand cause of the postmodern worldview. The point of interest here is that the reassertion of space in social theory meant an increasing recognition that, as Henri Lefebvre remarked in his pioneering work *The Production of Space*, 'Social relations ... have no real existence save in and through space.'[5] Crucially, not only is space seen to be a social construct, subject to the ever-changing ways in which we imagine our environment, but also society is found to be *spatially* constructed: an insight that grounds social theory in the actualities of local life.[6]

Thus understood, places are not 'passive', but actively generated by the routines and practices of purposeful human agency, as Anthony Giddens has argued.[7] Giddens's influential theory of 'structuration' highlights 'structuring properties' that bind together spatial practices to form social systems or common ways of life. These comprise not only political, economic and legal constraints and influences upon human action, but also what he calls 'symbolic orders': the more implicit structures of meaning – the parochial ideal, for example – that govern social conduct. Although Giddens's stress on the reciprocal, 'dual' nature of social systems is extremely helpful (essentially, that our concepts of place generate local action, while local action, in return, shapes our concepts of place), his analysis is so systematic that it can be hard to translate in more than a general way to the peculiarities of different locations and social groups.[8]

For the renowned geographer Doreen Massey, this rigidity is one of the features of the whole movement of structuralism which, although acknowledged to be one of the most significant contributory factors in the revival of space in twentieth-century social theory, inadvertently denigrated space (especially in the work of Henri Bergson) by over-associating it with *representation* – through which, critically, it (that is, space) was deprived of dynamism, and radically counterposed to time.[9] The dynamism of space is a guiding theme for Massey's work, and the central contention of her 2005 study *For Space*. Three central features underlie this view: that space, first, is constituted by *interrelations* and *interactions*, 'from the immensity of the global to the intimately tiny'; second, that space is inherently open to multiple possibilities – indeed, it defines the sphere of 'contemporaneous plurality'. Because of this, Massey concludes, third, space is always being reproduced, ever 'under construction'. As she expresses it: 'It is never finished; never closed. Perhaps we could imagine space as a simultaneity of stories-so-far.'[10]

The dominance of fixed notions of space has, for Massey, enabled it to be pressed into the service of political ideology: viewed as a commodity, ripe for conquest and containment. This, she argues, is to radically misrepresent space, which always evades capture and representation by its very fluidity. There is a great deal in Massey's approach that is both illuminating and refreshing for an understanding of the parish, not least its emphasis on the transformational nature of local practice. Nevertheless, the question needs to be raised as to whether she pushes her point too far. For Massey, space is a river, ever slipping beyond one's grasp, never the same when one returns to it, never, one might say, 'ours'.[11] The danger of this position is of space never being truly or fully *personal* – the opposite of her intention, ironically, which is to liberate space from domination so that it may become the context for free human relatedness. Her ambivalence towards spatial boundaries is really an extension of this, when to be bounded (it will be argued) is a precondition of being personal, being incarnate.

The practice of everyday space

In seeking to do justice to place, therefore, contemporary spatial theory pursues a route through static, 'structured' interpretations of society and the more dynamic, 'fluid' concepts characteristic of postmodernity. This is a tension felt keenly in current debate about the future of the parish system, where the latter's perceived fixity is often compared to freer networks of association that characterize new forms of church. For geographers and social theorists exploring this theme, an important tool has been the analysis of 'ordinary' patterns of action and interaction – what Pierre Bourdieu called the 'habitus'[12] of personal routines and preferences that govern rhythms of everyday behaviour.[13] Ordinary ways of life, such as where we choose to shop, or the localities we might avoid or gravitate towards, all conspire to produce a particular quality of place that would be otherwise, had we made an alternative range of choices.

Of particular interest to parochial theology are considerations of everyday life that adjust the focus on to micro-level aspects of local social behaviour – the plain fact, as Erving Goffman put it, 'that there are people out there moving about'.[14] In his influential work *The Practice of Everyday Life*, Michel de Certeau has written powerfully of the way in which everyday spatial practices such as walking or eating create social narratives. Likewise, he explains, a culture's stories are inherently spatial, serving to circumscribe the 'theatre of actions' defining cultural boundaries.[15] Such frontiers abound in the stories of Jesus wherein countless significant, though everyday, practices (breaking of bread, washing, journeying) become transforming signs of the kingdom of God. More often than not, these practices radically challenge accepted local norms (concerning ritual cleanliness, for example) to include those people who found themselves marginalized according to material parameters of religious and cultural tradition.[16]

Geography thus directs our attention towards what French thinker Georges Perec calls the 'infra-ordinary': those actions often overlooked by virtue of their sheer normality. In this vein, Erving Goffman's series of popular 'micro-studies' of human community are of great interest. By their finely focused attention – for example, on bodily posture when two people meet in the street, or one opens a door for another – his work interprets the minutiae of coded behaviour that influence local encounters. In *Relations in Public*, Goffman describes the 'territories of the self' – the spatial protocols that, by unspoken consent, mark out human interactions. He identifies, for example, the 'use space' – the room that a person requires in front of them – and the 'stall' – 'the well-bounded space to which individuals can lay claim to',[17] such as the chair, parking space or, it might be added, pew.

Where Goffman's (not uncontested) theories and classifications are of special interest here is in analysing the rules and norms that govern everyday human interaction. He suggests that normal conditions may be suspended in times of what he calls *crisis* and *festival* – scenarios familiar to all who, for example, have noticed the remarkable outbreak of cordial conversation with strangers that often accompanies extreme weather in England. Where what Goffman calls 'normal appearances' are violated, certain coded 'alarm signals' are given off, such as the responses in a supermarket queue (quiet huffing, looking around[18]) when someone pushes to the front.

All of which is extremely helpful in decoding and making visible the often elusive quality of social life that might be deemed 'parochial' – for example, the habitual encounters and greetings on familiar routes to work; the motivations to adventurous love and neighbourliness that prompt a disruption in these routines. Curiously enough in a secular age, parish priests – as key signifiers of 'parochial' behaviour – often retain a *carte blanche* to act as if normal appearances were permanently suspended – being hailed by strangers; permitted to call in to people's homes. In such ways, parish ministry retains (though by no means everywhere) vestiges of the old idea of the 'parson': the personification of otherwise disembodied ideas and associations. As William Blackstone expressed it in his *Commentaries on the Laws of England* (1765): 'He is called parson, *persona*, because by his person the church, which is an invisible body, is represented; and he is in himself a body corporate.'[19]

Especially when adorned with clerical collar, the parish priest is by definition approachable. If he or she were to respond to the myriad 'neighbourly' approaches from parishioners in an aggressive or ignorant manner, 'alarm signals' denoting the breaking of an unspoken social contract would be quick to follow. For better or for worse, the priest embodies the neighbourly ethics of the parish – they are expected to act, as it were, 'parochially'. The fact that social norms are, in such ways, locally and historically conditioned – and may be suspended under certain conditions – proves that, to employ Doreen Massey's maxim for places, 'they might be otherwise': a fact of crucial importance in the framing of parochial space. The challenge to the parish church is thus to play a distinctive part in framing and changing the norms that govern human interaction; to use micro-space as a means of growing Christian neighbourhood.

The geography of home

Potent association with nostalgic conceptions of place requires pastoral space to encompass also the private, 'interior' geographies influencing broader patterns of settlement and interaction. While 'geography tends to stop at the garden gate', as David Sibley put it,[20] the domestic landscape is by no means sealed off from these. Noting how homes, for example, can be as much places of exclusion and conflict as of belonging, Sibley explains: 'Living with others confronts us with the possibility, or not, of being an "other". It is not simply ... a matter of being able to accept the other, but of being in his place, and this means to imagine and make oneself other in his place.'[21] Thus the psychological and emotional need for 'belonging' and 'home' also comes to the fore in more aesthetic considerations of space and place – in which vein, de Certeau writes: 'Places are fragmentary and inward-turning histories, pasts that others are not allowed to read ... symbolizations encysted in the pain or pleasure of the body. "I feel good here": the well-being under-expressed in the language it appears in like a fleeting glimmer is a spatial practice.'[22]

In his study *A Place to Be*, Paul Tournier has considered the links between psychology and need for place in the formation of human identity. He presses that mental and spiritual *displacement* or dysfunction cannot be abstracted from the actual spatio-temporal context in which that condition is experienced. According to Tournier, 'Deprivation of love and deprivation of place overlap' – that is, secure roots in the psyche relate directly to security in locale. He cites the childhood home as illustrative here; the security of womb, cot, room and home nurtures the child's growing ability to deal with life.[23] Taking up this theme, in her 1999 study *Geography of Home*, Akiko Busch highlights 'return migration', the social-scientific term for the tendency of the 'baby-boom' generation to return from major urban areas to the smaller hometowns in which they were raised,[24] a trend in which, empirical evidence suggests, nostalgia plays an active and motivating role. There is, Busch concludes: 'a host of ... *interior systems,* a network of social and cultural currents, those habits, beliefs and values that also make it (the home) function ... it is by being attuned to these systems that we might arrive at some genuine understanding of what it is that gives power to the places where we live'.[25]

'Private' interior landscapes, therefore, spill out into the 'public' spatial patterns and social encounters that map the wider community, just as the latter currents flow directly into the home. Parish ministry patrols this threshold between home and community. While explicitly communal aspirations such as those prompting a Christening request are more obviously 'parochial' in their linking of personal and affective attachments to traditional modes of belonging, there is an equally close interplay of kinship, nostalgic desire ('the longing to belong') and bounded, territorial attachment in, for example, the spatial praxis of urban gangs, as recent studies have made abundantly clear.[26] Affective parochialism – the desire for personal 'settlement' – is not, it must be stressed, unique to rooted or 'traditional' communities: indeed, it may more accurately be seen as a powerful and universal motive for myriad forms of local behaviour.

Place as an imaginative construct

If, following Lefebvre, each society 'produces a space, its own space',[27] and if, furthermore, the resulting social space has a plasticity deriving from the interplay of culture and location, it follows that place is profoundly *ideological*: an imaginative concept as much as a physical practice.[28] Hence the traditional geographical preoccupation with cartography which, from the *Mappa Mundi* onwards – 'a Christian metaphor in which time and space are indivisible'[29] – has revealed maps to be culturally conditioned expressions and impressions of space. While in the modern era maps began as mere symbolic representations of space, useless for any kind of navigation, they developed not only into representations of space as it 'was', but *prescriptions* of space, as it 'ought to be'. Thai historian Thongchai Winichakul expresses it thus: 'A map anticipated spatial reality, not vice versa. In other words a map was a model *for*, rather than a model *of*, what it purported to represent. It had become a real instrument to concretize projections on the earth's surface.'[30]

In his seminal study on nationalism, *Imagined Communities*, Benedict Anderson presses that such bounded 'imaginings' (particularly the perceived bonds of kinship and affinity within and between cultures) were and remain determinative of geopolitical shifts in conflict and alignment: 'All communities', he asserts, 'are to be distinguished ... by the style in which they are imagined.'[31]

That the place practised is a function of the place conceived is a central claim of this book, strongly evident in the English context. But how is imagination translated into action? Lefebvre writes that the construction of social space involves a triad of relations: *spatial practice*, in particular locations; *representations of space* – the symbolic 'ordering' of these practices (a mix of 'ideology' and 'understanding' Lefebvre suggests, epitomized by the work of architects and planners);[32] and *representational spaces*: the lived intersection of the former two, 'overlaying' physical space and sustained by 'more or less coherent systems of non-verbal symbols and signs'.[33] The parish, it is suggested, involves the integration of all three – practice, imagined concept, and their intentional, lived integration. Taking up Anderson's point above, the lengthy historical process of systematizing and *mapping* the parish – in particular the imposition on the landscape of borders and boundary lines – may thus be seen as an imaginative exercise, circumscribing local praxis and impelling it in a specific cultural direction. Such mapping, it should be added, must be constantly *re*imagined if it is to be socially constitutive – maps do not hold space 'still' in time, they merely represent and condition the ongoing situation of relationships.

The social formation of landscape

Cartography captures the basic interrelation of human society and physical topography – a fundamental task of geography, described by one practitioner as 'the art of not dividing what nature brings together'.[34] The recognition of this symbiosis provides an important corrective to what Carl Sauer saw as the anthropocentrism of much geographical analysis, which tended only to highlight those elements of physical space that were 'of use' to human society – what he calls its 'habitat value'.[35] However, he insists: 'One has not fully understood the nature of an area unless one comprehends land and life in terms of each other.'[36]

Writing from an anthropological perspective, Eric Hirsch records the way in which landscape has long been a mere 'framing convention' in anthropology and argues that it must instead be both the foreground and background to social life. He distinguishes between two forms of landscape: the one initially perceived, and a second produced through local practice. This production of landscape, he contends, involves a relationship between 'everyday lived experience' and the 'ideal, imagined existence'.[37] Far from being the mere 'stage' or 'scenery' on which the human drama is played out, territory is, therefore, increasingly portrayed as dynamically involved in the performance, as the groundbreaking work of geographers Denis Cosgrove and Robert Sack has demonstrated.[38] Central to Cosgrove's thesis in his seminal work *Social Formation and the Symbolic Landscape* is the contention that landscape is a – uniquely European – 'way of seeing' the natural world and the human relationship to it: 'the external world mediated through subjective human experience'.[39] Being a social construction as much as a physical reality, the land emerges as a principal medium through which human expressions of meaning in narrative, myth and memory are framed.[40] 'It is in land', Cosgrove asserts, 'that perhaps the most deeply rooted myths are to be discovered. Indeed, the most powerful of these concern rootedness, ideas of home and belonging.'[41] Charting its seventeenth-century origins in art as 'landskip', the framed portion of land that forms a fitting scene for depiction, Cosgrove describes how the emergence of landscape as an artistic idea 'had the effect of making the countryside a picture'.[42] The idea of the 'picturesque' that arose in eighteenth-century art – typified by the 'Claude-glass', the small, mirrored device employed to depict the landscape, literally with one's back to it – not only introduced an artificial separation between human subjects and their landscape, but became associated with a particular view of 'landed' society, which has been subject to much criticism.[43]

In portraying landscape as, in essence, a social construct, Cosgrove arguably weakens an appreciation of the reciprocal ways in which society is, in turn, a terrestrial construction – a common shortcoming in the resurgent interest in landscape studies and one that risks perpetuating the old idea of human civilization as in effect 'the conquest of nature'.[44] Nevertheless, his case that the natural world is the perpetual partner for narratives of human identity is of great relevance to this study, as will be seen in the concluding chapter. If 'culture' is, on one level, what human practice makes of the earth,[45] more than one thousand years of parochial life amounts to a unique cultural inscription into the landscape.[46]

The ethics of territoriality

The contemporary focus in geography has thus moved away from seeing space as a blank canvas for the temporal portrayal of human society and towards its conception as something dynamic and malleable, more akin to sculptor's clay. As such, spatial practices have profound political, ethical and ecological consequences, which practical theologians increasingly recognize.[47] Within a 'vocational' theology of place, these may be seen as revealing or concealing the particular local calling of the Anglican parish, which is a geographical compound of territory, deeply traditioned 'idea' and committed social-ethical praxis.

The conviction that place may be 'shaped' according to vocation is, Walter Brueggemann insists, central to the Christian narrative. In an essay for the inter-disciplinary collection *Rooted in the Land*, he writes that the covenantal nature of Israel's relationship with the land enabled God's people to believe 'that this land of promise, distorted by exploitative social relationships, could be transformed'. He continues:

> This remarkable faith-claim has been decisive for Western culture. The place is not fated: it can be brought into an alternative destiny by the intentionality of the new vision-driven inhabitants. The land as a social reality ... takes on a different quality depending on the attitude, conduct and policies of its inhabitants.[48]

The dynamic integrity of spatial practice, social structure and the symbolic landscape brings into sharp relief the political and ethical potency of place. Thus understood, 'everyday life' is revealed not as something passive, predictable or theologically irrelevant, but subject to myriad political, moral and 'structural' forces. Crucially, also, it is shown to be the very sphere in which those forces may be resisted and reframed. Indeed, this conviction may be seen as the motive force behind the entire left-liberal narrative that has driven the reassertion of space in social science since the 1960s, a very definite and partial account

of political space that Doreen Massey to some extent acknowledges.[49] But the insights of the 'spatial turn' considered above
are not the intellectual property of any one cultural narrative: what is useful in analysing the means of production can
be equally valuable in decoding spatial practice in explicitly
Christian terms. Thus, the Church can learn directly from, for
example, the French Situationist movement of the 1950s (and its
derivatives in contemporary psychogeography),[50] in which the
pedestrian activity of walking through the city was transformed
– via the character of the 'flaneur' – into a revolutionary act,
through refusing to follow the accepted paths and attending to
the forgotten or demonized places. This is radical potential of
place: equally, as the next half of this chapter considers, it is the
theological potential of the parish.

The parish as a spatial ethic

If, in the Protestant tradition, Christ is the mediator of a new
place, in which created space-time is 'called back' to God – and if
this universal mediation is particularized by the Holy Spirit in all
places and times – then the dynamics of spatial practice outlined
above are of the greatest interest for the Church. If, furthermore,
the Anglican parish can be viewed as a particular cultural expression of 'Christ in our place', what may be the distinctive nature
and quality of 'parochial space'? In the second half of this chapter,
this question will begin to be answered by integrating the foregoing with an ecclesiological approach that takes seriously the
social space of the Church. Specifically, it will be proposed that
the parish not only represents a definite tradition of social ethics,
but – to adapt Stanley Hauerwas's ecclesiological phrase – that
it *is* a social (or, more accurately, *spatial*) ethic.[51] The distinction is an important one, because while its legal or constitutional
character may lend it a certain more or less recognizable frame,
this is secondary to the primary existence of the parish as a 'way
of life', its form sustained only by certain traditions of spatial
praxis emerging from a distinct theological purpose.

While associated with a brand of radical North American theology that might appear to stand at odds to the 'Christendom' model of the English parish, linked as it is to the nation state, Stanley Hauerwas emerges as a most useful interlocutor when attempting to understand its peculiar communal form. This is principally because of his concern to re-frame ecclesiological practice within what Stephen Toulmin calls 'the particular, concrete, timely and local details of everyday human affairs' – as opposed to the level of 'abstract, timeless, general and universal theories'[52] that dominated ethics after Kant. Accepting that, in Thomas Nagel's phrase, there is no 'view from nowhere', Hauerwas argues that, equally, there is no 'ethics for anyone'[53] and seeks to challenge modernity's tendency to universalize by portraying the Church as an alternative tradition, whose distinctive praxis can only be understood when lived as part of a localized community. The Christian narrative, he writes, 'is not primarily a set of propositions to be believed, but is rather the medium in which one moves, a set of skills that one employs in living one's life'.[54]

In *The Nichomachean Ethics*, Aristotle indicated that moral virtue 'comes about as a result of habit [*ethos*]', and that, therefore, 'legislators make the citizens good by forming habits in them'.[55] The cultivation of virtue thus requires an ongoing work of society, guided by a narrative tradition and the kind of community that is able to locate and sustain it. It is the development of such 'skills for living' that, for Hauerwas, binds Christian ethical formation to the communal, especially liturgical, life of the Church. While the Christian congregation is clearly not the focus of this book, the border between 'Church' and 'parish' is of real significance, particularly when the former is viewed (in Bonhoeffer's terms) as the place on earth where testimony is given to the reconciliation of all places in Christ.[56]

But what does it mean for the local church to 'be' a social ethic? Simply put, it means to be a community formed by the story of Jesus. For, as Hauerwas writes in *A Community of Character*: 'Jesus is, in his person and his work, a social ethic.'[57] Pursuing one will necessarily involve pursuing the other – hence the folly of trying to detach 'Christ' from 'culture' in academic theology. Being a social ethic finds the Church to be a producer of local culture, through its cultivation of virtue and distinctively Christian ways of life. For Hauerwas, this communal vocation is realized, above all, in worship – specifically, eucharistic worship, which acts as the heart of the body of Christ, impelling its moral and social circulation.

This approach – which defines ethics as 'informed prayer'[58] – has been amplified by Samuel Wells, whose work goes a long way towards rooting Hauerwas's approach in the Anglican context. Responding to criticisms that Hauerwas's ecclesiology is a 'fantasy', Wells contends that eucharistic liturgy 'trains Christians in the moral imagination',[59] citing numerous examples of how it does so. The simple habit of 'sharing peace' before Communion, for example, 'develops in the congregation ... the virtues of mercy and forbearance ... patience and courage, which help them to try once more with challenging relationships and risk rejection by trying to reconcile'.[60] This sacramental shape to Christian social ethics is further explored when Wells develops the notion of the Church as 'God's companions' who, by eating together, learn how to relate and so form a distinctive moral community. The Eucharist, he writes, 'makes the church visible' and 'is the key to locating the church in relation to the whole of creation'.[61] Baptism thus marks the boundary between old and new 'place', signifying: 'The passing over from a narrative bounded by birth and death to a narrative bounded by creation and eschaton.'[62]

By grounding it in local practice, Wells does much to refute the common charge that Hauerwas's ecclesiological ethic is idealistic.[63] His work in this respect is strongly resonant of the Parish Communion Movement of the mid-twentieth century, which looked to the re-creation of English social life through the Eucharist. With striking similarity to Hauerwas and Wells, the movement's architect, A. G. Hebert, wrote in the 1930s of worship 'moulding' people in community, rather than simply laying down a 'rule of ethics'.[64] Central to this local formation was the ideal that 'All those who live in one place should eat and drink together before God.'[65] Hebert was, of course, addressing a

'Christian England' in which the baptismal boundary was nothing like as conspicuous as it is in most parishes today. Hauerwas and Wells take up the Parish Communion ideal, but the challenge remains how it may be reconceived among a largely unbaptized populace without lapsing into a kind of sectarianism. Nicholas Healy, in reaction against what he sees as the 'blueprint' ecclesiologies of the modern era, which typically identified 'models' of church to be universally applied, has warned against viewing the Church as an 'independent society'. The Church, he writes: 'May be a society in the minimal sense that it is a group of people who share a distinctive goal, but ... [they] live out much of their lives within a society that is not Christian ... and they are influenced by their society at least as much as they influence their society as Christians.'[66] Though sharing much in common with Hauerwas in his desire for a 'concrete' ecclesiology, Healy is concerned that he downplays the extent to which this is formed through engagement with the non-church world. Maintaining that the 'character' of a congregation is particular to its cultural setting, Healy suggests that a process of ecclesiological ethnography might be applied in each parish, to tease out the points at which that character has been shaped in this symbiotic relationship between church and place.

Can a church established in law, whose local and national forms are closely allied to secular authority, be a truly distinctive social ethic? In a significant paper directly addressing the English parochial context, Hauerwas has written favourably of the parish as a 'form of resistance' to the 'false universals' of secular power, while maintaining his opposition to 'Constantinian' models of church. [67] To do so, he admits, 'takes some explaining', which he does by stressing the 'priority of the local' for the Church, whose catholicity does not smother local particularity (as modernity tended to), but is rather defined by it.[68] Parish churches can therefore critique the prevailing social narrative by telling a more accurate story about the places in which they are set. While acknowledging here the close identification between Anglicanism and territory, Hauerwas to a certain extent overlooks the fact that nations, being another form of locality, are just as particular as parishes. Viewing the kingdom of heaven as 'God's International', Hauerwas rarely acknowledges this potential. Because his critical horizon is fixed at the Enlightenment, he risks an unfocused view upon conceptions of nationhood that demand, at least, a more nuanced appreciation of the historic relationship with Christian faith – a theme that will be returned to in the next chapter.

The main target of Hauerwas's opposition, however, is not nations as such, but their perceived captivity of the Church – and, undoubtedly, the question of where to place the boundary between 'church' and 'world' is one of the most salient points his work raises for parish ministry. In the Anglican setting, 'church', in ministry of word and sacrament, establishes a Christian 'centre' through which the *whole* life of a place is offered to God and, in turn, God's life for that place is received. The tension for any local church, however, is that the Christ in whom this priestly movement is made 'stands at once at the centre and the boundaries of our existence', as Bonhoeffer wrote. While at heart this is a question of Christology, it is also, importantly, one of *holiness*: a key biblical term for unlocking the distinctive social ethic of God's people.

Negotiating the perimeter of holiness, it may be attested, is about perception as much as practice; vitally, in the teaching of Jesus, it is about 'seeing' oneself as a neighbour. Typically in the Anglican context, the congregational boundary is more feintly drawn than that of the parish, thereby highlighting a specific 'neighbourhood' in which holiness may be practised in relation to others.[69] For St Augustine, love of neighbour acted as a bridge between earthly and heavenly cities, relating these two realms across their eschatological boundary. Peace between them, he writes, may be 'viewed': 'in every good action it [i.e. the heavenly city] performs in relation to God, and in relation to neighbour, since the life of a city is inevitably a social life'.[70]

The British ethicist and theologian Oliver O'Donovan, whose work often stands in critical relation to that of Hauerwas, draws out Augustine's social ethic, focusing on the latter's assertion that community is shaped and defined by its 'common objects of love'. For Augustine, the 'character' of a particular people could be observed by examining whatever it loves – and, conversely, those things it chooses not to love.[71] Significantly, O'Donovan's focus here is upon the love that reaches beyond the community towards external 'goods', rather than the reciprocal love of members for one another. In the Augustinian schema, the two greatest social objects of love are God and neighbour, which together comprise the common life of the Church. The social ethic generated in worship must equally, then, be a *spatial* ethic, produced through adventurous love for the 'other' – a universal command that only becomes particular when placed within a 'neighbourhood' of proximate relations that allows for peaceable encounter with those who differ from us.

Neighbourhood is a complex space, however – and becomes ever more so as local ethics diversify. Addressing this theme, John Reader has employed sociologist Ulrich Beck's term 'zombie categories' to denote those practices that are still enacted by the Church, but that have long since ceased to live for the wider society. In particular, he pinpoints the danger of maintaining a nostalgic – essentially rooted and stable – view of space and place that no longer pertains.[72] Writing of the 'new theological space' with Chris Baker, Reader recognizes the 'increasingly blurred and overlapping religious and faith-based spaces' in a variegated and pluralistic society, citing as an example the controversies over the introduction of Sharia law in England.[73] Such tension between secularism and competing religious cultures, between the global and the local, behoves the Church, they venture, to embrace a far more fluid conception of place than it has hitherto displayed.

This welcome injection of reasoned, geographical thinking would fall short, however, if it failed to appreciate counter-cultural value and vocation of the parish, which, if not yet resurrected, is very far from 'undead'. In an era dominated by what John Reader calls the 'polygamy of space',[74] the most radical praxis may well be found by pursuing the idea of 'local monogamy'. Indeed, culturally complex spaces especially require the kind of faithful presence that fosters committed and trusting relationships over time and across social and religious boundaries. According to the Church of England's 2015 electoral statement, *Who is My Neighbour?*, 'People are not so much divorced from place as seeking a place where they can most be at home.'[75] This primal 'longing to belong' sounds straightforward, yet in practice is anything but, because concepts of belonging and 'home' are shaped by widely diverging – and sometimes incompatible – narrative traditions. Shared values – which come across as artificial and a little desperate when superimposed nationally – only grow from shared narratives, which likewise only emerge locally and gradually, often from the mutual experience of crisis and festival.

To conclude, if common prayer is the congregational heart of social ethics, its parochial counterpart must surely be described as 'common ground' – the field of proximate social relations in which the Christian ethic of love for neighbour is realized. As such, the social space – in Bourdieu's terms, the *habitus* – produced by the parish system has a vocational character, being conceived in response to the call of God in Christ. The very territoriality of the parish – its grounded, bounded nature – gives concretion (specific gravity, one might say) to this call and prevents neighbourly relations being subject to mere arbitrary selection.

Parochial space is thus the production of neighbourhood: a virtuous practice especially required of, but not limited to, the priesthood of believers. Anyone and everyone can view themselves as a parishioner and act parochially (that is, in neighbourly love), just as, in Jesus' teaching, anyone can and must view themselves as a neighbour and act accordingly. The parochial outlook ought therefore to be inherently collaborative, an outworking of the Church's belief that, in Christ, God draws us into his ministry of reconciliation. To claim the parochial (rather than the congregational) boundary as the Church's natural horizon is, therefore, a Christological assertion – for, as Bonhoeffer writes: 'God and the world are thus at one in Christ in a way which means that although the church and the world are different from each other, yet there cannot be a static, spatial borderline between them.'[76]

At the heart of the parochial tradition is thus a refusal of what Thomas Arnold, in his defence of the national church, called 'the pretended distinction between spiritual things and secular'.[77] As we proceed to Part Two of the book, this calling to 'common ground' will be appraised historically as well as geographically. For, whatever else it may be, the Anglican parish is a place long in the making.

Notes

1 Simon Jenkins in the London *Evening Standard*, 8 October 1998 (my italics).

2 Kenneth Clark, *Landscape into Art*, Harmondsworth: Penguin, 1956, p. 1. Clark concludes his thesis: 'Landscape painting, like all forms of art, was an act of faith' (p. 142).

3 See 'The Verdant Cross' in Simon Schama's magnificent *Landscape and Memory*, London: Fontana, 1995, pp. 214–26.

4 Derek Gregory and John Urry, *Social Relations and Spatial Structures*, London: Macmillan, 1985, pp. 10–11.

5 Henri Lefebvre, *The Production of Space*, Oxford: Blackwell, 1991, p. 228.

6 As Doreen Massey explains in Gregory and Urry, *Spatial Structures*, p. 19. Massey sees this, in part, as a recognition that 'the unique' (that is, the local and particular) is 'back on the agenda' (p. 12).

7 Anthony Giddens, *The Constitution of Society*, Oxford: Blackwell, 1984.

8 Nigel Thrift's criticism of structuration theory is partly that it lacks a sense of the *personal*: being too 'functionalist' to fully explain and interpret the concrete situations to which it is directed (in *Spatial Formations*, London: Sage, 1996, p. 65).

9 Doreen Massey, *For Space*, London: Sage, 2005, p. 21.

10 Massey, *For Space*, p. 9.

11 Massey, *For Space*, ch. 12: 'The Elusiveness of Space'.

12 For example, Nigel Thrift, in his critique of Giddens, employs 'habitus' as the mediating concept between 'structure' and 'human agency' (in *Spatial Formations*, London, Sage, 1996, pp. 69ff). See Jean Hillier and Emma Rooksby (eds), *Habitus: A Sense of Place*, Aldershot: Ashgate, 2005. Elaine Graham draws out this point in relation to specifically Christian social praxis, in her emphasis on the *performative* nature of faith, whereby *habitus* signifies the complex of social and historical

traditions both 'inherited and inhabited' by the Church (in *Transforming Practice*, London: Continuum, 1996, p. 139).

13 Pierre Bourdieu, *Outline of a Theory of Practice*, Cambridge: CUP, 1977, ch. 2. According to Derek Gregory, everyday life depends on highly routinized interactions between people who are *co-present* in time and space (in Derek Gregory and Rex Walford (eds), *Horizons in Human Geography*, London: Macmillan, 1989, ch. 14). For Lefebvre, these follow certain rhythms that form, in his words, 'the concrete modalities of social time' (Henri Lefebvre, *Rhythmanalysis*, London: Bloomsbury, 2013, p. 82).

14 Erving Goffman, *Relations in Public*, Harmondsworth: Penguin, 1971, p. 13.

15 Michel de Certeau, *The Practice of Everyday Life*, Los Angeles: University of California Press, 1984, ch. 9.

16 Mary Douglas notes how such borders are intrinsic to religious communities in *Purity and Danger*, London: Routledge, 2002. Robert Schreiter argues that 'local theology' necessitates a deep appreciation of cultural semiotics (in *Constructing Local Theologies*, New York: Orbis, 1985, pp. 78ff). For the impact of poverty on material parameters of everyday life, see John Eyles in Gregory and Walford (eds), *Horizons*, pp. 103ff.

17 Goffman, *Relations*, ch. 2.

18 Kate Fox gives a perspicacious and often hilarious analysis of this in *Watching the English*, London: Hodder & Stoughton, 2005.

19 William Blackstone, *Commentaries on the Laws of England*, book 1 chapter 11: http://www.lonang.com/exlibris/blackstone/bla-111.htm, accessed 29/6/15. Tate notes the interpretation of the 1894 Parish Councils Act as being that the incumbent is a 'corporation sole' (in *The Parish Chest*, 3rd edn, Cambridge: CUP, 1969, p. 13).

20 David Sibley, *Geographies of Exclusion*, London: Routledge, 1995, p. 97.

21 Sibley, *Geographies*, p. 112. Robert Schreiter picks up on the critical importance of liminality in semiotics, noting how the sense of belonging – being 'in place' – has as its counterpart the possibility of being 'out of place' (in *Local Theologies*, p. 54). Compare Elaine Graham on 'alterity' in Christian praxis (in *Transforming Practice*, pp. 168ff).

22 De Certeau, *Practice*, p. 108. Likewise, Gaston Bachelard writes that 'all really inhabited space bears the essence of the notion of home' (in *The Poetics of Space*, Boston: Beacon Press, 1994, p. 5).

23 Paul Tournier writes of how 'the place is a sort of mirror of the person' (in *A Place for You*, London: SCM Press, 1968, p. 27). See also David Canter, *The Psychology of Place*, London: Architectural Press, 1977.

24 Akiko Busch, *Geography of Home*, New York: Princeton Architectural Press, 1999, p. 20. See also Alain de Botton, *The Architecture of Happiness*, London: Penguin, 2006, ch. 4: 'Ideals of Home'.

25 Busch, *Home*, p. 163.

26 The 2008 Joseph Rowntree Foundation report 'Young People and Territoriality in British Cities' is especially pertinent here, demonstrating how territorial gangs function as an alternative to 'family and household affiliation'. http://www.jrf.org.uk/system/files/2278–young-people-territoriality.pdf, accessed 6/7/15. See also P. Jeffrey Brantingham, George E. Tita and Martin B. Short, 'The Ecology of Gang Territorial Boundaries', *Criminology*, 50.3 (2012), pp. 851–85.

27 Lefebvre, *Production*, p. 31.

28 Thus Massey: 'The nature of geographical imagination – our view of the world – can be of fundamental importance to how we act within it' (in John Allen and Doreen Massey (eds), *Geographical Worlds*, Oxford: OUP, 1995, p. 41).

29 Massey in Allen and Massey (eds), *Geographical Worlds*, p. 27.

30 Quoted by Benedict Anderson in *Imagined Communities*, London: Verso, 2006, pp. 173–4. Rachel Hewitt notes the Romantic movement's objection to modernist cartography as being inimical to the spirit of place – epitomized by Blake's depiction of Urizen in *The Ancient of Days*, poised over the globe with a pair of dividers (in *Map of a Nation: A Biography of the Ordnance Survey*, London: Granta, 2010, pp. 206–7).

31 Anderson, *Imagined Communities*, p. 6.

32 Lefebvre, *Production*, p. 41. Lefebvre accentuates the link between physical and mental space – what he calls 'logico-epistemological space including products of imagination such as symbols and utopias', p. 12.

33 Lefebvre, *Production*, p. 39.

34 Vidal de la Blache, quoted in J. B. Mitchell, *Historical Geography*, London: English Universities Press, 1954, p. 325. Similarly, Doreen Massey notes how 'space, place and nature are central to the geographical understanding of the world' (in Allen and Massey (eds), *Geographical Worlds*, p. 14).

35 In this vein, Robert Macfarlane writes: 'we are good at saying how we shape place, less good about saying how place shapes us' (in *The Old Ways*, London: Hamish Hamilton, 2012, p. 27).

36 Carl Sauer, 'The Morphology of Landscape', in John Agnew, David N. Livingstone and Alasdair Rogers (eds), *Human Geography*, Oxford: Blackwell, 1996, pp. 300ff. Likewise, Richard Chorley defines geography as a 'human ecology', which 'concerns itself with the tangible spatial manifestations of the continuing intercourse between Man and his habitable environment' (in *Directions in Geography*, London: Methuen, 1973, p. 158).

37 Eric Hirsch (ed.), *The Anthropology of Landscape: Perspectives on Place and Space*, Oxford: OUP, 1995, p. 1.

38 Denis Cosgrove, *Social Formation and the Symbolic Landscape*, Wisconsin: University of Wisconsin Press, 1998. For Cosgrove, 'terrestrial space is both subject and object of human agency' (in *Symbolic Landscape*, p. 15). See Robert Sack, *Human Territoriality: Its Theory and History*, Cambridge: CUP, 1986; also, Sack's article, 'The Power of Place and Space', *Geographical Review*, 83.3 (1993), in which Sack insists that landscape is not secondary to social process, but *interactive* in the formation of meaning that gives rise to place. Doreen Massey notes how even geological formations are not static, but constantly evolving in relation to natural processes (in *For Space*, p. 141).

39 Cosgrove, *Symbolic Landscape*, p. 13. Likewise, Simon Pugh affirms that 'landscape and its representations are a "text" and are, as such, "readable" like any other cultural form' (in Simon Pugh (ed.), *Reading Landscape*, Manchester: MUP, 1990, pp. 2–3).

40 An approach elaborately developed by Simon Schama in *Landscape and Memory*.

41 Cosgrove, *Symbolic Landscape*, p. xxx.

42 Cosgrove, *Symbolic Landscape*, p. 212. Russell Chamberlin gives a good account of the origins of the term in *The Idea of England*, London: Thames & Hudson, 1986, ch. 5.

43 See especially Raymond Williams, *The Country and the City*, London: Chatto & Windus, 1973, ch. 4. Williams castigates this sense of detachment as morally and socially ignorant, preserving both 'the myth of the happier past' and an image of the landscape in which working communities are effectively made invisible.

44 Keith Thomas's phrase, in *Man and the Natural World*, Harmondsworth: Penguin, 1984, p. 25. Thomas is referring to the prevailing view of the landscape up to the eighteenth century.

45 The agricultural origins of 'culture' are noted by Kelton Cobb in *Theology and Popular Culture*, Oxford: Blackwell, 2005, p. 41.

46 In relation to parochial customs, Nicola Whyte affirms that 'relations are always material and social at once ... human relations are created through the medium of landscape' (in 'Landscape, Memory and Custom: Parish Identities c.1550–1700', *Social History*, 32.2 (2007), pp. 166–7).

47 See Elaine Graham, Heather Walton and Frances Ward, *Theological Reflection: Methods*, London: SCM Press, 2005, ch. 7.

48 William Vitek and Wes Jackson, *Rooted in the Land*, Newhaven: Yale University Press, 1996, p. 125.

49 In Gregory and Urry, *Spatial Structures*, ch. 2. Massey here gives a helpful account of the narrative basis for human geography between the 1960s and 1980s.

50 See Ian Sinclair, *Lights Out for the Territory*, Harmondsworth: Penguin, 2003. A useful introduction is found in Merlin Coverley, *Psychogeography*, London: Pocket Essentials, 2010.

51 Stanley Hauerwas, *A Community of Character*, London: University of Notre Dame Press, 1981; *The Peaceable Kingdom: A Primer in Christian Ethics*, Notre Dame: University of Notre Dame Press, 1983, p. 99.

52 Stephen Toulmin, *Cosmopolis: The Hidden Agenda of Modernity*, Chicago: University of Chicago Press, 1990, p. 35.

53 Cited in Samuel Wells, *Transforming Fate into Destiny: The Theological Ethics of Stanley Hauerwas*, Carlisle: Paternoster Press, 1998, p. 39.

54 George A. Lindbeck, *The Nature of Doctrine*, Louisville: Westminster John Knox Press, 2009, p. 21.

55 Aristotle, *The Nichomachean Ethics*, Oxford: OUP, 1980, pp. 28–9.

56 For example, Dietrich Bonhoeffer, *Ethics*, London: SCM Press, 1964, pp. 200–2. Bernd Wannenwetsch notes how, in worship, this recognition 'produces' a world at peace with God (in *Political Worship*, Oxford: OUP, 2004, p. 249).

57 Hauerwas, *Community of Character*, p. 40.

58 Stanley Hauerwas and Samuel Wells (eds), *Blackwell Companion to Christian Ethics*, Oxford: Blackwell, 2004, ch. 1. A version, possibly, of Coleridge's 'he prayeth best, who loveth best', in *The Rime of the Ancient Mariner*.

59 Samuel Wells, 'How Common Worship Forms Local Character', *Studies in Christian Ethics*, 15.1 (2002), p. 66.

60 Wells, 'How Common Worship Forms Local Character', p. 71.

61 Samuel Wells, *God's Companions: Reimagining Christian Ethics*, Oxford: Blackwell, 2006, p. 129.

62 Wells, *God's Companions*, p. 57.

63 Wells, *God's Companions*, p. 66.

64 A. G. Hebert, *Liturgy and Society*, London: Faber & Faber, 1961, p. 193.

65 Hebert, *Liturgy and Society*, p. 93.

66 Nicholas Healy, *Church, World and the Christian life: Practical-Prophetic Ecclesiology*, Cambridge: CUP, 2000, p. 167.

67 Stanley Hauerwas, 'A Particular Place: The Future of Parish Ministry', in *War and the American Difference*, Grand Rapids: Baker Academic, 2011, ch. 11.

68 In similar vein, William Cavanaugh refers to globalization as 'false catholicity' in *Theopolitical Imagination: Discovering the Liturgy as a Political Act in an Age of Global Consumerism*, Edinburgh: T&T Clark, 2002, p. 6.

69 In the biblical narrative, Leviticus 19 envisages love of neighbour and social justice combining in a local setting. On the role of boundaries in this practice, cf. Richard B. Miller, in John A. Coleman (ed.), *Christian Political Ethics*, Princeton: Princeton University Press, 2008, pp. 68–70.

70 Augustine, *City of God*, Harmondsworth: Penguin, 1972, p. 879.

71 Augustine, *City of God*, p. 890.

72 John Reader, *Reconstructing Practical Theology*, Aldershot: Ashgate, 2008, ch. 2.

73 John Reader and Christopher R. Baker, *Entering the New Theological Space*, Aldershot: Ashgate, 2009, pp. 7–8.

74 Reader, *Reconstructing Practical Theology*, p. 11.

75 *Who is My Neighbour?*, London: CHP, 2015, p. 22.

76 Bonhoeffer, *Ethics,* p. 207.

77 From 'A Fragment on the Church', included in David Nicholls's collection entitled *Church and State in Britain Since 1820*, London: Routledge, 1967, p. 34.

PART TWO

Common Ground: The Anglican Parish in History and Practice

4

Another Country: Parish and the National Myth

Some day, there will be a history of England written from the point of view of one parish.

Edward Thomas, *The South Country*

Standards raised click smartly into place. The soft thud of unsoldierly soles on tarmac; the drill and snap of military drums; a ripple of uncoordinated limbs and our parade is under way. From the leatherette couches of the British Legion and up Church Lane to the memorial, dedicated, like so many, 'to the men of this parish, who ...' Unexpectedly mild is the morning as we muster, just ahead of time. The rector checks his watch, chief execs and head girls red-wreathed, Beavers shuffling up, everyone conscious of their position.

Remembrance Sunday brought me up like a salute when we first moved to Oxted. As a tradition, in south London, it seemed almost to have expired: a mere 15 miles away in Surrey, it displayed all the vital signs and drew diverse hundreds to watch and worship. The common view is that Armistice rituals are inherently conservative. In the sense that conservatism reveres the patient construction of social institutions and despises their easy dismantling, this is probably true. However, such traditions don't merely conserve: they reassemble both past and present in creative ways. In his influential work *The Past is a Foreign Country*, David Lowenthal argued that, while preservation 'segregates a tangible past required to be unlike the present', remembrance, by contrast, denotes living conversation with a history that isn't set hard like memorial concrete, but as malleable as Flanders mud to our interaction with it.

Remembrance calls for a peculiarly pastoral patriotism: not only in the need to tread softly on personal territory but also in attending to local notions of nationhood. None of us knows our country (or town, come to that) as a whole; we know the parts of it with which we are familiar, projecting from there our wider senses of belonging. Any idea of England, or Britain, or the world as a whole, is at heart an extension of one's local experience, however complex: millions of worldviews, each from a particular standpoint. If we are 'at home' parochially (in the loosest sense), we ought perhaps to be 'at home' nationally. In this way, when local battalions in the Great War fought for King and country, they were truly fighting for their own backyard. With that patriotic bond long blasted apart, however, our present-day relation to nationhood is, to put it mildly, complicated. For many, local or regional belonging (as a Londoner first, for example) leap-frogs the national wall altogether as an expression of global citizenship: inverting Wesley, our parish has become the world.

Back on parade, the Kohima Epitaph is engraved again: 'for your tomorrow we gave our today'. Not only is the past what we make it to be, but quite clearly we are also what the past makes of us. If, therefore, our national traditions become rusty and as restrictive as medieval armour, they can be remade – 'if you do not like the past, change it', as William L. Burton advised. Remembrance Sunday may feel like an anachronism, our civvy separation from armed service all too evident in the mare's nest of a marching stride that most of us can manage. But, as Lowenthal writes, 'nothing that survives is wholly anachronistic. Every generation disposes its own legacy, choosing what to discard, ignore, tolerate or treasure, and how to treat what is kept.' Our autumnal parade and its devotees, halting the SUVs, breathes new life into the past. Always poignant, always a privilege, it is a living thing: and still one of the finest things we who live can do to remember the generous dead.

The Anglican parish, as the basic constituent form of the Church of England, is the local expression of a national idea. A flawed idea, perhaps: being but one, singularly self-possessed, politically belligerent part of a bigger idea still – the universal or catholic Church. Nevertheless, it is one that has proved highly versatile over an extraordinarily long period, and that the parish has proved capable of regenerating as our experience of place and nationhood changes.

Having explored the formation of place in both Christological and geographical terms, we have arrived at a provisional, theoretical description of the Anglican parish as a form of 'common ground' – both as an expression of neighbourhood and (in the Christian symbolic world) between the 'kingdoms' of heaven and earth. In Part Two of this book, attention turns to the practical experience of parish and an account of its contours and calling in the English setting. Evidently, such a portrayal is both blurred and enhanced by the richness of 'parish' as a word, and the multiple resonances that arise from being embedded in the broader social landscape.[1] In order to understand this deposit of meanings – to weigh 'parish' as a concept against what 'really happened' – social history becomes an essential tool, employed now as the following chapters explore the parish's vocation in three intersecting dimensions: national, communal and natural.

Gathering the nation in

There is, as is often observed, a world of difference between 'being the church *of*' and 'being the church *in*' a particular place – indeed, for parish churches to be 'of' Mayfair or Maidenhead is, in an important sense, the very definition of the national Church. Yet it is continually surprising how little analysis exists of the Church's '*of England*' ascription. In part, this is due to reservation among Christian writers about the idea of nationhood as such – in particular, its recurrent tendency to demand a godlike level of allegiance and sacrifice.

Whereas 'state' is a slightly clinical term, highlighting the legal and political aspects of shared territory, 'nation' is subject to what geographer David Storey calls more 'nebulous' associations, being 'a collection of people bound together by some sense of solidarity, common culture and shared history'.[2] As such, he continues, a nation is a 'mental construct as much as a physical reality', echoing Benedict Anderson's assertion that nations arise from shared perceptions of common life and a 'deep horizontal comradeship'.[3] The symbolic roots of nationhood are essential, then, to understanding its purpose, or vocation. Arguing from a Marxist perspective, Anderson insists that contemporary ideas of nationhood recognize the cultural systems that preceded and shaped them, of which he identifies two: the 'dynastic realm' and 'the religious community'.[4] While he draws out the signifi-cance of 'Christendom' for the emergence of the modern nation state, other commentators go further in emphasizing the explic-itly Christian origins of nationhood. In *Christianity, Patriotism and Nationhood*, an unusually positive contemporary study of the theme, Julia Stapleton suggests that Christian doctrine con-tains within itself receptivity to a certain kind of national feeling. Uniquely among the religions, Julia Stapleton writes: 'Christian-ity accommodated the local and particular within the universal ... by the doctrine of incarnation through the sanctity of place.'[5]

What was the effect of this 'sanctity of place' as the parish system became established? In the British situation, without question, it meant the infusion of Christian meaning into both pagan culture and the national myth. England has been singu-larly susceptible to this kind of mystical history, epitomized by the Glastonbury and Grail legends that, via Blake's *Jerusalem*, retain traces of their folkish resonance.[6] In large part, this is down to the historical coincidence of national formation and Christian conversion. Against the prevailing (socialist) account of nationhood advanced by Hobsbawm and others in the latter part of the twentieth century, which viewed the nation state essentially as a modern construct, Adrian Hastings has argued for a much earlier genesis, with England as the prototype nation, by virtue of its peculiar blend of sacred and secular organization. While not disputing the acceleration of national consciousness across Europe and the United States in the modern era, Hastings proceeds to demonstrate how, in England, this grew from an explicitly biblical narrative, without which the concept of nation-hood *per se* simply would not exist.[7] In this process, the creation of a national Church under Henry VIII and Elizabeth I may be viewed as giving particular political shape to an already long-established self-perception.

There are echoes here of a well-rehearsed narrative of European history, which sees the Christian Church as, in John Macmurray's phrase, 'the motive force behind the development of [Western] civilization'.[8] For the English context, however, the key issue is that, as Patrick Wormald affirms, 'England was united ecclesiastically well before it was united politically'.[9] This point is made in reference to Bede's *Ecclesiastical History*, a pivotal document for such an assertion. According to Wormald, England's 'unparalleled' early sense of national identity was a direct consequence of Bede's integrated vision. His conclusion is unequivocal: 'It was Bede who gave "Englishness" a manifesto of unique grace and power.'[10]

This is clearly a focal insight for the origins of 'national' Christianity. Yet rarely do scholars develop this further to demonstrate its essential link to specifically *local* church organization.[11] The first great synod of the English Church, the Council of Hertford of 672, convened by Archbishop Theodore of Tarsus, is significant here in two ways. First, as medieval historian John Godfrey asserts, because it marked:

> the first occasion on which representatives of the English met together for common discussion and decision ... The Anglo-Saxons would continue for a considerable period to be organized politically in separate kingdoms, but their church was now legislating as one body ... *and the way towards national unification had been shown*.[12]

Second, the meeting at Hertford laid the foundations for local forms in which this national unity was to be administered, establishing rules for the bishops' jurisdiction within their own *parochia*.[13] The vital counterpart to England's national formation was thus the development of a cohesive system of local communities, from whose varying Anglo-Saxon forms the parish gradually emerged as the principal one. However accurately or otherwise it was lodged in fact, Bede's *Ecclesiastical History* was instrumental in fixing the new national narrative that came to define Anglicanism. Historians have subsequently struggled with categorizing Bede's *History*, tending to view it either as 'church' history or 'national' history. However, as J. N. Stephens notes, it proved a seminal – and unprecedented – document because, in a sense, it was neither of these: 'Bede's *History* does not concern the English "Church", but the *gens anglorum*. Nor is it an ecclesiastical history, if we understand thereby that it concerns only one part of the *gens* – its ecclesiastical part. It is a history of that life itself, interpreted from a particular conception of God.'[14]

The narrative synthesis Bede achieved was further fused by the *Anglo-Saxon Chronicle*, which plotted the points of national emergence by their relation to the commencement of the Christian era. When the English kingdoms became unified under King Alfred, not only were his foundations for common law prefaced with excerpts from the Mosaic Law ('modified for application to Christian nations'),[15] but also his extension of civil society relied upon the 'parochial' bishops – as seen, for example, in their dissemination to local, secular leaders of Alfred's own translation of Pope Gregory's *Pastoral Care*.[16]

Just as the adoption and promotion of the Christian narrative in Anglo-Saxon society was playing a central role in the unification and formation of England, it simultaneously began to transform the way in which *local* society was perceived and governed. As noted in the Introduction, any attempt to trace the origins of the parochial system is fraught with challenges, not least because of the interchangeable forms of nomenclature given to different types of medieval community and the variable way in which key documents are translated.[17] Nevertheless, the slow emergence of a parochial system from the eighth to the thirteenth centuries carried with it the same integration of sacred and secular life that defined the nation. In part this was due to its inheriting and adapting patterns of land ownership from the pagan era that preceded it whereby, it has been suggested,[18] a new parish would effectively be the estate of the converted chieftain and the payment of tithes continued (albeit in somewhat altered form) the tribute from the glebe – 'a legacy from the heathen days' according to Hartridge.[19] Certainly the 'ownership' of the ecclesiastical parish by the local landowner was a dominant feature until what has been described as the 'Magna Carta of the parish priest', the Fourth Lateran Council of 1215, which freed the appointment of parish priests from control of the landowner and placed their oversight more firmly in the hands of the diocesan bishop.[20]

The growth of a parochial system in the Middle Ages had, it may be argued, a cohesive effect upon the emerging bond between national and local identity, even if the terminology of 'nation' and 'country' would not appear in dictionaries until the sixteenth century. Asserting that, by the mid-fourteenth century, 'all the requirements' were in place for an English national self-perception, Robert Colls describes how '9,000 parishes *gathered the nation in*', presenting the parish as a form of social fabric, clothing a newly self-conscious nation.[21]

Thus, it may be seen that, from the early medieval period, English local administration was a hybrid of ecclesiastical and civil forms: a unity derived not simply from methods of land tenure but a cosmology that, as has been well-documented, did not delineate between sacred and secular, or 'church' and 'state' in the manner that emerged after the Reformation.[22]

A curious compound

Perhaps it is surprising, then, that the English Reformation ('the biggest single transformation in the history of the English parish', according to Beat Kumin),[23] rather than drawing apart these strands, endowed them with greater strength. Powicke puts the matter well, expressing how the new national Church 'seemed to acquire new energy from a living principle which could not be defined either as ecclesiastical or secular, but was a curious compound ...'[24] Just as it had in the age of Bede, the English Church played a formative role in the emergence of the nation state during this period: legitimizing the break with Rome while simultaneously baptizing the concept of an independent

'Christian nation'.[25] The equation of English Christianity with nascent nationalism grew steadily throughout the sixteenth century, Liah Greenfeld argues, flourishing in the lyrical patriotism of Elizabeth's reign, epitomized by Shakespeare's 'This England' soliloquy,[26] and tellingly revealed in the King James Bible's emphatic preference for 'nation' as the 'translation of choice' for numerous regional terms in the vulgate. 'It was', she concludes, 'England's religious standing which was the basis of the nation's distinctiveness and uniqueness.'[27]

As with its origins in the Dark Ages, however, historians rarely explore the role of the parish in sealing and sustaining this 'curious compound' of national ecclesiology.[28] For at the heart of both the Henrician Reformation and the Elizabethan Settlement, which together framed the national Church, was a simultaneous strengthening of parish as the essential local component of what was often referred to as the 'English Commonwealth' – the resonant early modern term for national welfare and society. The first Poor Law, passed in 1536 as part of the sweep of reforms pioneered by Thomas Cromwell following the 1534 Act of Supremacy, established this local principle, and later expanded it in the Elizabethan Acts of 1598 and 1601 which, in Elton's words, 'borrowed the parish from the old ecclesiastical organization of charity' – thus setting in place a local welfare system that lasted for the next two and a half centuries.[29] The social cost of an emerging national polity was, in part at least, underwritten by the parish.

In a perceptive historical study Joan Kent argues that, in contrast to the prevailing view of the 'powerless' authority of the state in the localities in early modern England, the parish proved to be the essential local counterpart to state-formation in the period 1640–1740. Citing, among other factors, the local establishment of workhouses following an Act of Parliament in 1723 and the growing strength of the vestry meeting as a representative and effective form of parochial administration, Kent concludes that: 'To understand the growing power of the English in the later seventeenth and early eighteenth century England, it is thus necessary to appreciate not just the role of county elites or the state's new bureaucrats, but also to take into account the often willing compliance of parish vestries and their officers.'[30]

Although Tate's description of the parish as 'the cradle of our liberties' is stretching the case,[31] it was undoubtedly the main local point of access to the national *polis*, affording a form of basic democratic participation denied to the majority of people at the national level.[32] Not only did the Poor Law effectively localize the emergence of the nation state, but it arguably also *nationalized* the local – as evinced by the Report of the Poor Law Commissioners in 1834 who, tellingly, considered each parish to be 'in respect of parochial management, *an independent nation*'.[33]

By the early nineteenth century, however, there is the distinct sense that too much was being asked of – and claimed for – the parish in this respect. Outweighing all other governing authorities in terms of its levels of taxation, the parish system became an expensive burden: by 1835 absorbing nearly one-fifth of the entire national budget.[34] The high tide of Victorian secular parochialism is marked by Toulmin Smith's magisterial work from 1857, *The Parish*: in essence a handbook detailing its powers in law, but with an extensive, polemical introduction in which Smith argues that, despite being the form 'on which the chief part of the social and public relations of every neighbourhood ... depends', the parish 'is not ecclesiastical either in origin or purpose'.[35] Ecclesiastical powers were a later accretion, he emphasizes, and, in making his point, gives an often-erudite summary of the parish's early medieval origins in secular land use and local government, while at the same time studiously avoiding its evident integration with religion. With its resistance to the infusion of the ecclesiastical with the political, *The Parish* appears as a distinctly modern work, in which the seismic movements of European society through Reformation and Enlightenment loom large in the background.

In a fascinating theological study, William Cavanaugh considers this context in relation to the Church, arguing for the religious wars of the sixteenth and seventeenth centuries being viewed as the 'birthpangs' of the secular state, which first 'absorbed' the Church before eliminating it from the public sphere. The creation of 'religion' as a concept, Cavanaugh argues, was itself a means of circumscribing – and thereby controlling – church power.[36] In any consideration of territory, power is, of course, a guiding dynamic: territoriality being the innate drive to make claims over space. The fact that Anglican political power, as grounded in its Establishment in law, has manifestly not been wholly ejected by the state may be remarkable, but its resilience – and fate – is inextricably bound together with the parochial ideal, which has crested every wave of debate about disestablishment since the nineteenth century.[37] It is hard to overstate the centrality of the parish in this discourse, both practically and symbolically, and an interesting equivalence exists between what Wesley Carr calls 'high' Establishment – denoting affairs of symbolic national ceremonial, such as the monarch's role as Defender of The Faith – and 'low' Establishment – the Church's local responsibility, legally enshrined in the 'cure of souls', given to each parish incumbent.[38] The bond between these two may be increasingly hard to sustain, but it is telling, to say the least, that Bagehot, in his classic exposition of the English constitution, describes 'local holiness' as the consequence of the monarchy's fusion of religious and worldly power.[39]

Germ of civilization

Unsurprisingly, perhaps, given its pertinence in local welfare, the most fervent apologies for the parish as 'Christian England' in microcosm appear in the first half of the nineteenth century, a period of fierce disestablishmentarianism. In this climate, the Poet Laureate Robert Southey, writing in 1820 about the expansion of the new cities, argues for an extension of the 'old parochial system' into urban areas and describes 'every parish being in itself a little commonwealth'[40] – a fascinating encapsulation of the term, suggesting a reciprocal sense of the nation as, in effect, a 'large parish'. The spectre of urbanization filters through this narrative for, as Henry William Wilberforce presses in his impassioned pamphlet from 1838, *The Parochial System:*

An Appeal to English Churchmen, the idea of the self-contained parish had become, by the early nineteenth century, 'little more than a delusion' in large cities – Wilberforce noting how that of Bethnal Green, for example, now contained over 62,000 souls.[41] Arguing that the parish is 'part and parcel of the ancient laws of this land', he calls for an urgent reconfiguration and subdivision of parochial boundaries, asking: 'Why was the ancient custom discontinued (a custom coeval with the parish and almost a necessary part of it) so that our old parishes were not subdivided as occasion required?'[42]

Such appeals for the reappraisal of the parish (then, as now) invariably begin by sketching an imagined parochial ideal; observe how far this has fallen, then employ nostalgic concepts of common life and welfare to inspire present action.

Coleridge's abstruse, though influential, defence of the Established Church from 1829, *On the Constitution of Church and State*, epitomizes this approach and is particularly interesting for its lyrical evocation of the parish's place within the nation: 'That to every parish throughout the kingdom there is transplanted a germ of civilization: that ... there is a nucleus around which the capabilities of the place may crystallize and brighten ... This it is which the patriot and philanthropist ... cannot estimate at too high a price.'[43] While idealistic to the point of fiction, Coleridge's 'germ of civilization' comes close to describing the parish's imagined encapsulation of national welfare, to which legislators and social commentators alike make endless returns, up to the present day.[44] Leaving aside the question as to whether Coleridge fully appreciated the harsh reality of parish life, this, his last published work, shows an instinctive appreciation that it expressed, as no other concept, the bond between the national and local 'soul' – and, presciently, that this must needs be reimagined in secular terms for an era in which uniformity in religion was already a thing of the past.

The Church of England's peculiar national status is, then, an indispensable key to unlocking its enduring local role – and vice versa. In a significant work, Frank Prochaska has argued forcefully for viewing Christianity as the very engine of social action in Britain until its localized systems of charity and welfare were, in his view, surrendered to the agencies of an increasingly centralized state, to which the Church gave willing deference.[45] Addressing the remarkable upsurge in Christian charitable enterprise during the Victorian era, Prochaska's concern is the way in which Christian voluntarism then receded in direct proportion to the advance of state provision during the first half of the twentieth century. He observes that: 'While central government was little noticed in the 1850s, the tendrils of the state were everywhere to be seen a century later, from the local surgery to the unemployment office on the high street.'[46] The simultaneous contraction of 'Christian society' and expansion of the welfare state was, he argues, far from coincidental. Indeed, as he writes: 'The expansion of government into education and the social services was both cause and effect of Christian decline.'[47]

When seeking to trace the decay of specifically *Anglican* social action, however, Prochaska's account is somewhat perplexing – the main issue being that it becomes lost in his necessarily broad, interdenominational sweep of 'Christian social service'. This would be reasonable if his conclusions regarding its decline were not so firmly fixed on the Church of England. Though thorough in his analysis of the causes for decline – he cites, in particular, the devastating effect of the two world wars and the rise of a less voluntary attitude to social service through agencies like the Charity Organization Society – the culmination of his case rests upon an exhausted Anglican Church, which effectively 'sold out' to the state in the years immediately prior to and following the end of World War Two. In particular, he highlights as significant the resolutions made at the Lambeth Conference of 1948, the pivotal year that saw, in Derek Fraser's words, 'the whole apparatus of what came to be called the Welfare State move into operation'.[48] Homing in on this conference's resolution that the state was 'intended [by God] to be an instrument of human welfare', he concludes: 'Obeisance to the "omnicompetent" state was an abdication of a historic responsibility, and it reflected a social and cultural transformation ... as great as any since the eighteenth-century religious revival.'[49]

A close reading of the 1948 Lambeth report, however, shows its conclusions to be far more nuanced than Prochaska would admit. Though acknowledging the process of extending state control as 'inevitable' and 'not likely to be reversed', the conference recognizes the 'delicate problem' this presents for the Church.[50] Emphasizing the latter's need 'to be vigilant to warn the state against treating persons as means to ends', the report resolves, crucially, that:

> The Church must not allow the State to disregard or throw away the experience and the good will which are found in voluntary social service ... Some forms of welfare and educational work are better done under voluntary auspices than by state agencies, provided they are efficiently done, and especially by the Church within the fellowship of the Body of Christ.[51]

This is certainly not the language of 'abdication'. What, then, does such ambivalence towards the state represent? Between the wars, the Church of England resembled, to some extent, an actor in search of a new role, owing to its growing autonomy from national government – a process that had culminated in the Enabling Act of 1919 and the creation of the Church's own legislative assembly (and, for the first time, parochial church councils).[52] Pre-eminent in negotiating this new role was the figure of William Temple who, as leader of the 'Life and Liberty' movement from 1917, secured the Church's partial separation from government and later, as Bishop of Manchester then Archbishop (York, then Canterbury), reckoned with its implications for the 'national mission' of the Church and likely relationship to the nascent welfare state.[53]

Temple's thought – hammered out in his numerous publications and the seemingly endless succession of national conferences that typified Church of England debate in the interwar years[54] – may thus be seen as the late flowering of an idealistic Anglicanism that sought a re-identification of church and state: viewing the latter as, in Stephen Spencer's words, 'an extensive and powerful social structure that would bring its citizens to their true end'.[55]

Temple's bestselling *Christianity and Social Order*, published in 1942, is the mature summary of this position, in which his 'derivative social principles' of Freedom, Social Fellowship and Service are commended by Temple for realizing 'the fullest possible development of individual personality in the widest and deepest possible fellowship'.[56] Though a detailed assessment of his case is not desirable here, Temple's writings and ministry epitomize the paradoxical forces that underlay Anglican social service in the first half of the last century. These may be summarized in terms of a threefold tension: between the desire for both self-governance *and* union with the state; between collectivist socialism and a deeply paternalistic Anglicanism (a contradiction that Temple personified)[57] and, lastly, that between an increasingly state-based agenda and the desire to preserve what remained of 'voluntary society'.

The net result was not a withdrawal from local social service: rather, it was a concerted attempt, under Temple, to baptize in infancy the state provision over whose growth it had decreasing control. This could not help but involve an eclipse of the local in favour of the national, which now presents the years between 1918 and 1948 as something of a 'lost period' for the Anglican parish. For Keith Snell, this period marked a profound shift in the idea of *settlement* at the heart both of the parish system and English life as a whole. He writes: 'Developing from and using the Anglican parish, the settlement system delivered and nestled a Christian welfare system that was benevolent and encompassing when seen in international terms, one whose *mini-statehoods* laid expectations and groundwork for the broader welfare state of the twentieth century.'[58]

The move after 1948 to a concept of, in effect, 'national settlement', while profoundly beneficial in many ways, arguably denuded the local attachment that preceded it, leaving the ecclesiastical parish shorn of all secular powers but its enduring mandate for the 'cure of souls' as a vestigial token.

Conclusion: Little England?

The Irish poet Patrick Kavanagh, in his 1967 essay 'The Parish and the Universe', makes the provocative claim that 'All great civilizations are based on parochialism – Greek, Israelite, English.'[59] Continuing, 'it requires a great deal of courage to be parochial', Kavanagh's point is that parochialism involves recognition of, and pride in, the authenticity of local experience, which requires no constant comparison with, or recourse to, neighbouring forms of expression. As such, he writes:

> Parochialism and provincialism are [direct] opposites. The provincial has no mind of his own; he does not trust what his eyes see until he has heard what the metropolis – towards which his eyes are turned – has to say on any subject ... The parochial mentality, on the other hand, is never in any doubt about the social and artistic validity of his parish.[60]

While he is writing primarily about creative expression, Kavanagh's conclusion that 'parochialism is universal: it deals with fundamentals' is a valuable insight into the shifting nature of English national identity, whose 'universal' definition has, it is being argued, directly derived from a sense of local self-possession. The unavoidable problem for the Church of England, though, is that the seeds of its legitimacy are set in the historic core of political power: the resulting sense of 'entitlement' makes the parish in its Anglican form deeply ambivalent for many and noxious to some.[61] In the current situation, the account of England as a 'Christian Nation', as one narrative among many, remains highly contested – not least because, to borrow Massey's phrase about space in general, 'its symbolism is endlessly mobilized in political argument'.[62] Similarly, in the topical question of whether England is a nation at all, such descriptions tend to be heavily freighted by those intending to re-create a sense of 'Englishness' in the wake of a resurgent nationalism across the British Isles.

Like all political positions, this one has besetting strengths and weaknesses: the latter always being various shades of nostalgic xenophobia – and, under certain conditions, their more chilling progeny. Its contrasting strengths, however, are communal cohesion and the resulting confidence to engage openly with those beyond our borders. Whenever received wisdom insists on the contrary – that social conservatism and attachment to territory are necessarily a symptom of something sinister – then extremism and insularity become self-fulfilling prophecies, being the only lens people are offered to view these allegiances through. England, owing to its imperious role in the formation and governance of the United Kingdom, is chronically prone to this condition – unlike the Scots, for example, whose commitment both to 'Little Scotland' and radical social inclusion is something the English can only watch with envy and a heavy measure of despair.

Given this weighting, localized terms such as 'parish' inevitably list towards the past rather than the future, frustrating a balanced view in the present of their value and validity. Therefore, it is vital to recognize that neither parish nor nation are subject to any one geographical narrative, but are – and have been – constantly reconceived, according to the times. It is a commonplace that evocations of Christian society are returned to in times of crisis or national instability, but the fact that they are extremely ancient does not mean they are incapable of renewal. With characteristic plainness, Bishop Hensley Henson, writing nearly a century ago, stated that 'a national church in the old sense ... is definitely and irretrievably obsolete'.[63] The 'old sense' he was referring to was that which assumed the nominal Anglicanism of every person in the country: a conceit, which, if ever true, was strictly so only between the Religious Settlement of 1559 and the Act of Toleration in 1689. In particular, Henson singles out the 1919 Enabling Act which, in his view, wrought 'a revolutionary change in the parochial system ... [because] the territorial basis of church membership, which is the necessary assumption of a national church, was abandoned'.[64]

This assumption had long been an illusion, however, as the 1851 Census had dramatically revealed. Writing of the plurality of place and religious practice with which Anglicans now reckoned, H. C. Darby observed that, by 1851, 'the parish was not even the sole territorial unit of *religious* life'.[65] Nevertheless, successive crises reveal the parish to be both adaptive and resilient, demonstrating how the territorial basis of the Church may be redefined without being abandoned. To take one articulation of this, Rowan Williams has written that, by asserting the public and political nature of religious affiliation, the 'vestiges of a confessional polity' retained by the state find the Church of England in a unique position to form local society in ways that provide far more than 'a cheap pool of labour for projects of social integration'.[66] Indeed, as the surviving embodiment of 'local settlement', the parish, both civil and ecclesiastical, remains an agent of the kind of social cohesion unavailable at the national level. As Patrick Kavanagh further reflects: 'It is not by the so-called national dailies that people who emigrate keep in touch with their roots ... So it is for these reasons that I return to the local newspaper. Who has died? Who has sold his farm?'[67] This comes strikingly close to what Ben Quash calls the 'polity of presence' at the heart of the Church of England's national vocation. In his essay of the same name, Quash notes the marked contrast between the presentation of Anglicanism in national and local media: 'In the local press, the Church's role in community life – providing care, taking responsibility, focusing local activities, and all the rest of it – is described and acknowledged. In this context there is nothing *odd* about the place of the church.'[68]

Parochialism is the boon and bane of English politics. Yet despite its significant drawbacks – wistful exceptionalism and reactionary jingoism not least among them – the 'England-ness' of the parish must be reckoned with if the Anglican vocation is to be fully understood. At heart, it expresses a vision for common life that is an integral strand in the complex weave of contemporary English identity: one that, in Julia Stapleton's words, 'defies categorization in simple cultural or civic terms, one that is not lightly dismissed as an inferior or deformed expression of nationhood, or as the thin end of the "ethnic" nationalist wedge'.[69]

If, as Krishnan Kumar notes in the same collection of essays, it is more accurate to speak not of English *nationalism*, but of an

English national *tradition*, the parish has not only had the 'hallowing' effect on territory described above, but made national tradition inseparable from local description – has made England, as well as the Church, parochial. This has meant not only that national life was imbued from the outset with a localized form of secular Christianity, but also ensured that Anglican ecclesiology has an inescapable secularity to it.[70] While this doubtless contributed towards the separation of Christian social ethics from their source in God,[71] and thus the growing secularization of English society, it has also enabled a form of what Simone Weil described as 'that mutual penetration of the religious and the profane which would be the essence of a Christian civilization'.[72] There is, in conclusion, an unavoidable perichoresis to the terms 'nation' and 'parish', which has existed from the earliest foundations of English society. Largely because of this, the parish embodies a similar mutual indwelling of 'religious' and 'secular' that has long endowed English life with a highly localized form of civil Christianity: even if, for many, this remains only as a trace element of cultural identity. One cannot sound the word 'parish' without both sacred and secular resonance, which gives unambiguous credence to the 'of England' definition of the national Church. To style oneself as, for example, the rector *of* Oxted (rather than 'of St Mary's Church') is, on one level, just as presumptuous and obsolete as the Church's claim to be *of* England; but it can only aspire to the latter if it begins as the former. Indeed, the Church's view of England is unavoidably an imagined projection or extrapolation of its parochiality – and if the national Church falters it is usually when presuming a kind of strategic independence of the localities in which it still makes a peculiar kind of sense.

This symbiosis with place represents more than the outworn husk of religious hegemony (although it may be that, too): it reveals an ecclesiology that cannot conceive of a church without its corresponding neighbourhood. To be the Church 'in' a particular place suggests a degree of detachment and self-sufficiency – the congregation as colony – whereas to be 'of' declares that place to be more than just functionally valuable (the hackneyed 'best boat to fish from' view of low church parochialism): in the Anglican imagination it becomes an integral part of the Church itself. So, then, there can be no truly 'secular space' for an Anglican, because they live as if every place has been reconciled to God in Christ – especially, it may be added, those where all evidence is to the contrary. This commitment is also an assertion about priesthood, in a broad sense. If the local church (not only its ordained ministers) is truly priestlike, then its liturgical purpose is to offer the world to God and vice versa, as a witness to that reconciliation. Regardless of denominational tradition, the Church can never be the Church unless it is also a 'bit' of the world.

Given that the English parish is defined by this interpenetration, it is curious that such a chasm exists between the study of its historic role in English society and the theology, which – albeit complicated by alliance with secular power – is its motive and momentum.[73] The unity of sacred and secular in the Anglican mind was never only political expediency – it was, at origin, a conscious synthesizing of the Protestant conception of 'two kingdoms', mentioned in Chapter 2. In a rather more realized application of their union, the architect of Anglican polity, Richard Hooker, could write of church and commonwealth as being 'personally one societie' – a perspective that underwrites the curious compound of parochial Christianity with far greater theological potency than the accidents of history might suggest.[74] In their lingering embrace of locality, Anglicans are channelling Hooker still, whose view that 'England did not *have* a church, England *was* a church'[75] has gradually come to be applied in missional rather than confessional terms. While, from the world's viewpoint, the Church of England's institutional influence has long been shrinking like a balloon, this slow puncture has not, by contrast, shrunk the Church's own view of its worldly reach and responsibility. National allegiance to the Church may be in freefall, but the Church's allegiance to the nation remains as lofty as ever. In this, the Church is not so much clinging to the myth of its own significance as to that of the places it exists to serve.

Notes

1 In its rural setting alone, Herron, Jackson and Johnson have, in a recent study, identified four such qualitative uses: a feudal or historical settlement; a form of religious or ecclesiastical organization; a form of secular or civic government and, lastly, a 'community planning process'. Each of these meanings, they write, employs a different 'organizing principle' (in Rebecca Herron, Jennifer Jackson and Karen Johnson, 'Rural Parishes and Community Organization', in Gary Bosworth and Peter Somerville (eds), *Interpreting Rurality*, Abingdon: Routledge, 2014, ch. 5).

2 David Storey, *Territories: The Claiming of Space*, Harlow: Pearson, 2001, p. 71.

3 Benedict Anderson, *Imagined Communities*, London: Verso, 2007, p. 7.

4 Anderson, *Imagined Communities*, p. 12.

5 Julia Stapleton, *Christianity, Patriotism and Nationhood*, Maryland: Lexington Books, 2009, p. 217.

6 The seminal account of this mythical narrative remains *King Arthur's Avalon* by Geoffrey Ashe, London: Fontana, 1973.

7 Adrian Hastings, *The Construction of Nationhood: Ethnicity, Religion and Nationalism*, Cambridge: CUP, 1997, p. 4. See also 'God's Firstborn: England', in Liah Greenfeld's *Nationalism: Five Roads to Modernity*, London: Harvard University Press, 1992, pp. 27–88.

8 John Macmurray, *The Clue to History*, London: SCM Press, p. ix. More recently, Tom Holland has argued for a Christian basis to liberal secularism in 'Uncomfortable Origins', *The New Statesman*, 20/11/2008.

9 Patrick Wormald, 'The Venerable Bede and the "Church of the English"', in Geoffrey Rowell (ed.), *The English Religious Tradition and the Genius of Anglicanism*, Wantage: IKON, 1992, p. 21. This is a view echoed and endorsed by Adrian Hastings in *Nationhood*, p. 36.

10 Wormald, 'The Venerable Bede and the "Church of the English"', p. 21. He notes that this 'exceptionally creative' integration of nationality and Christianity was to have a 'long future' (p. 27).

11 While Adrian Hastings does not address the parish, he does highlight the significance of the shire in England's national formation (in *Nationhood*, p. 40).

12 John Godfrey, *The Church in Anglo-Saxon England*, Cambridge: CUP, 1962, p. 133 (my italics). Similarly, Sherley-Price in his introduction to Bede's *History*: 'a common belief in Christ gradually drew together the peoples of Britain into the English nation' (in *A History of the English Church and People*, trans. Leo Sherley-Price, Harmondsworth: Penguin, 1955, p. 23).

13 H. Bettenson (ed.), in *Documents of the Christian Church*, Oxford: OUP, 1956, p. 215, translates *parochia* here as 'diocese', as the term at this stage denoted the wider sphere of the bishop. D. H. Farmer avers that the Synod of Whitby unified Celtic and Roman forms of organization by 'the consolidation of local centres of diverse origin into a united nationwide church, under territorial bishops' (in *The Age of Bede*, Harmondsworth: Penguin, 1983, p. 15).

14 J. N. Stephens, *History*, 62.204 (1977), p. 12. Cf. also Benedicta Ward, *The Venerable Bede*, London: Geoffrey Chapman, 1998, pp. 113–14.

15 *Alfred the Great*, trans. Simon Keynes and Michael Lapidge, Harmondsworth: Penguin, 1983, pp. 39, 40.

16 Robert Colls notes how Alfred's laws were 'encrusted with Christian references' (in *Identity of England*, Oxford: OUP, 2002, p. 18).

17 Principally township and 'vill'. For a clear summary of these and their relation to the parish, see Angus Winchester, *Discovering Parish Boundaries*, Princes Risborough: Shire, 2000, ch. 1. Throughout this discussion, it is important to remember that, as it were, 'other forms of locality are available'.

18 For example, in E. A. Greening Lamborn, *The Parish Church*, Oxford: OUP, 1929, p. 68. See also John Godfrey, *The English Parish: 600–1300*, London: SPCK, 1969, ch. 2.

19 R. A. R. Hartridge, *A History of Vicarages in the Middle Ages*, Cambridge: CUP, 1930, p. 3: 'Glebe was a legacy from the heathen days'.

20 Hartridge, *History of Vicarages*, p. 21. See Godfrey, *The Church in Anglo-Saxon England*, pp. 319ff, for analysis of medieval ownership of parishes. Notwithstanding episcopal administration, the patronage system, in many places, remains as an ancient link to 'secular' territory.

21 Robert Colls highlights the following marks of this symbiosis of national and local place in England: a distinctive sense of territory; an English Church, a sense of the 'state' and its laws; a common language and shared 'national fables' (in *Identity of England*, Oxford: OUP, 2002, pp. 17–18). For the emergence of 'nation' terminology, see Greenfeld, *Nationalism*, p. 31.

22 Oliver O'Donovan finds that 'church' and 'state' did not emerge as separate entities until the late seventeenth century. See *On the Thirty-Nine Articles*, Exeter: Paternoster Press, 1986, p. 94. For a winsome explanation of the pre-Renaissance worldview's synthesis of sacred and secular, see C. S. Lewis, *The Discarded Image*, Cambridge: CUP, 1964. Writing of medieval literature, he attests (p. 94): 'the old language continually suggests a sort of continuity between merely physical events and our most spiritual aspirations'.

23 Beat Kumin, *The Communal Age in Western Europe, c 1100–1800*, New York: Palgrave Macmillan, 2013, p. 47.

24 Maurice Powicke, *The Reformation in England*, Oxford: OUP, 1941, p. 135.

25 Greenfeld, *Nationalism*, ch. 1. Keith Wrightson notes the significance of the Reformation for state-formation – and its effects on parochial community in his essay 'The Politics of the Parish in Early Modern England', in Paul Griffiths, Adam Fox and Steve Hindle (eds), *The Experience of Authority in Early Modern England*, London: Macmillan, 1996, ch. 1.

26 Greenfeld, *Nationalism*, pp. 60ff. Greenfeld notes how the King James Bible promoted this equation, with 454 uses of the word 'nation' as opposed to only 100 of 'natio' in the vulgate. The high (or low) point of Elizabethan exceptionalism was undoubtedly Bishop Aylmer's blank assertion that 'God is English'. See Donald Horne, *God is an Englishman*, Harmondsworth: Penguin, 1969, p. 264. Horne questions whether this is more than 'a special form of vanity'. See also Cole Moreton's more recent consideration of the same theme in *Is God Still an Englishman?*, London: Abacus, 2010, p. 17.

27 Greenfeld, *Nationalism*, p. 62.

28 Keith Wrightson, for example, concludes that Early Modern England saw an 'intensified interaction between the locality and the larger society', but only implies the pivotal role of the parish as the fulcrum of this dual identity (in *English Society 1580–1680*, London: Routledge, 1982, pp. 223ff; see also his essay, 'The Politics of the Parish', in Griffiths, Fox and Hindle (eds), *The Experience of Authority*, p. 31.

29 A. G. Dickens remarks of Elizabeth I that 'her religion was deeply permeated by a secular idealism' (in *The English Reformation*, London: Fontana, 1964, p. 403).

30 Joan R. Kent, 'State Formation and Parish Government', *The Historical Journal*, 38.2 (1995), p. 403. K. J. Kesselring describes a similar congruence between local and national in '"Berwick is our England": Local and National Identities in an Elizabethan Border Town', in Norman L. Jones and Daniel Woolf, *Local Identities in Late Medieval and Early Modern England*, Basingstoke: Palgrave Macmillan, 2007.

31 W. E. Tate, *The Parish Chest*, Cambridge: CUP, 1969, p. 9.

32 David Fletcher notes: 'Although parish life, and English society more generally, was far from democratic, parish boundary marking provided an opportunity for widespread involvement of the "lesser sort"' (in 'The Parish Boundary: A Social Phenomenon in Hanoverian England', *Rural History* 14.2 (2003), p. 192).

33 Quoted by Fletcher in 'The Parish Boundary', p. 179 (my italics). Steve Hindle, in a similar tone, remarks that the parish in this period became a kind of 'welfare republic' (in Alexandra Shepard and Phil Withington (eds), *Communities in Early Modern England*, Manchester: MUP, 2000, pp. 98ff).

34 This figure is identified by Sidney and Beatrice Webb in *The Parish and The County: English Local Government Volume 1*, London: Frank Cass & Co., 1963, p. 4.

35 Joshua Toulmin Smith, *The Parish*, London: H. Sweet, 1857, p. 4.

36 William Cavanaugh, *Theopolitical Imagination: Discovering the Liturgy as a Political Act in an Age of Global Consumerism*, Edinburgh: T&T Clark, 2002, p. 22.

37 See David Nicholls, *Church and State in Britain Since 1820*, London: Routledge & Kegan Paul, 1967, ch. 1. Also usefully surveyed in E. R. Norman, *Church and Society in England 1770–1970*, Oxford: Clarendon Press, 1976, ch. 3.

38 In Wesley Carr, 'A Developing Establishment', *Theology*, 102.805 (1999), pp. 2–10. See David McLean's exposition of this in 'The Changing Framework of Establishment', *Ecclesiastical Law Journal*, 7.35 (2004), pp. 292–304. John Inge presses that this provides not only an 'earthed' establishment, but also continues to ensure the 'protection' of the parish principle at the national level (in 'Theological Reflections on the Place of the Sacred in Society', *Ecclesiastical Law Journal*, 7.35 (2004), pp. 397–8).

39 Walter Bagehot, *The English Constitution*, Oxford: OUP, 1928, p. 35. Such intriguing theological concepts often crop up in apologies for the national Church, especially in their Victorian dress. In *The Old Church: What Shall We Do With It?*, London: Macmillan, 1878, Thomas Hughes asserted its demonstration of the theological unity of earthly and heavenly kingdoms thus: 'Protestant revivalism, like Roman Catholicism, sets the other world against and above this, and to Nationalism is reserved the task of properly reconciling the two ...' (p. 159).

40 Robert Southey, from B. I. Coleman (ed.), *The Idea of the City in Nineteenth-Century Britain*, London: Routledge & Kegan Paul, 1973, p. 41.

41 Henry William Wilberforce, *The Parochial System: An Appeal to English Churchmen*, Memphis: General, 2012, p. 3. Recent historical studies show this had long been the case in the London suburbs. Boulton notes how parochial administration had been slow to respond to urban expansion: parishes in Southwark and the East End, for example, were on an 'unwieldy scale' even by the seventeenth century (in *Neighbourhood and Society: A London Suburb in the Seventeenth Century*, Cambridge: CUP, 2005, p. 263).

42 Wilberforce, *Parochial System*, p. 6.

43 S. T. Coleridge, *On the Constitution of Church and State*, London: J. M. Dent, 1972, p. 60. For a reprise of his position, see also Hughes, *The Old Church*.

44 See, for example, 'In Praise of ... Civil Parishes', an editorial in *The Guardian*, 16 May 2011.

45 Frank Prochaska, *Christianity and Social Service in Modern Britain*, Oxford: OUP, 2006, ch. 1.

46 Prochaska, *Christianity and Social Service*, p. 148.

47 Prochaska, *Christianity and Social Service*, p. 150.

48 Derek Fraser, *The Evolution of the British Welfare State*, Basingstoke: Palgrave Macmillan, 2003, p. 261. Fraser gives a comprehensive overview of the 1944–8 legislation in ch. 9.

49 Prochaska, *Christianity and Social Service*, p. 151.

50 *Lambeth Conference 1948: Encyclical Letter from the Bishops together with the Resolutions*, London: SPCK, 1948, p. 17.

51 *Lambeth Conference 1948*, p. 18.

52 Keith Robbins observes that the Church 'occupied a puzzling position' between 1918 and 1939, which led it 'deep into the thickets of social policy' (in *The Eclipse of a Great Power: Modern Britain 1870–1975*, London: Longman, 1975, p. 156).

53 For Temple's formative role in Anglican life during this period, see John Kent, *William Temple: Church, State and Society in Britain, 1880–1950*, Cambridge: CUP, 1992, ch. 1; also F. A. Iremonger, *William Temple, Archbishop of Canterbury: His Life and Letters*, Oxford: OUP, 1948.

54 See Kent, *William Temple*, chs 2 and 3 for an analysis of these.

55 Stephen Spencer, 'William Temple's Christianity and Social Order: After Fifty Years', *Theology*, 95.32 (1992), p. 34.

56 William Temple, *Christianity and Social Order*, Harmondsworth: Penguin, 1942, p. 74.

57 Captured in his wartime correspondence concerning the Beveridge Report. See F. S. Temple (ed.), *William Temple: Some Lambeth Letters*, Oxford: OUP, 1963, pp. 91–5.

58 K. D. M. Snell, *Parish and Belonging*, Cambridge: CUP, 2006, pp. 160–1 (my italics).

59 Included in Patrick Kavanagh, *A Poet's Country, Selected Prose*, Dublin: Lilliput, 2003, p. 237. Likewise, Julia Stapleton: 'nations that endure are those that build upwards from smaller associations' (in 'The Voice of Chesterton in the Conversation of England', *The Chesterton Review*, XXXV, 3 and 4, pp. 622–3).

60 Kavanagh, 'The Parish and the Universe', *A Poet's Country*, p. 237.

61 Cole Moreton records the view of one parish priest: 'The whole parish system is underpinned by the assumption that we have a right to be there. That approach has been a huge failure' (in *Is God Still an Englishman?*, p. 328).

62 Moreton, *Is God Still an Englishman?*, p. 5. The most recent occasion being a flurry of articles in April 2014, following the Prime Minister's

assertion that Britain is a 'Christian country'. For example, 'Yes, Britain is a Christian Country' by Toby Young, *The Spectator*, 26 April 2014. Jonathan Chaplin (2009) has observed how, in contemporary debates, the term 'Christian nation' is often employed polemically by those (both Catholic and Reformed) seeking a restoration of the 'essentially Christian corporate character' of national life (in 'Can Nations be "Christian"?', *Theology*, CXII, 870 (2009), p. 420).

63 Herbert Hensley Henson, *The Church of England*, Cambridge: CUP, 1939, p. 175.

64 Hensley Henson, *The Church of England*, p. 169.

65 H. C. Darby (ed.), *A New Historical Geography of England*, Cambridge: CUP, 1973, p. 533 (my italics).

66 Rowan Williams, 'Convictions, Loyalties and the Secular State', *Political Theology*, 6.2 (2005), pp. 156, 164. Jeremy Morris has questioned whether it is 'theologically responsible' for the Establishment to depend on 'residual functions' (in 'The Future of Church and State', in Duncan Dormor, Jack McDonald and Jeremy Caddick (eds), *Anglicanism: The Answer to Modernity*, London: Continuum, 2003, p. 181).

67 Kavanagh, 'The Parish and the Universe', p. 237.

68 Ben Quash, 'The Anglican Church as a Polity of Presence', in Dormor, McDonald and Caddick (eds), *Anglicanism*, p. 49. This lack of 'oddness', which finds, for example, the parish priest still to be the inevitable first point of journalistic call in situations of local crisis or tragedy, is the key to the parochial calling, and is explored by Edmund Newey in Samuel Wells and Sarah Coakley (eds), *Praying for England: Priestly Presence in Contemporary Culture*, London: Continuum, 2008, ch. 4.

69 In Arthur Aughey and Christine Berberich (eds), *These Englands*, Manchester: MUP, 2011, p. 234.

70 The counterpoint of which is F. D. Maurice's view that both church and nation were, in different senses, 'anti-secular' (in *The Kingdom of Christ*, London: SCM Press, 1958, ch. 5:III, p. 228).

71 What Erdozain, quoting Clement Attlee, names 'Christianity without the mumbo-jumbo' (in *Christianity Without the Mumbo-Jumbo: The Making of a Secular Outlook in Modern Britain*, address to KLICE conference, 2009. http://www.klice.co.uk/uploads/Erdozain%20secular%20outlook.pdf, accessed 15/6/2015).

72 Simone Weil, *The Need For Roots*, London: Routledge & Kegan Paul, 1978, p. 285.

73 Timothy Jenkins argues that, in the country parish, sacred and profane spheres have no clear separation (in *Religion in English Everyday Life: An Ethnographic Approach*, Oxford: Berghahn, 1999, p. 70).

74 Richard Hooker, *Of the Laws of Ecclesiastical Polity*, London: J. M. Dent, 1954, Book 8.1.4. David Edwards affirms Hooker's synthesis of the 'two kingdoms' doctrine in *Christian England*, vol. 2, London:

Collins, 1983, pp. 100–1. For in-depth analysis, see Torrance J. Kirby, *Richard Hooker's Doctrine of the Royal Supremacy*, Leiden: Brill, 1990.

75 A. S. McGrade's expression, in his excellent introduction to the 1975 edition of Hooker's *Laws*, London: Sidgwick & Jackson, 1975, p. 32.

5

Good Fences: Parish as Neighbourhood

Like the first hatching of midges, Anglicans gathered outside today to celebrate Rogationtide: four spring days when, according to ancient custom, the fields are blessed and processed and the parish bounds beaten. Here in Oxted, we spilled outdoors to find the five sheep in our churchyard had, with Summerisle abandon, swiftly become eleven sheep, the lambs tottering like models over the tombstones.

For centuries, beating the bounds was a fundamental way in which social space was both practised and produced in this country. In his classic work from 1973, *Religion and the Decline of Magic*, Keith Thomas calls it the 'corporate manifestation of the village community', in which natural, spiritual and social strands were closely interwoven – fist fights and ale-gatherings breezily mixing with hymn singing and the recital of Psalms. Before the advent of accurate mapping techniques, it was an equally vital means of 'knowing your place': the practice of beating key landscape markers with sticks (or, if a child, being beaten yourself, as a helpful aide-memoire), imprinting the limits of community upon each member.

The marks of this social mapping are as indelible as they are invisible – and influence contemporary life in some surprising ways. I became keenly aware of this in my former parish, at Crystal Palace in south-east London, whose central triangle of roads stands at the intersection of five London boroughs. In *The Phoenix Suburb*, his fine local history, Alan Warwick unearthed one particular Rogation Day in 1560 that marked the culmination of a longstanding territorial dispute, played out in their annual beating of the bounds, between 'the Croydon men' and the 'Penge men', over the precise location of their respective parish borders. During his Rogationtide perambulation of the bounds, Richard Finch, the vicar of Croydon ('a man of not very determined character'), encountered the equivalent party from Penge and backed down following aggressive accusations of trespass, thus conceding to them a significant portion of land, which remains as the borough boundary to this day.

Further details aside, two features of this case are particularly noteworthy: first, that the practical peculiarity of the current Croydon borough boundary – running along the middle of Church Road in Upper Norwood, to the confusion of municipal dustcarts – is, as Warwick writes, 'to some extent the outcome of the perambulations of a vicar in the reign of Queen Elizabeth I who was not sufficiently resolute'. Second, and perhaps of greater interest, is the way in which this particular Church Road has consistently proved to be a site of social tension and boundary conflict: becoming something of a 'front line' in the 2011 riots and also the site of a notorious current planning dispute, regarding the conversion by a Pentecostal church of a former cinema site along the same stretch of road. The Crystal Palace Cinema Campaign has come to be viewed as a test case for determining equal access to the planning process for divergent community groups.

Recent research by Nicola Whyte and others suggests that this kind of psychogeographic recurrence may not be an isolated example of how the accidents of parish history converge to influence and, to some degree, explain, present-day patterns of social inclusion. In other words, the routes we take now yield an unavoidable harvest in the future. Tudor clergy should, it seems, have been more careful where they walked.

Parish is the nearby community: its vocation is to proximity. This 'nearness' in spatial terms is the key to most of the perceived blights and benefits of parochial life – its equal suggestion of settled support and suffocating pettiness. The biblical command to love our neighbour – literally, the one who is near or 'nigh' – invests social proximity with divine potential. In the teaching of Jesus, when people perceive themselves as neighbours, their environment is transformed into a potential theatre for acts of love and service. Through such encounters, the kingdom (the eternal place simultaneously close to, and at the boundaries of, everyday experience) nearly comes, on earth as in heaven.

Historically, as one case study puts it, 'parishes have often been described as places where people recognized each other'.[1] The Anglican parish is, then, the field of proximate social relations, the 'common ground', in which this mutual recognition takes place: where neighbourhood is both acknowledged and practised. Indeed, given its historic role in shaping local communities, one might go further to say that, in the English context, the parish represents the *archetypal* neighbourhood, to which other local forms inevitably refer. In large part, this may be seen as a consequence of what the social historian Keith Snell calls the 'enormous saliency' of the Anglican parish to systems of welfare in England from 1700 up to 1950.[2] As he remarks: 'I can think of no ... community focus that had anything approaching the administrative, legal, social and cultural importance of the parish ... *Community* for most people *was the parish*.'[3]

There can be little question that this role extends well back into medieval society and the bridging centuries covered by an increasing range of historical studies that have emerged in the last 25 years, which have reoriented local social history by their 'discovery' of the English parish.[4] In the collection of essays *The Parish in English Life, 1400–1600*, Katherine French makes a strikingly similar observation to Snell's assessment of its significance in a later era:

> It was the level of most collective social behaviour. Poor relief, religious worship, neighbourhood and village celebrations, the collection of taxes and a myriad of cultural interactions and negotiations were all organized and conducted within this fundamental unit. English society and culture between 1400 and 1600 ... simply cannot be understood without taking the parish into account.[5]

Despite this welcome redress, contemporary social historians rarely acknowledge the persistence of the ecclesiastical parish to the present day as a fundamental agent of local welfare. In Derek

Fraser's standard text *The Evolution of the British Welfare State*, the ongoing role of the Church of England in social service beyond the Victorian age barely merits a mention – omitting, for example, any reference to William Temple, in whose writings the phrase 'welfare state' was coined.[6] What we 'see' in history, however, is largely determined by narrative tradition, so this invisibility requires those from other traditions to reveal what, hitherto, may have been overlooked: namely, the enduring vitality of the parish as an agent of social formation. This is not to say that its role has been a consistent one. In terms of historical influence, the parish emits a somewhat fluctuating signal whose reception fades in and out according to its shifting associations with political power and, importantly, the equally motile perspective of historians on the social significance of the Church. Both of these aspects mean that changes in the social role of the Anglican parish cannot be considered in isolation from broader questions regarding the increased secularization of modern British society and the historic decline of all Christian denominations in terms of their membership and influence. Jeremy Morris has usefully identified three strands to this process: first, 'institutional marginalization' or 'the progressive disentanglement of established religion ... from structures of local and national government'; second, 'institutional attenuation' – a reduction in the Church's overall membership; and, third, 'cultural displacement', whereby alternative forms of morality and common life have come to occupy the role formerly filled by the Church.[7] As Morris observes, such changes have been 'a work long in the making' and the question of their origin, extent and local variegation remains a focus of intense interdisciplinary debate.

Critical for the historian are the questions of *when* and, to a lesser extent, *where* such decline began to take effect. Surveying recent (although writing in 2003) scholarship, Morris categorizes its progress in terms of a 'modernist' position – which tended to take a pessimistic view of the churches' response to modernity and a more recent 'revisionist' position which, over the last 40 years, has come to challenge the assumption of rapid church decline from the mid-nineteenth century onwards. For

Morris, the high-water mark of revisionism was reached with the publication in 2001 of Callum Brown's *The Death of Christian Britain*, which asserted the vitality and resilience of British Christianity until the 'long 1960s' (1956–73) when the churches experienced rapid and terminal decline. Despite its narrative bias towards urban, nonconformist experience, Brown's thesis has proved highly significant, as much for its shortcomings as its strengths. Indeed, by simultaneously prolonging the life and hastening the death of British Christianity it provokes an uncertain response from Christian practitioners and church historians alike.[8] Whenever the date for decline is set, what Brown calls the 'endgame' of British Christianity[9] becomes extremely important, determining whether twentieth-century church history is seen principally as a matter of life or death. Complicating any such diagnosis is the plain fact that, as Matthew Grimley has pointed out in a recent appraisal of Brown's thesis, 'the victim is not actually dead. There is no corpse in the library ...'[10] As the previous chapter indicated, the persistence of a national Church, for example (albeit in a denuded state), leaves the question open and frustrates every attempt at autopsy.

Admitting this broader historiographical context, the purpose of the present chapter will be to 'home in' on the ecclesiastical parish's definitive role in forming local neighbourhood. The potential historical ground being vast, I shall highlight five stages in its history that, I believe, both demonstrate this enduring vocation and display how it has been 'made flesh' in the English context.

The sacred community, 1215–1536

The parish, as already observed, took several centuries to become a 'system' in the sense of comprehensively covering the English social landscape. Its establishment as such a network appears to reach a level of completion by the time of the Fourth Lateran Council of 1215,[11] which, to some extent, marks its 'victory' over other forms of local organization. Hartridge, for example, notes how, during the long period of its foundation, the parish 'came to replace the *villa* as a unit, and to prepare for, even create, the village'.[12] The social historian Katherine French explains that this creative role was only strengthened after the Black Death in the mid-fourteenth century and what has been seen as a decline of village community during this period. 'After the plague', she writes, 'local life revolved more around the parish.'[13] It is vital to recognize, however, that within a national framework, there was huge regional and local variation in the structure and function of medieval parishes – as French recognizes in her study of late medieval parochial life in the Diocese of Bath and Wells: 'Each parish's unique resources, location, status, wealth and needs distinguished it from all others. Such local characteristics and priorities evolved into local religious cultures that became forums for community identity.'[14] Central to French's analysis is the idea of the pre-Reformation parish as a form of sacred community, in which the role of church governance (especially by bishops) was particularly evident. Successive episcopal reforms in pastoral oversight in the twelfth and thirteenth centuries concerning revenue collection, and more consistent patterns of local organization – especially through the church courts – meant that the social influence of English parishes grew steadily.

This influence not only concerned the *coercive* ways in which the Church penetrated medieval society (attendances at mass, 'tithe gatherings' and so on), but, importantly, the *voluntary* dimensions of parochial life, such as parish guilds, church ales and the local celebration of saints' days – a recognizable mix of 'conviviality and charity', in Judith Bennett's words.[15] The ongoing need for local fundraising bridged both of these: it was coercive to the extent that growing legislation in the thirteenth century required parishes to shoulder extensive responsibilities for the financial upkeep of the church building and grounds – and it was voluntary, because (then, as now) these demands became the occasion for wide-ranging local expressions of communal life, as French has demonstrated in her detailed studies of parochial fundraising in late medieval Somerset.[16]

In this context, the parish guild is particularly instructive as a gauge of the medieval parochial system's ability to accommodate more dynamic forms of social space that spilled over its territorial boundaries. The guilds – fraternities inaugurated via papal licence, often in response to the aforementioned demands of local fundraising – proliferated across late medieval Europe, before their demise by statute in 1547, along with much of the apparatus of the 'religious' parish. Because of the decline in creating new parishes after 1300 (such that they remained largely unchanged for some 600 years), the guild, as a form of voluntary association, could respond to more unsettled patterns of relationship – in commerce, for example. In his case study of the Hertfordshire town of Baldock, Gervase Rosser challenges the 'myth of parochial stability' in the late Middle Ages, demonstrating how guilds enabled the limitations of fixed geographical boundaries to be transcended where occasion demanded.[17] This medieval 'mixed economy' of place has much contemporary relevance and reveals parochial guilds to be a church-sponsored response to spatial change that integrated successfully with its existing territorial arrangements. Indeed, in some settings, it is doubtful whether parish institutions would have survived without them.

The strongly 'religious' nature of local society in pre-Reformation England, unsurprisingly, comes across plainly in recent scholarship – an aspect that can easily depict the parish as an exalted form of overtly Christian society, from which it descended into the mundane apparatus of local government during the Tudor period. While the close interplay of Catholic doctrine and local society were the explicit cause behind, for example, the outlawing of parish guilds ('for devising and phantasinge vayne opinions of Purgatorye'),[18] the harmonious integration of secular and sacred in the medieval parish should not be overplayed. Its undoubted capacity for assimilating pagan customs and hallowing 'profane' society could frequently become the source of significant local tensions, as instructions given to fourteenth-century parish priests not to allow 'markets and fairs in churchyards, or games or stone-throwings, or those dissolute dances and inhonest songs customarily performed on the vigils of certain feasts' rather enjoyably suggest.[19]

The secular parish, 1536–1834

During the English Reformation, the very changes that dismantled the medieval 'sacred' parish simultaneously transformed and enhanced its secular role. The 'poor laws', as they are usually termed, comprised a series of legislative reforms that began in 1536 as part of Thomas Cromwell's reorganization of local government, culminated in the Elizabethan Poor Law Act of 1601, but continued for an extraordinarily long span until its successor arrived – the so-called 'New Poor Law' of 1834. In the intervening centuries, the parish (and its executive, the vestry) accrued a bewildering array of social services (the licensing of public houses, for example, or the provision of fire engines) in addition to basic obligations like the repair and upkeep of highways and church buildings.[20] Crucially it was also responsible for the funding and allocation of 'indoor' and 'outdoor' poor relief – the former requiring the recipient to enter an institution such as a workhouse and the latter offering relief in the form of money, food or clothing without the need for the recipient to be thus installed. Successive legislation meant that substantial authority and discretionary power was devolved to parochial officers and the parish itself became the very keystone of local government.

In his study of social life in Tudor London, social historian Gary Gibbs affirms that 'when Londoners organized responses to the many formidable problems which beset their city, it was usually at the parish level'.[21] As an index of the transition from the pre-Reformation period, Gibbs highlights the City of London budget, of which, in the fifteenth century, over half had, staggeringly, been spent on 'ecclesiastical items' for the decoration of churches and chantries. 'All this had changed' by the mid-sixteenth century, he concludes.[22] South of the River Thames, a similar situation pertained, according to Jeremy Boulton, whose research into the London Borough of Southwark reveals the bewildering diversity of roles accorded to vestry officers, including keeping the marketplace clear and whipping beggars from the parish.[23] A similar study of south London in the Elizabethan era, by Ian Archer, also charts the emergence of the parish vestry as what he terms 'the cockpit of local government', but offers a helpfully nuanced account of the overlapping communities of which the parish was but one.[24] The degree to which the parish accommodated or deferred to other local forms clearly varied substantially according to region, so it would be mistaken to assume its general dominance at any historical stage. Because of this, Archer warns:

> There are serious problems in regarding the parish as defining the boundaries of local community, particularly in an urban context. No geographical area will satisfactorily describe the boundaries of a local social system in the sense of the area within which the social relationships of inhabitants were constructed because it will not include all the termini of the social relationships involved.[25]

In similar fashion to the parochial guilds in the preceding centuries, the livery companies emerge in Archer's account as offering a more network-based, associational form of common identity, alongside other territorial divisions – notably precincts and wards. Yet among these other bonds of fellowship and locality, Archer is compelled to acknowledge that 'there is a strong case for asserting the primary importance of ties to the parish',[26] especially in binding people to a sense of local belonging. Interestingly, this could serve as a means of opening such community to those who might otherwise be, in effect, placeless – as Boulton displays, again with regard to seventeenth-century Southwark: 'Such an institution by fulfilling its role as "a gathering of neighbours" may have counteracted the dislocating influences of heavy immigration by acting as a "home from home" for first generation immigrants.'[27]

The contemporary resonance of this historic function is powerful, and clearly provides one of the keys to the parish's renewal in our own day. At the heart of such local pre-eminence lay a fairly unassailable complex of welfare and governance, combined with social customs and rituals of behaviour ('neighbourliness' being paramount among them)[28] that not only reflected or enhanced, but also *produced*, neighbourhood in early modern English communities. The result, proposes Steve Hindle, was an 'internalized' sense of place:

> The parish was the locale in which community was constructed and reproduced, perhaps even consecrated ... If, as the new sociology insists, society is a process constantly reproduced by its members, then in early modern England the parish was *the* arena in which structure, ritual and agency combined to create and maintain (and perhaps even to challenge) a highly localized sense of belonging.[29]

Especially in rural areas, the confluence of these currents was the enduring idea of *settlement*. In governmental terms, settlement was not, it may be stressed, some idyll of local rootedness, but defined purely and simply as 'the eligibility to receive poor relief in a parish or township where one had gained that status (i.e. *of* settlement)'.[30] From their institution in the late seventeenth century, to their abolition in the mid-nineteenth century, the settlement laws (with the accompanying vagrancy legislation that effectively tied landless poor to a particular parish) generated, argues Keith Snell, a complex and deeply hierarchical system of belonging in which, he writes, '"home" was a term of parish attachment'.[31] What Snell calls the 'eligibility to belong' in parochial terms proved an exceptionally durable component of English society, surviving, as we have seen, the reconfiguration of poor relief in the nineteenth century right up to the formation of the welfare state. Snell notes how, as late as 1932, a handbook for local welfare officers states: 'The place of settlement is the place to which a person "belongs". To such a place he may be removed; from such a place he may not be removed.'[32]

The settlement system, which did not finally disappear from the statute book until 1948, was, however, riddled with paradoxes and irregularities that resist any easy equation of 'parish' with 'neighbourhood'. It gave definition to local allegiance, unquestionably, but also corralled the poor into an enforced and dependent place within the community – the shadow side of parochial administration, in which the Church of England, as agent of the state, was bound to be complicit. Steve Hindle describes this dual effect as the 'dark parish'. His eloquent summary is worth quoting in full:

> In all these respects, the unit of obligation and control was the little commonwealth of the parish, which effectively became a welfare republic, the moral and physical boundaries of which had to be effectively policed. Of course the ancient settled poor of the parish lay at the heart of the community and were accordingly treated benevolently and with sympathy by their rate-paying neighbours. But if the local community was compassionate its compassion had a hard edge, and the realities of relief at the margins (where communities are always tested and new social identities formed) were grudging, mean and tainted by fear and suspicion.[33]

At the other end of the social scale, notes Snell, 'core belonging' had, by the end of the nineteenth century, increasingly come to be defined and demonstrated by ownership of property.[34] Among the ironies of the settlement system was the fact that the gradual repeal of settlement law between 1795 and 1876 – especially the abolition of the poor's 'removability' – in many cases had the opposite of the desired effect, fostering the growth of a mobile urban working class (who felt that they now had greater social security away from the parish) and often relocating those who 'belonged' in one parish to another, by virtue of the new Poor Law Unions.[35] As Charles Dickens was to parody to such effect in *Oliver Twist*, the already frayed fabric of parochial welfare was beginning to unravel.

The unsettled parish, 1834–94

It was in urban areas that the cracks in the Anglican consensus first made its monopoly of local government seem untenable. As Jonathan Barry explains, in his study of parishes in eighteenth-century Bristol:

Both the city and parish held a dual role (i.e. both secular and religious) and some kind of church establishment to express this unity seemed desirable to most. But religious pluralism, and the political divisions this engendered, increasingly meant that the ... parish administration became the focus of conflict, which seemed to threaten civic unity. This encouraged initiatives to bypass the parish in various areas of town life.[36]

The pattern of medieval parishes, largely unchanged by the middle of the nineteenth century,[37] not only became hopelessly inadequate for the purposes of local administration in the modern era, but was also marked by glaring regional inequalities. The 1851 census verified this in no uncertain terms, remarking: 'Parishes are, in many instances inextricably intermingled; and they vary in population from single families to tens of thousands of families; in extent, from a few hundreds of acres to many thousands of acres.'[38] And yet, because of the considerable variance, both in size of parishes and the efficacy of their governance, it is almost impossible to generalize about their positive or negative effect upon local communities. The parish of Liverpool, which had been formed in 1699 from the still larger parish of Walton, is an excellent case in point. By the year 1801 it contained a staggering 80,000 souls, which might be thought to have made its parochial administration unwieldy to say the least. Nevertheless, the efficiency and co-operation modelled by the Vestry (and its executive, the Parish Committee) presents Liverpool as a kind of proto-democracy – to the extent that Sidney and Beatrice Webb, the great Fabian chroniclers of English local government, assert that: 'To have crystallized in a general statute applying to all populous parishes the working constitution of Liverpool ... would have gone a long way to democratizing English home affairs.'[39]

The irony was that, when the long overdue creation of new parishes began in the nineteenth century, this often had the effect of loosening such effective and long-established communal bonds. Snell explains the paradox of such reforms thus:

In some ways they underline the vitality of the parish as a reconceivable and adaptable entity ... Yet they disrupted relatively clear-cut, integrated units of local attachment, in which lay affairs had a spiritual overlay ... They complicated and confused ideas of parish belonging, they undercut the parish as a moral ideal, and they splintered hitherto reciprocal and conjoint features of local life.[40]

While setting in motion a legislative process that gradually eroded parochialism, the New Poor Law of 1834 (and the protracted problems of its implementation) epitomized the contradictory forces to which the parish was subject in the nineteenth century. Although its amalgamation of parish-based relief into regional Poor Law Unions[41] marked the partial detachment of welfare from the parish, the persistence of the settlement laws and parish-based 'outdoor' relief (that is, welfare based on financial or other donations, rather than the workhouse) indicated the continued dependence of the state upon the parochial system as the nucleus of social service.

Despite the fact that, in rural areas especially, the old blend of sacred and secular persisted, the legislative current neverthe-less continued to head in only one direction during the Victorian era.[42] From the Sturges-Bourne Act of 1819, which required of parish vestries a measure of local democracy in decision-making, through to the 1836 Tithe Commutation Act, ending almost 1,000 years of tithe payments to the Church (the Church's right to receive tithes had been granted by King Ethelwulf in 855), to the abolition of church rates (the taxes levied locally for the upkeep of the parish church) in 1868, a series of bills gradually cut off from the parochial authorities both the autonomy and revenue necessary to govern as they had governed hitherto. This slow 'strangling of the parish', as the Webbs luridly refer to it, may have been inevitable but, they argue, it also:

> Unwittingly threw away ... the immemorial right of the inhab-itants in Vestry assembled to tax themselves for any purpose of public utility; and incidentally abandoned such public right as existed to the interesting and valuable public buildings which had, from the very beginning of English history, served as the secular as well as the religious meeting-place of the parish.[43]

The 1894 Local Government Act was the high-water mark of this process. Dubbed 'a bill for the spoliation of the Church of England' by critics,[44] it is particularly significant for the question at hand because of its effective separation of the secular and ecclesiastical functions of the parish. This Act, tackling what Snell calls 'all the confusing geographical miscellanea of Victorian local government', sought clarity by transferring to the civil parish (or district, in urban areas) the bulk of the Anglican Church's statutory responsibilities – for example, in the management of burial grounds or the appointment of local constables. With the incumbent relieved of his obligation to be chairman of the parish council and the Vestry shorn of its powers, the 1894 Act represents a hinge between eras which, according to R. W. Ambler, 'officially ended the close interrelationship between religious and civil affairs that had characterized the English parish from the 16th century ... [It] was, in effect, the local disestablishment of the Church of England.'[45]

Instrumental in this secularizing process, perhaps ironically, was the challenge brought by the rise of other Christian denominations. The Catholic Relief Act of 1829, the extension of the franchise, after 1832, to include nonconformists, and the vitality of dissenting churches, especially in the new towns and cities, made increasingly unfeasible the Elizabethan ideal of 'uniformity and conformity' in religion – and, by extension, the Anglican control of local social service.[46] In an unprecedented empirical study, Keith Snell offers gravestones in parish churchyards as an index of the shifting sense of parochial affiliation during this period. In particular, he alights on the phrase 'of this parish' (a common epigram to the deceased's name) as, he argues, a more precise indicator of belonging than the parish registers more commonly employed in local research.[47] While marriage registers, for example, tend simply to indicate residence at the time of marriage, Snell considers 'of this parish' to sound deeper echoes of local belonging:

When we read gravestones which say 'of this parish', we are surely receiving a stronger message: this seems to indicate greater rootedness to locality than underlay some parish-register usage of the term. Nobody dying and being buried in a parish which they were a temporary sojourner would have any obvious motive to have 'of this parish' inscribed on a monumental stone, nor would their relatives. A very certain, enduring and meaningful attachment to place was being chipped into stone and inscribed to posterity by such a memorial statement.[48]

Charting the incidence 'of this parish' in selected graveyards, Snell notices fascinating fluctuations in epitaphs linking people with place: from about 10 per cent of memorials in the first half of the eighteenth century (when, he argues, it would simply have been assumed that the deceased was 'of this parish', obviating the need for its inclusion), through a high of some 40 per cent in the period 1860–90 (when greater local mobility – and, no doubt, changing burial customs – encouraged parochial specification) to 'well below 10 per cent' by the late twentieth century.[49] In his explanation of this evidence, he concludes that: 'The parish, once the key unit of local governance and the organizing area of most people's secular and religious lives, has become a relic of its former self.'[50]

The invisible neighbourhood, 1894–1948

Perhaps the core of the parish's problems in the nineteenth century was a new approach to the idea of settlement which, especially with the rise of the new industrial cities, rapidly transformed the social landscape.[51] Considering the aforementioned decline in 'of this parish' inscriptions into the twentieth century, Snell remarks: 'Preoccupation after 1890 with national and imperial issues ... commonly made very local ties to place seem antiquated at all cultural levels. "Parochial", like "provincial", was one of the newly disparaging words of the later nineteenth century.'[52] Such pejorative associations of 'parish' were, he adds, compounded by the anti-parochialism of writers such as Dickens and Chadwick, for whom it was inextricably linked to the tyrannies of the

New Poor Law. In both church and society, then, the twentieth century saw the parish's growing invisibility as the acknowledged mainstay of English neighbourhood. Nevertheless, the picture is by no means one of inexorable decline – more one of evolution and adaptation, as has been demonstrated by a series of local studies over the last 30 years; these studies have considered in detail the impact upon churches of increased state welfare provision. While most of these concentrate on the years before 1914, are usually ecumenical in focus and are almost exclusively London-based, they shed useful light on the Church of England's changing role.

The fundamental matter arising from each of these is whether this *separation* of sacred and secular agencies at the local level necessarily involved a *decline* in the social service offered by the parish. It altered it, without doubt – perhaps immeasurably – but did it *reduce* the 'community value' of the Church of England? After all, the partial separation of church and state following the 1919 Enabling Act (which instigated the Church's own National Assembly and Parochial Church Councils) had been, for William Temple and his reformers, a matter of 'life and liberty' (as their movement was named), not the opposite.

In his study of the south London borough of Lambeth, Jeffrey Cox notes that the demise of the Vestry, while reducing its civic role, also 'provided an opportunity for the Church of England to strike out on its own'.[53] Although his overall portrayal is of a church in retreat which, especially in the interwar years, found itself merely plugging the holes in state provision, Cox is clear in resisting what he calls 'the inadequate generalization' that 'the welfare state killed off religion'.[54]

A similarly nuanced picture is painted by Jeremy Morris, in his study of the neighbouring London borough of Croydon, *Religion and Urban Change: Croydon 1840–1914*. Like Cox, Morris also emphasizes the processes of social differentiation, here accompanying the rapid suburbanization of Croydon in the mid-nineteenth century and its transition from semi-rural parish to metropolitan borough. Morris underlines the 'sheer weight of Anglican dominance' in Croydon's local government, in which the Vestry existed as 'the nexus of religion and political activism under the parochial system'.[55] The increasing redundancy of this system, owing to its combination of intransigent landed interest and unrepresentative leadership, saw the rise of a new breed of 'local state' that saw the old 'Anglican oligarchy' superseded by a separate municipal elite. One inevitable consequence of thus shifting the centre of local political gravity away from the Church of England was, Morris suggests, 'to set firmer boundaries to what was to be regarded as the legitimate sphere of religious activity'.[56]

An increasingly sectarian outlook for the Church of England was therefore unavoidable, and a significant conclusion of Morris's case is that the early twentieth century found the churches tending towards social programmes that were concerned with *endogenous* rather than *exogenous* growth – typically the 'softer' communal programmes (uniformed organizations, for example) that leavened parish life rather than 'hard' responsibilities – poor relief, in particular – delegated to the Church from without. To some extent the historical geographer Rex Walford takes up the story where Morris leaves it, in his fascinating study of suburban Middlesex between 1918 and 1945. Rare in viewing the parish church in the interwar years as more than merely a postscript to its Victorian heyday, Walford argues that, on the contrary, the Church of England fared surprisingly well in adapting to the rapid extension of Greater London, 'not only sustaining its presence in new districts (sometimes against considerable odds) but also recovering some lost ground from former generations and playing a key role in the development and maintenance of new communities as they formed'.[57]

Three things in particular strike home from his account: the first being the robustness and speed of the Anglican Church's response to suburban growth, which saw some 49 new parishes being created between 1923 and 1944. Second, the scale and pace of the mission – echoing that of a century earlier to urbanization, and with no evident loss of zeal or sense of communal responsibility – is matched by the vitality of the social programme being offered. One of the new churches considered in detail, St Alban's

North Harrow, appears typical – from which Walford records the comment of one new parishioner: 'We were pleased to find the new church so lively. It was the centre of life in the district. There were all sorts of organizations to belong to.'[58]

Third, while such observations are endorsed elsewhere in the region, from Walford's analysis it is clear that the social service so energetically embarked upon by Middlesex parish churches principally falls within Morris's category of 'endogenous growth' – that which is concerned, in other words, with the radial spread of church life into the community rather than the 'exogenous' sharing of civic administration which symbolized the parish's role in the former period. As he acknowledges in conclusion: 'What was lost was a general visibility for parson and church in wider community issues – and into the vacuum would eventually step the new borough authorities.'[59] Such visibility, however, was arguably not 'lost' in the 'New London' suburbs, because it had never existed there. The absence of its historic role in local government, while serving to excise the parish from most secular social histories of the period, plainly did not destroy Anglican social service in these communities: rather, it regrouped it around the liturgical and communal centre that, in Middlesex at least, continued to be a vital force in the formation of neighbourhood.

While such studies counter the Webbs' premature claim (from 1906) that the nineteenth century brought the 'death of the parish', an accurate diagnosis of its vitality in the twentieth century is hampered by what Keith Snell and Paul Ell see as an inadequate grasp of spatial patterns of religion among secular academics, whose 'predilection for national rather than local description' undermines their assessment of the Church's declining social influence. The latter, they contend, in their perceptive study *Rival Jerusalems*, is usually dismissed as 'a local matter'.[60] The parish evidently did not die, but has certainly been afflicted by three ailments, common to old age, which tend to explain its fading from the historical foreground. These may be characterized, first, as *amnesia* – the 'editing out' of the distinctive contribution made to civil society by the parish church in the twentieth century, not only by secular sociologists and historians, but by the Church of England, whose horizons, as we have seen, shifted to the nation state during the era of the two world wars; second, by a peculiarly Anglican *nostalgia* that can skew a true reading of parish history; and which, third, is regularly accompanied by a certain *hypochondria* – the Church's obsessive checking of its own pulse (again, predominantly at the national, not parochial, level), which has impelled statistical analysis of religion in Britain since the census began.[61]

A snapshot of the parochial history of Christ Church, Gipsy Hill, one of the Lambeth parish churches cited in Jeffrey Cox's study, yields telling evidence of at least two of these conditions at play. Christ Church's centenary history, for example (published in 1967), describes the interwar years wistfully as 'the golden age of church going',[62] in which: 'A Christian community whose whole life was concerned ... not only [with] spiritual sustenance, but their social life as well ... would that it might now be so!'[63] The parish magazines from that halcyon time, however, bristle with warnings from the vicar of that community's impending moral collapse. Displaying what Patrick Wright has called 'the grieving hindsight of the 1930s', the incumbent writes, in August 1937, 'As I look out upon the parish, I realize that the church is definitely in touch with only a small minority of the people.' Commenting on the 'prevailing indifference' to the 'precious old paths' of Christian society, he concludes, bleakly, 'The fact remains that the people of England are living apart from the church.'[64]

The parish records suggest that the truth lay, in all probability, somewhere between these twin poles of exaltation and despair. Indeed, the chief impression given is of *continuity*, not least in relation to social service. An interesting index of the latter appears in the progress of the Gipsy Hill 'Poor and Parochial Fund', the 'general purse of the parish' which, according to the 1917 parish accounts, 'dispenses to needy homes with the best judgement that the vicar and the district visitors can exercise and gives a great amount of practical relief and comfort in this way'.[65] Two things are notable about this fund during the period in question: first, that despite the concerns of the Vestry about falling receipts, the budget remained at a healthy level, standing at £298 in 1900 and £328 in 1933. Second, the accounts show, from 1919, an increasing proportion of the Poor and Parochial Fund as 'administered through the agency of the Charity Organization Society' rather than the direct control of the vicar. Though fragmentary, such evidence strengthens the impression that gradual separation of local welfare provision from the Church of England meant the *realignment*, but not necessarily the *decline*, of its charity. The secularization of social institutions, then as now, by no means indicates the withdrawal of Anglican presence from them.

The persistent parish, 1948–

Its relative obscurity in twentieth-century scholarship is one reason why, as David Martin acknowledged in the 1980s, 'Sociologists have not done a great deal of work on the parish.'[66] Certainly it barely merits mention in his significant 1967 study *A Sociology of English Religion*, although this does admit the need for future research into England's 'local ecclesiastical history and religious social geography'.[67] Perhaps, as David Clark proposed, in one of the very few studies of the theme, the dual identity of the parish as both a civil and ecclesiastical entity has deterred sociological inquiry. Clark considered that parochial studies were hindered by the parish's existence as something of a contradiction in terms, whereby: 'The sociologist who is asked to study the parish today is faced with investigating a unit which in many places is of declining ecclesiastical viability and frequently of little secular relevance.'[68]

Paying insufficient attention to the local character of English Christianity only reinforces the mistaken impression of its irrelevance: for one is, quite simply, 'looking in the wrong place'. This is especially troublesome given that attention to a particular territory is a defining feature of Anglican tradition and practice. When the academic focus on locality is restored, it is telling how the parochial emerges from obscurity – as the various, albeit few, sociological studies of postwar parish life have revealed. Perhaps unsurprisingly, the idea of 'neighbourhood' again comes to the fore in these, as Neal and Walters pick up in their recent ethnographic study, 'Rural Social Belonging and Rural Social Organizations', which notes how the creation of one 'parish map' enhanced 'the convergence of locality and sociality' among those interviewed.[69] Another rural study, by Winter and Short (from 1994), is significant in avoiding the usual criteria for religiosity and focusing instead on attitudes towards the Church of England, and its clergy in particular. Their sample survey, drawn from village parishioners in five rural dioceses, revealed a high level of identification with the Church – with 62 per cent considering that they 'belonged' to the Church of England.[70] The authors conclude that, by using such indices, 'we have revealed a relatively, and perhaps surprisingly, low level of secularization'.[71]

While acknowledging the enduring 'social fact' of the English country church, Anglican priest and social anthropologist Timothy Jenkins also provides a fascinating account of Christian society persisting in a suburban community – the parish of Kingswood, in Bristol. Jenkins argues that the prevailing 'narrative of decline' is inadequate because it herds empirical data into 'objective' external categories that these may not fit. A social-anthropological approach, by contrast, is *indigenous* to a particular community and releases local data to define its own meanings and categories. Thus 'religion', for Jenkins, is not necessarily a helpful category to use: regarding the parish in question, his overriding question is instead 'What is it like to live in Kingswood?' This is answered through an extended study of 'The Kingswood Whit Walk', a local church custom in which 'personality, territoriality and local history' all combine. Although the walk is an 'act of witness' by the local churches, Jenkins emphasizes how: 'All Kingswood is present, the respectable and rowdy, in a celebration of local identity ... [which] has different meanings for different members of the community.'[72] 'Religion' is deliberately kept in the background of this study – not because it is unimportant, but in order to appreciate its local dimensions more clearly. Through the lens of the Whit Walk, Jenkins perceives how issues of belief, belonging and social ethics (characterized here by the terms 'fecklessness' and 'respectability') all converge in a manner that is peculiar to this parish. Only after such careful attention, Jenkins later reflects, can religion 're-emerge' in a way that is locally authentic.[73] This case study is extremely useful (even if now a little dated) in being a rare example of a single parish being studied as a microcosm of English parochialism in practice – a contemporary analogy to the boundary perambulations of a former era. In so doing, Jenkins underlines the need for local particularity to inform general-izations about religious trends, and not vice versa. Commenting on their 'misrecognition' in modern social studies, he concludes, drily: 'Communities of the kind studied here were supposed to have disappeared ... [but] have long existed behind the appear-ance of "being about to disappear".'[74]

Such examples should, of course, be set alongside others where the picture was not quite so encouraging for the Church, such as research by Geoffrey Ahern (from 1987) and Laurie Green (from 1995) into Anglican belief and practice among white working-class residents in east London, and Malcolm Torry's useful collection of reflections on contemporary parish ministry in the Diocese of Southwark. From his work with the South London Industrial Mission, Torry observes that, despite a 'distancing' of ecclesiastical institutions from secular agencies: 'The parish, understood as a patch of ground, as the people who live and work on it ... has been and still is a bulwark against secular-ization in ways that other styles of religious organization cannot be.'[75]

Conclusion

Drawing conclusions from the foregoing, three points are imme-diately clear. First, that throughout an extremely long tenure the parish occupied an unrivalled position as the archetype of English neighbourhood: a fact warmly endorsed by historians from medieval to modern periods. Second, despite (and perhaps because of) its deep rooting, the parish proved both resilient and surprisingly adaptive to the changing cultural and political climate, redefining and reasserting its peculiar blend of territory, community and Christian ethics at successive stages when it might otherwise have been abandoned.[76] Third, that while society at large became, from the nineteenth century onwards, more secular in its vision, the Church did not, interestingly, become *less* secular in its own: making the most of its remaining mandate for the 'cure of souls' in a persistent work of place-formation.[77]

This much is evident. Nevertheless, if 'neighbourhood' is not simply another word for an area or district, but an *ethos* – a way of living locally – there is a deep moral ambivalence about the parochial record that has to be acknowledged. In particular, this derives from the parish's bounded nature, which has always been both its strength and weakness. In the present time, this becomes increasingly problematic, partly due to a narrative within the Church that characterizes the existing parochial model as inherently archaic and restrictive of growth,[78] but also because of a postmodern geographical account that has asked serious questions of the use and abuse of boundary in social structures. Two aspects of this important critique are of special pertinence here, the first being that territorial boundaries, as social constructions, are inevitably 'exercises of power' imposed in order 'to establish outsiders – those who do not belong', according to Doreen Massey.[79] Thus it follows that a large part of the work of a human geographer lies in *deconstructing* the social forces that determine where the lines are drawn: a process in which cartography emerges as vitally significant in revealing the multiple means by which space is culturally and politically represented.[80]

The second relevant aspect of the postmodern critique argues, as already observed, for a more fluid conception of social space than traditional concepts of boundary might allow. Doreen Massey's *For Space* is perhaps the most convincing appraisal of this movement, in which she not only notes the transition from a structuralist approach that robbed space of its dynamism by equating it with a negation of time, but equally criticizes post-structuralism for not liberating space sufficiently from this straitjacket. The modernist tendency to *contain* space by means of boundaries, local and national, is, Massey argues, innately conservative, all too often gazing back to a non-existent past. The counterpart of this is a 'persistent tendency to exonerate the local' without regard to the 'flows' of interconnectedness that form any local community.[81]

To what extent does this salvo hit home when aimed at the Anglican parish? Certainly, to defend historic parish boundaries as if they represent a kind of ecclesiastical Rourke's Drift is unlikely to serve their survival. However, the danger (as with the earlier consideration of Stanley Hauerwas's account of nationalism) is that the postmodern critique misses the mark because its target – usually modernity – is set too close and so never quite 'lands' on the English situation, whose positions begin much further back. Unquestionably effective as a criticism of, for example, the land enclosures of the eighteenth and nineteenth centuries, the fact is that many parish boundaries had already existed for a millennium by that stage, in an unmapped and altogether different form.[82]

This said, it is vital that the often-bitter reality of parochial life is recalled and, to the extent that it was ever a 'structure' in a sociological sense, deconstructed, in order to forestall the idealism that all too easily clouds this theme. Incontestably, power interests have been at the heart of parochial definition since the earliest times, as the previous chapter demonstrated. Furthermore, there is a strong case for viewing the parochial system – via the Tudor Poor Laws and, in particular, the 1662 Settlement Act that tied the landless poor to their parish – as a tyranny of locality, a parody of neighbourhood. In his landmark essay *The Country and the City*, Raymond Williams argued powerfully that, while the parochial arrangement of poor relief was 'rationalized as the duty of people to care for their own, for their neighbours', the reality of its restrictions on movement were 'insolent indifference to most people's needs'.[83] Its idealization of parochial 'settlement' was, Williams claims, particularly damaging: 'Settlement is indeed easy ... for those who can settle in a reasonable independence. For those who cannot ... it can become a prison: a long disheartening and despair, under an imposed rigidity of conditions.'[84]

While the moral force of Williams's case must be heard, there have appeared since his work was published a growing number of other, more nuanced, assessments of the bounded nature of the traditional parish. Among these, two recurrent themes emerge: the high degree of local variation in, for example, the application of settlement laws (including the long-running historical distinction between 'open' and 'closed' parishes)[85] and, second, the surprisingly adaptive nature of the parochial system to changing social circumstance. Arguing that the enduring idea of the 'self-contained community' is 'at best, a half-truth', social historian Keith Wrightson urges that 'the real strength of social ties must not be held to imply that local communities were either bounded or static'.[86]

In assessing the nature and role of the parish boundary in early modern England, Nicola Whyte has made the important contention that, contrary to the prevailing opinion that these constituted an essentially stable system between 1200 and 1800, parish boundaries were, within limits, flexible and negotiated by social relationship. Contending that the Ordnance Survey's selection of the parish boundary as the basic administrative unit 'diverted attention away from the existence of a complex, multi-layered web of territories', Whyte considers that it was essentially a locally enacted reality, often contested and open to a degree of adjustment, even after the introduction of modern cartography.[87] This certainly appears to have been the case with the neighbouring parishes of Tooting and Streatham whose Vestries, as late as 1808, formally agreed to exchange various parcels of land and housing without any apparent thought that such a decision concerned an external authority.[88]

The principal theatre for establishing these mutual arrangements, over many centuries, was the annual Rogationtide 'beating of the bounds'. It is hard to overestimate the significance of these annual perambulations, which will be considered further in the final chapter. Considering them to be 'the principal means by which the local community was defined in early modern England', Steve Hindle deftly explains their peculiar significance as 'one of those fleeting moments when society might be observed in the act of describing itself'.[89] Both symbolically and practically, beating the bounds was as much about defining relationships with neighbours outside the boundary as those within. In an insightful article, 'The Parish Boundary: A Social Phenomenon in Hanoverian England', David Fletcher acknowledges the ambivalence of the boundary as agent of, simultaneously, 'territorial threat and social cohesion', noting how boundary perambulations served not only to enhance collective identity but also prevent incursions into the parish from neighbouring paupers.[90] The paradox seems to be that, in the traditional parish, social inclusion was generated by a measure of social exclusion, a fact suggested in Fletcher's concluding remarks: 'Adversity, in the form of external threat to the territorial integrity of a parish, was perhaps the most socially binding process. The dividing function of a parish boundary at one spatial scale could have a bonding role on the people contained within it at the most local level.'[91] While, plainly, that boundary could foster the kind of local xenophobia to which parochialism has always been prone, Fletcher nevertheless finds that perambulations were, on balance, 'a force more for social cohesion than for division, at least at the intra-parish level; a notion at odds perhaps with the spatial characteristic of the boundary line as literally a division'.[92] The risk that bounded locality will involve pulling up the communal drawbridge is vital to recognize. However, in Massey's phrase, it would be 'a failure of spatial imagination' to consider the limits of the parish only in defensive terms, rather than, to borrow a biological metaphor, a kind of 'permeable membrane' that affords the necessary boundary conditions for the very kind of dynamic interrelation she espouses to flourish.[93]

In his early poem *Mending Wall*, Robert Frost uses the gruff refrain 'good fences make good neighbours', repeated by the old man living next door, to explore the paradox that boundaries are necessary in order for people to live together. 'Before I built a wall', Frost reflects, 'I'd ask to know what I was walling in or walling out'. Such physical boundaries give concrete form to a much less visible social contract. Though shaped by landscape, gated and punctuated by signs, lines and barriers, a community begins, essentially, as an idea: its border a meniscus formed by the surface tension of people pulling together. When these are imposed from outside – witness the crude, imperial carve-up of Africa in the 1880s or Europe after the Great War – they tend to end in communal dismemberment. Enduring community is internally conceived and exists as the product of a shared imagination, or 'the common objects of love' – notwithstanding the fact that, when people love in common, the objects of their shared fear and hatred are never far away. So, then, to play borders down is not to belong: to love everywhere equally is to love nowhere very much.[94]

Contemporary human geography tends to encourage the view that heavily drawn national and local boundaries are, at best, socially restrictive and, at worst, geographically redundant. Doreen Massey's plea for a more 'messy' understanding of space and place is at its most winning in its desire that they should enable the 'thrown togetherness' that 'may set us down next to the unexpected neighbour'. Against the rigid mapping of human territory, she writes: 'On the road map you won't drive off the edge of your known world. In space as I want to imagine it, you just might.' But the vital counterpoint is that boundaries enable one to do just that – by delineating and describing the 'known world'. Indeed, there is arguably no such thing as a 'known world' without a boundary – personal knowledge always being limited. Boundaries are thus a necessary part of human physicality: communities require them as bodies require skin. They exist in order to enable social inclusion, not frustrate it. For the sake of a clear and pleasant worldview, there is a temptation to remove them from sight: to make each one a kind of cultural ha-ha, giving the illusion of free passage until you realize the ground has disappeared underneath you. As with neighbourhood: so with the nation. The philosopher Alasdair MacIntyre has disputed the liberal idea that to act morally 'is to learn to free oneself from social particularity' – to be, effectively, 'citizens of everywhere'. On the contrary, he argues: '"Where" and "from whom" I learn my morality turn out to be crucial for the context and nature of moral commitment, as any form of morality will be intimately connected with specific institutional arrangements.'[95] Loyalty to a particular community, he continues, is 'a prerequisite for morality', concluding: 'deprived of this community I am unlikely to flourish as a moral agent'. In *Mending Wall*, Robert Frost questions the wisdom of bricking up a boundary where none seems to be needed – especially when there is so much that 'wants it down'. As for his neighbour, he reflects:

> He is all pine and I am apple orchard.
> My apple trees will never get across
> And eat the cones under his pines, I tell him.

Nevertheless, the shared task of reconstructing the wall – dismissed at first as 'just another outdoor game: one on a side' – becomes both the occasion and the fulcrum of his relationship to the old man next door. The pressing contemporary challenge is thus not how to dismantle borders, but instead reconfigure them so that both 'inside' and 'outside' relationships are enabled in morally positive ways. Fundamentally, this requires starting not at a community's limits but at its centre, for boundaries are merely the extension of our core vision and purpose. If a society's borders have gone haywire, we can be sure something is badly wrong at the centre. When, however, the 'soul' of a community is secure, the borders can afford to be less so, paradoxically, because – to employ the familiar trope of neighbourhood – this is the kind of place where you can leave your door open.

Notes

1 Rebecca Herron, Jennifer Jackson and Karen Johnson, in Gary Bosworth and Peter Somerville (eds), *Interpreting Rurality*, Abingdon: Routledge, 2014, p. 75.

2 K. D. M. Snell, *Parish and Belonging*, Cambridge: CUP, 2006, p. 499.

3 Snell, *Parish and Belonging*, p. 499.

4 Katherine French assesses the development of this strand of social history in the introduction to *The Parish in English Life, 1400–1640*, Manchester: MUP, 1997.

5 French, *Parish in English Life*, p. 3.

6 Derek Fraser, *The Evolution of the British Welfare State*, Basingstoke: Palgrave Macmillan, 2003. William Temple coins the term 'welfare state' in *Christianity and the State*, London: Macmillan, 1928; for commentary, see Matthew Grimley, *Citizenship, Community and the Church of England: Liberal Anglican Theories of the State between the Wars*, Oxford: Clarendon Press, 2004, pp. 1ff.

7 Jeremy Morris, 'The Strange Death of Christian Britain: Another Look at the Secularization Debate', *The Historical Journal*, 46.4 (2003), p. 972.

8 Discussed in Jane Garnett, Matthew Grimley and Alana Harris (eds), *Redefining Christian Britain: Post-1945 Perspective*, London: SCM Press, 2007.

9 Callum Brown, *The Death of Christian Britain*, London: Routledge, 2001, p. 7.

10 See Garnett, Grimley and Harris (eds), *Redefining Christian Britain*, p. 289.

11 For concurrence regarding this date for establishment of the parish 'system', see D. M. Palliser, in Susan Wright (ed.), *Parish, Church and People: Local Studies in Lay Religion 1350–1750*, London: Hutchinson, 1988, p. 9.

12 R. A. R. Hartridge, *A History of Vicarages in the Middle Ages*, Cambridge: CUP, 1930, p. 2.

13 Katherine French, *The People of the Parish: Community Life in a Late Medieval Diocese*, Pennsylvania: University of Pennsylvania Press, 2000, p. 43.

14 French, *People of the Parish*, p. 21.

15 Judith Bennett considers the role of 'parish ales' in this respect in 'Conviviality and Charity in Medieval and Early Modern England', *Past & Present*, 154.1 (1997).

16 French, *Parish in English Life*, ch. 7; French, *People of the Parish*, ch. 4.

17 Gervase Rosser observes 'a common impetus ... to transcend the limitations, geographical or institutional, of the parish' – especially apparent 'in social contexts characterized by a relatively high degree of mobility, such as the parish could not accommodate' (in 'Communities of Parish and Guild in the Late Middle Ages', in Wright (ed.), *Parish, Church and People*, p. 33).

18 Wright (ed.), *Parish, Church and People*, p. 45.

19 Noted by Palliser in Wright (ed.), *Parish, Church and People*, p. 11.

20 Tate notes (in *The Parish Chest*, Cambridge: CUP, 1969, p. 14) scholarly disagreement regarding the origin of the Vestry, but supports the Webbs' dating of its inception to 1507. According to Tate, the parish thus became 'the territorial basis for community service' (*Parish Chest*, p. 5).

21 In French, *Parish in English Life*, p. 163. For accrual of power by parish officers, see also Steve Hindle, 'A Sense of Place? Becoming and Belonging in the Rural Parish 1550–1650', in Alexandra Shepard and Phil Withington (eds), *Communities in Early Modern England*, Manchester: MUP, 2000, p. 98.

22 French, *Parish in English Life*, pp. 168–9.

23 Jeremy Boulton, *Neighbourhood and Society: A London Suburb in the Seventeenth Century*, Cambridge: CUP, 1987, p. 266.

24 Ian W. Archer, *The Pursuit of Stability: Social Relations in Elizabethan London*, Cambridge: CUP, 2003, p. 169.

25 Archer, *Pursuit of Stability*, p. 82. This local variegation is endorsed by other commentators, for example: Nicola Whyte, in 'Landscape, Memory and Custom: Parish Identities, c. 1550–1700', *Social History*, 32.2 (2007), and Angus Winchester, 'Dividing Lines in a Moorland Landscape: Territorial Boundaries in Upland England', *Landscapes* 1.2 (2000), pp. 16–32. Winchester demonstrates how, in the 'Northern uplands', parochial organization was much more complex, interwoven with and subdivided by townships and other settlement patterns.

26 Archer, *Pursuit of Stability*, p. 83.

27 Boulton quotes Wrightson in this excerpt (in *English Society 1580–1680*, London: Routledge, 1982, p. 213).

28 Keith Wrightson underlines the centrality of 'neighbourliness' in early modern social ethics in Paul Griffiths, Adam Fox and Steve Hindle (eds), *The Experience of Authority in Early Modern England*, London: Macmillan, 1996, ch. 1.

29 Hindle, 'A Sense of Place?', p. 96.

30 Snell, *Parish and Belonging*, p. 85.

31 Snell, *Parish and Belonging*, p. 87.

32 Snell, *Parish and Belonging*, p. 159.

33 Hindle, 'A Sense of Place?', p. 99.

34 Snell, *Parish and Belonging*, p. 158.

35 Snell, *Parish and Belonging*, pp. 158–9.

36 Jonathan Barry, 'The Parish in Civic Life: Bristol and its Churches 1640–1750', in Wright (ed.), *Parish, Church and People*, p. 171.

37 K. D. M. Snell and Paul S. Ell note 'significant parochial discontinuities' of only 5 per cent between the 1676 'Compton' census and that of 1851 (in *Rival Jerusalems*, Cambridge: CUP, 2009, p. 251).

38 Census of 1851, cited in H. C. Darby (ed.), *A New Historical Geography of England*, Cambridge: CUP, 1973, p. 531.

39 Sidney and Beatrice Webb, *English Local Government. The Parish and County*, London: Frank Cass & Co., 1963, p. 146.

40 Snell, *Parish and Belonging*, p. 370.

41 For a useful survey, see Derek Fraser, *The New Poor Law*, London: Macmillan, 1976.

42 E. R. Norman usefully weighs this legislation in *Church and Society in England 1770–1970*, Oxford: Clarendon Press, 1976, pp. 109–22; also Owen Chadwick, *The Victorian Church Part II*, 2nd edn, London: A&C Black, 1972, pp. 194–6. Woodward (1938) saw the 1868 Act as the point after which 'the parish as a unit of government fell into decay' (in *The Age of Reform: 1815–1870*, Oxford: OUP, 1938, p. 451).

43 Webb, *Parish and the County*, p. 172.

44 In Chadwick, *The Victorian Church*, p. 196.

45 R. W. Ambler, *Churches, Chapels and Parish Communities of Lincolnshire, 1660–1900*, Lincoln: History of Lincolnshire Committee, 2000, p. 2. Cf. also Snell, *Parish and Belonging*, p. 446. Nevertheless, E. R. Norman notes how the idea of the 'secular' parish lingered on post-1894 (in *Church and Society in England*, p. 54).

46 For Callum Brown, the critical contribution of evangelical piety in this loosening of establishment ties lay in its stress upon the individual as free moral agent. This it was that gave Victorian voluntarism its primary motive force and, in Brown's words, 'broke the mental chains of the *ancien regime*' (in *The Death of Christian Britain*, London: Routledge, 2001, p. 36). Frank Prochaska concurs: 'evangelicals ran perhaps as many as three out of four voluntary societies during the second half of the nineteenth century' (in *Christianity and Social Service in Modern Britain*, Oxford: OUP, 2006, p. 13).

47 For the genealogical potential of parochial studies, including maps of each parish in England, see also Cecil Humphery-Smith (ed.), *The Phillimore Atlas and Index of Parish Registers*, Chichester: Phillimore, 1984.

48 K. D. M. Snell, 'Gravestones, Belonging and Local Attachment in England', *Past & Present*, 179 (2003), p. 101. This study was later incorporated into Snell's *Parish and Belonging*.

49 Snell, 'Gravestones', p. 116.

50 Snell, 'Gravestones', p. 121.

51 See P. J. Perry, *A Geography of 19th-Century Britain*, London: Batsford, 1975, pp. 44–8.

52 Perry, *A Geography*, p. 127. Julia Stapleton notes this early-twentieth-century anti-localism in 'The Voice of Chesterton in the Conversation of England', *The Chesterton Review*, XXXV, 3 and 4, pp. 617–34.

53 Jeffrey Cox, *English Churches in a Secular Society: Lambeth, 1870–1930*, Oxford: OUP, 1982, p. 183.

54 Cox, *English Churches*, pp. 210–13. The process of social differentiation, central to secularization theory, finds strong endorsement in Cox's account of Lambeth, being particularly evident in his description of a developing professionalism in social work – especially through the evolving role of the Charity Organization Society, which came to replace the amateur philanthropy of the parish visitors.

55 Jeremy Morris, *Religion and Urban Change: Croydon, 1840–1914*, Woodbridge: Boydell Press, 1992, p. 107.

56 Morris, *Religion*, p. 155.

57 Rex Walford, *The Growth of 'New London' in Suburban Middlesex and the Response of the Church of England*, Lampeter: Edwin Mellen Press, 2007, p. 324.

58 Walford, *Growth of 'New London'*, p. 155.

59 Walford, *Growth of 'New London'*, p. 380.

60 K. D. M. Snell and Paul S. Ell, *Rival Jerusalems: The Geography of Victorian Religion*, Cambridge: CUP, 2009, pp. 2ff, pp. 395ff. This, despite the fact that, as Coleman affirms, local variegation has been a defining feature of English religion. See B. I. Coleman, *The Church of England in the Mid-Nineteenth Century: A Social Geography*, London: The Historical Association, 1980. See also John Gay, *Geography of Religion in England*, London: Duckworth, 1971.

61 See Brown, *Death*, ch. 2, for evidence of the Church's misplaced statistical pessimism.

62 Christ Church Gipsy Hill, *Centenary 1867–1967*, p. 6.

63 *Centenary*, p. 6. Jeffrey Cox notes the diversity and activism of the Christ Church social programme at this time in *English Churches*, p. 41.

64 *Christ Church Gipsy Hill Parish Magazine*, 1936–44.

65 *Christ Church Financial Reports*, 1917–33. This relic of the 'secular' parish was only recently wound down.

66 In Giles Ecclestone (ed.), *The Parish Church?*, Oxford: Mowbray, 1988, p. 44.

67 David Martin, *A Sociology of English Religion*, London: Heinemann, 1967, p. 123.

68 David Clark, 'The Sociological Study of The Parish', *The Expository Times*, 82 (1971), p. 296.

69 Sarah Neal and Sue Walters, 'Rural Social Belonging and Rural Social Organizations: Conviviality and Community-making in the English Countryside', *Sociology*, 42.2 (2008), pp. 285ff.

70 Michael Winter and Christopher Short, 'Believing and Belonging: Religion in Rural England', *The British Journal of Sociology*, 44.4 (1993), p. 641.

71 Winter and Short, 'Believing and Belonging', p. 648.

72 Timothy Jenkins, *Religion in English Everyday Life*, Oxford: Berghahn, 1999, p. 99.

73 Timothy Jenkins, *An Experiment in Providence*, London: SPCK, 2006, p. 101.

74 Jenkins, *Religion*, p. 216.

75 Malcolm Torry (ed.), *The Parish: People, Place and Ministry*, Norwich: Canterbury Press, 2004, p. 10. Geoffrey Ahern and Grace Davie, *Inner City God*, London: Hodder & Stoughton, 1987, p. 131; Laurie

Green in Peter Sedgwick (ed.), *God in the City*, London: Mowbray, 1995, pp. 72–92. Green's study of 'Christian religious experience' in Poplar also reveals what he calls 'a deeper hidden life' closely linking a 'sense of God' to a 'sense of place'.

76 Beat Kumin observes that, for the parish, 'adaptation and resilience appear as the underlying themes throughout the centuries' (in *The Communal Age in Western Europe c. 1100–1800*, New York: Palgrave Macmillan, 2013, p. 52).

77 In F. D. Maurice's terms, while the nation arguably lost its 'anti-secularity', the Church did not. Maurice writes: 'A nation is anti-secular in one way, just as much as the church is anti-secular in another' (in *The Kingdom of Christ*, London: SCM Press, 1958, vol. II, V, iii, p. 241).

78 The most historically well-informed of these critiques is Nick Spencer's *Parochial Vision: The Future of the English Parish*, Carlisle: Paternoster Press, 2004.

79 Doreen Massey and Pat Jess (eds), *A Place in the World? Places, Cultures and Globalization*, Oxford: OUP, 1995, pp. 69 and 99. See also David Sibley, *Geographies of Exclusion*, London: Routledge, 1995, chs 5 and 6.

80 See David Harvey, *The Condition of Postmodernity*, Oxford: Blackwell, 1990, ch. 15. For the territorial 'rules' that define being 'in place' or 'out of place', see Robert Sack, 'The Power of Place and Space', *Geographical Review*, 83.3 (1993), p. 17; Robert Schreiter, *Constructing Local Theologies*, New York: Orbis, 1985, p. 54; also Michel Foucault, *Power/Knowledge: Selected Interviews and Other Writings, 1972–1977*, New York: Pantheon, 1980.

81 Doreen Massey, *For Space*, London: Sage, 2005, pp. 102–3. Interestingly, Beaver records that nonconformists in early modern England rejected the parish boundary as sinful and man-made (in *Parish Communities and Religious Conflict in the Vale of Gloucester, 1590–1690*, Harvard: Harvard University Press, 1998, p. 325).

82 According to Angus Winchester, parish boundaries are 'among the most durable legacies from the Anglo-Saxon period' (in *Discovering Parish Boundaries*, Princes Risborough: Shire, 2000, p. 5). David Harvey notes how enclosures 'forcefully transformed the English landscape' – and local society along with it (in *The Condition of Postmodernity*, Oxford: Blackwell, 1990, p. 254).

83 Raymond Williams, *The Country and the City*, London: Chatto & Windus, 1973, p. 84.

84 Williams, *Country and City*, p. 85. Wrightson remarks how, in early modern England, 'neighbourliness was confined to the more settled inhabitants' (in *English Society 1580–1680*, London: Routledge, 1982, p. 57).

85 Much-discussed historical terms, relating to the rural labour market and the 'openness' or otherwise of particular parishes to receiving potential incomers. Snell gives a good summary in *Parish and Belonging*, pp. 127–8.

86 Wrightson, *English Society*, p. 48.

87 Whyte, 'Landscape, Memory and Custom', pp. 170ff; Nicola Whyte, *Inhabiting the Landscape: Place, Custom and Memory 1500–1800*, Oxford: Windgather Press, 2009, ch. 3. See also Keith Wrightson, *Politics of the Parish*, ch. 1.

88 Webb, *Parish and the County*, p. 53. They cite further examples from the same period.

89 Steve Hindle, 'Beating the Bounds of the Parish: Order, Memory and Identity in the English Local Community, c 1500–1700', in Michael J. Halvorson and Karen E. Spierling (eds), *Defining Community in Early Modern Europe*, Aldershot: Ashgate, 2008, p. 206.

90 David Fletcher, 'The Parish Boundary: A Social Phenomenon in Hanoverian England', *Rural History*, 14.2 (2003), pp. 187–9.

91 Fletcher, 'The Parish Boundary', p. 192.

92 Fletcher, 'The Parish Boundary', p. 192. Hindle finds that parish boundaries marked an ethical as well as physical delimitation by depicting those beyond the bounds as 'strangers', and thereby unsafe (in Shepard and Withinton (eds), *Communities in Early Modern England*, p. 97).

93 Timothy Gorringe, in conversation with the author, comments that 'all boundaries bleed at the edges, they always have'.

94 An adaptation of Oliver O'Donovan's phrase 'to love everyone equally is to love no one very much' (in 'The Loss of a Sense of Place', *Irish Theological Quarterly*, 55.1 (1989)). The nature writer Roger Deakin picks up this theme, with reference to John Donne's poem *The Good Morrow*: 'A parish accommodates to the imagination because it is framed or contained ... by ancient boundaries, natural and supernatural.' As in Donne's poem, Deakin writes, the parish 'makes one little room, an everywhere' (in Sue Clifford and Angela King (eds), *From Place to PLACE*, London: Common Ground, 1996, p. 27).

95 Alasdair MacIntyre, *Is Patriotism a Virtue? The Lindley Lecture for 1984*, Kansas: University of Kansas, 1984, p. 9.

6

A Handful of Earth: Parish, Landscape and Nostalgia

Stumping around the massive tower of Oxted church at dawn. This squat trunk, recorded by some footsore scribe in the Domesday Book, is more geological feature than building – an extrusion or outcrop, an ecclesiastical crag reforming the terrain. Here, local ironstones pepper the exterior of walls so thick that the belling clock wells time deeply into space, lending the land an implanted musical pulse. 'The earth has a way of absorbing things that are placed upon it', wrote Richard Jeffries, 'of drawing from them their stiff individuality of newness and throwing over them something of her own antiquity'.

Yet each of the trio of medieval churches under my care is a stripling next to the pair of ancient yew trees in the grounds of two of them, Tandridge and Crowhurst. Tautly banded like a Leonardo muscle and with a rippling girth of 34 feet, the Tandridge Yew must be just about the oldest living thing in England. Or perhaps the second oldest: by an odd quirk of local competition, its senior stands in the graveyard of our neighbouring parish of Crowhurst. This leviathan broke the soil well before King David penned his first Psalm and is said to approach a breathtaking 4,000 years old.

Hollowing out as they age, yews are anatomized while still alive, so you can enter the blackened belly and be swallowed whole, like a dry Jonah. To be chambered thus is an intensely mortal moment: birth, breath and death – all feel close. In a nice domestication of its primal power, teas were once served from within the Crowhurst Yew, which reputedly also hosted parish meetings of up to a dozen people. Standing sciatically inside, that seems a bit far-fetched, although the Hobbit-hole impression is enhanced by the addition of a slanting door about four feet tall, wedged into the dirt.

The door was constructed in the early nineteenth century, a refurbishment that liberated a cannonball from the English Civil War, wedged deeply into the flesh of the tree. The Tudor pile opposite the churchyard was a Royalist stronghold during that conflict, so the bullet must have slammed into the tree during a skirmish, gradually becoming pearled into the trunk, as pink sinews of wood enfolded the wound.

The graveyard fogged in a gunpowder haze, the offensive blow absorbed, neutralized – a leaden own-goal, saved in the tree's embrace: this story stirs a Dream of the Rood worth a season of sermons. In that early English visionary poem, the cross tells its own tale of the Lord's Passion: 'the soul's sweet dwelling-place'. Felled, then pressed into divine service, the tree describes its own grievous duty to bear the blows alongside Christ:

> I was raised up a Rood, a royal King I bore.
> The High King of Heaven: hold firm I must.
> They drove dark nails through me, the dire wounds still show,
> Cruel gaping gashes, yet I dared not give as good.

I next visit Crowhurst for Plough Sunday: winter in reverse and the farmers' work blessed ahead of the growing season. I'm joined at the front of the church by a huddle of bantams domed in wire, a milk churn and a hefty ploughshare: all in place for the ancient grace, 'God speed the plough!' Lambeth was never like this. Taking an opportunity to survey the ordnance, I discover that their yew tree's gallstone still exists: 'there is a cannonball in the vestry', confirms the churchwarden. Heavy in my hands, shortly after, is held a pitted brown ball like a small planet: the world hurled against itself.

Perhaps the most valuable lesson the Church can learn from geographical study is its most basic insight: that human community and the natural landscape are intimately connected. Although physical and human geography used to be presented almost as parallel tracks, they comprise one routeway and neither can fully be understood without the other. Any place, rural or urban, is an ecology that mixes each aspect of human community (commerce, transport, patterns of settlement and so on) with the physical processes (climate, landscape, natural resources) undergirding and permeating it. In the Bible, human destiny is bound up with that of the creation and so, truly to understand Adam, we also need to know the land from which he takes his name. While the relationship between 'Christ' and 'culture' came to the fore in twentieth-century scholarship, recognition of Christ as the pioneer of a new earth – the last Adam, as St Paul calls him – may prove to be the present century's theological burden. With environmental debate increasingly turning to a more integrated view of sustainable communities – in which not only food, housing and energy but also common life and political ethics are locally sourced – this becomes ever more apt.

Parish is a threefold cord of soul, soil and society. In this last main chapter, that relationship will be explored with particular attention being given to the enduring union between the parochial system and British topography. Because all places are produced by what Raymond Williams described as 'common meanings … writing themselves into the land',[1] this must involve a certain amount of historical geography, together with theological reflection upon the idealistic overtones of 'parish', whose meaning evokes a particular kind of relation to landscape, both social and physical. If the parochial system is to be free, both from the negative aspects of this association and for a newly meaningful future, this is essential groundwork.

Gleba

The Local Government Act of 1894, an unexciting but none the less pivotal piece of legislation that divided its civil and ecclesiastical forms, defined the parish as 'that circuit of ground which is committed to the charge of one person or vicar'.[2] This groundedness was deeply set within the territorial origins of the Anglo-Saxon *parochia*: from the smallest 'field church' (the phrase in Anglo-Saxon law for churches newly established on lands recently brought under cultivation) to the regional 'head

minsters' or cathedrals.[3] As Anthea Jones remarks: 'The territorial pattern of English parishes ... had roots in agricultural
practices probably ancient when Augustine landed on the Kent
coast in 597.'[4]

The parochial bond with the land derived at first not from
any overt application of theology, but from the endowments and
revenue required for the upkeep of each type of church: 'soul-scot'
(effectively a burial fee), 'plough alms' (the penny paid within a
fortnight of Easter in respect of each plough-team working in a
parish) and also direct donations of territory, often to monas-
teries or dioceses, which harnessed the Church's growing wealth
to land tenure. Principal among parish fees was the tithe, the
portion of the harvest given – at first voluntarily and, from the
tenth century, enforced by secular fines – to the Church. Tithing
served to etch the emergent parochial system into the landscape,
as Pounds explains: 'While most of the obligations to the church
were personal, the tithe was territorial. It was generated by land,
and parishes had to be bounded in order to determine where
tithes should be paid.'[5]

The other vital constituent of the early parochial 'field economy' was the original endowment of land given to each church,
known as the glebe. From the Anglo-Saxon *gleba,* meaning 'soil'
or 'earth', glebe was intended for the subsistence of the parson,
who was expected to cultivate it himself. Glebe fields, where they
survive, are among the most striking relics of the ancient landscape. Green islands in improbable places, some have acquired
fresh totemic force as symbols of local entrenchment against addi-
tional housing: disputes that find Anglicans implicated still in the
negotiation of territory. Eventually incorporated into the jumble
of rights or 'rectory' that supported the local priest (including
the 'benefice' – the incumbent's material reward, derived from
beneficium, another landholding term), glebe lands helped root
the pastoral economy of the Anglo-Saxon parish firmly into the
soil upon which its livelihood already depended. The ecclesiastical benefice, still founded upon the economic subsistence of
each parish, is, Godfrey writes, 'essentially a variant of this ...
feudalistic practice'.[6]

The contingencies of manorial history thus played a leading role in defining the bounded 'shape' of parishes – which in turn gave distinctive form to the English landscape. In his book *Landscape and Community in England*, Alan Everitt examined how regional variations in landholding affected the types of parish and, thereby, the kind of landscape formed. He distinguishes between 'manorial' parishes, such as those in Northamptonshire, where two-thirds of the territory formed part of great estates under landed magnates and 'freeholding' parishes in other areas, such as Kent, where a far higher proportion of the land came to be owned by yeoman freeholders, well into the modern era. Varying parish typologies, he concludes, left a varying social and physical 'footprint' according to region.[7]

What appears as singular, however, is not simply the continuity into the present of many parochial boundaries – their astonishing age a generally recognized feature of the landscape – but the way in which their subtler, more 'invisible' effects upon communal behaviour also persist. The ancient practice of beating the bounds, highlighted in Chapter 5, provides fascinating examples of this. As the embodied circumscription of neighbourhood, boundary perambulations were of fundamental significance for the traditional parish: 'corporate manifestations of the village community', in Keith Thomas's words, which required of local parsons a keen sense of landscape and topography.[8] This was, of course, essential before accurate printed maps, at a time when knowledge of parish boundaries often resided solely in folk memory, but also meant that the parish became what Fletcher calls the 'basic reporting unit' in the development of local mapping of England in the nineteenth century.[9]

In *Religion and the Decline of Magic*, Keith Thomas argued that this practice, originally a kind of mystic cartography directed towards the material benefit of abundant crops, had by the sixteenth century become mere custom, in keeping with his thesis about the progressive disenchantment of English life. While the Reformation doubtless accelerated the decay of the practice's more 'Popish' or, indeed, pagan overtones,[10] Thomas rather overlooks its evident and ongoing value in enabling communities to internalize and maintain agreed limits – and the subtle ways in which these can influence the present. Indeed, Nicola Whyte's recent research suggests that, against the prevailing view of their decline, parish perambulations continued in many areas – depending partly upon the rate and extent of common land enclosures – to be a principal means of defining territory.[11] Beating the bounds thus appears as a fundamental way in which 'parochial space' was both recalled and produced, through a combination of natural, spiritual and social engagement.[12] Whyte describes the physicality of this process – recognizing, touching and hatching marks in familiar natural features – as a 'mnemonic language' through which the limits of landscape and local community were learned.

English pastoral

The 'Christianization of the landscape' at such an early stage, through the rapid proliferation of church-building in medieval England,[13] when allied to the narratives of national religion and local welfare already described, made the parish into a fairly unassailable symbol of cultural belonging. Church buildings soaked up these associations into their stonework, with an iconic function only heightened when burial grounds – 'God's Acre' according to custom – surrounded them. Sam Turner's archaeological research into South West England reveals that England's conversion to Christianity was, so to speak, a monumental 'landscape event' that transformed the physical appearance of the country. By the late pre-Conquest period, he contends: 'The influence of Christian ideology had reached out to the edges of the cultivated land and into the rough ground beyond.'[14] This topographical 'reach' of the English church was extended, Turner claims, not only through the physical construction of churches, crosses and burial grounds, but also through the altered social practices instigated by such a shift in the belief system. In particular, he discerns in the relationship between church and landscape a Christian 'grammar' of community, claiming that 'the ideology of "settlement" that helped shape the medieval landscape encompassed a Christian view of the world'.[15]

Part of this social grammar clearly includes place-names, which give cultural personality to the physical environment and enable it to evoke distinctive kinds of belonging. In this vein, Alexandra Walsham, in her recent study of early modern England, *The Reformation of the Landscape*, describes how the Christianization of places was 'superimposed on the surface of the British and Irish countryside, by "rechristening" towns, villages and hamlets'.[16] The word 'superimposed' jars a little, suggesting as it does that there existed, somehow, an authentic substratum of place, immune to the social processes Walsham so effectively explores. The Christianization of place was only one – albeit highly significant – layer in this topographical formation, no more or less socially constructed than the pagan landscapes that preceded it.[17] However, Walsham's central thesis is that, while transforming the medieval 'hallowed landscape', the Reformation in fact served to regenerate it in an altered form: as a means of discerning divine handiwork, such that the landscape became 'God's great book in folio'.[18] The point is well made and, within this paradigm, the parish continued both to reflect and shape the landscape, physical and imagined, with the result that it came to occupy a unique position within what John Lowerson calls 'the mystical geography of the English'.[19] In the extensive literature about this inheritance, it is common to find the church building, especially in its 'country' setting, portrayed as an almost organic thing, a quasi-natural feature of the landscape, as if it were an extrusion or extension of the terrain. As rural writer Fraser Harrison expresses it: 'The church moves me too ... because it unifies the village and its landscape in a single, reciprocal creation.'[20]

In the mid-twentieth century, this suffusion of real and imagined parochial landscapes reached its zenith (or nadir, according to taste) in Arthur Mee's 'King's England' gazetteers which, alongside those of shelfmate Arthur Bryant, blended architecture and popular history with a malty nostalgia that can now seem as puffed up and pointless as a pipe rack. While the style of English

exceptionalism that these authors tended towards is redundant
in our day, they keenly sensed a native faith organically linking earth to altar. This is Mee from 1936, describing the village
church, in *The Enchanted Land*:

> ... a few yards down the lane and we feel that Browning is right
> – lo, we are at the heart of things. Always it has been at the
> heart of things, the Village Treasure House. Go where we will,
> the church has in it something of the eternal which knows no
> time. It is of the spirit of the hills about or the green meadows
> in which it rises naturally, as though it has always been there.
> It is of the past and of the future and in the present it is ours.[21]

Bucolic and hyperbolic (that 'lo' says it all), this demands decon-
struction, of course: *Why 'village'? How is it 'ours' – and who
are 'we'? What if there are no 'green meadows'?* And so on.
Nevertheless, if topography is continually being reproduced in
the social imagination – if, as Massey claims, 'landscape is provisional; it changes and it could be otherwise'[22] – then there are
myriad ways in which these keynotes of territory and memory
can be reconceived for other cultural locations.

The Church's failure to transfer such principles into the newly
urbanized communities of nineteenth-century England is a matter
of lively historical debate, though with a degree of consensus
that the Anglican parish lost the initiative in cities to nonconformist denominations, especially in the North, as the results of
the 1851 census gave salutary evidence.[23] The geographical rootedness of the parish system, while fundamental to its resilience
in an agrarian economy at a time of rapid and complex social
change, was ponderous and far too 'landed' (with all of the social
and economic associations of that term) to respond effectively.[24]
Coleman, analysing this process and its regional differentiation,
remarks: 'Only in a largely static society could a church slow to
adapt and highly dependent on habit, convention and traditional
forms of influence hope to survive unscathed.'[25] Inescapably,
both the concept of 'parish' and its built embodiment, the parish
church, became – and arguably remain – deeply associated with

an idea of the 'pastoral': the aesthetic tradition that drank deeply from classical imagery of an idealized topography. In its various forms, from sixteenth-century renaissance poetry through to the paintings of Constable, pastoral infused the present landscape with symbolic visions of both past and future that were wittingly illusory, according to Laurence Lerner, embodying the contrast between 'seeing nature as it is' and a 'mediated vision' shaped by human expectations, 'wishes, fears and hopes'.[26] As such, it was inherently nostalgic in tone – Peter Bishop affirming that 'all nostalgia is pastoral', in the sense of being rooted in 'a sense of place and landscape, yearning and loss'. 'To encounter nostalgia', he writes: 'is always to enter a particular landscape ... in a specific mood: the pastoral'.[27]

Like the churchyard in Gray's *Elegy* or Coleridge's *Ancient Mariner*, returning to the kirk at the end of his voyage, the Anglican parish is deeply implicated in this myth of belonging to the land. This is, of course, exceedingly problematic: not only in perpetuating the fallacy that 'God made the country, man made the town', but also in presenting an equally fallacious view of rural life, blind to the dynamics of power and poverty.[28] There is a dual irony to this, given the origins of the parochial idea in Graeco-Roman civic life and of Christianity as an 'urban cult' and that, as P. J. Taylor notes, 'the pioneer of industrialization and the most urbanized country in the world is idealized in rural terms'.[29] Periods of intensified cultural change, however, inevitably produce an equal and opposite reaction that seeks images of rooted permanence as reassurance in unsettled times and it is no coincidence that pastoral nostalgia flourished (and flourishes) in such circumstances.[30]

The secret parish

By any reckoning, the Reverend Gilbert White's *The Natural History of Selborne* – staggeringly, the fourth most published book in the English language – is an unlikely success story. Essentially a journal of the fauna and flora found in one eighteenth-century

Hampshire parish, its littleness is undoubtedly the clue to its appeal: 'England in close-up' as one author has it.[31] Unlike many clergy today, engrossed with global dynamics well beyond their influence, White's principal pastoral concern appears to have been the varying movements of toads across his rectory garden. Such micro-level attention – and his role as unwitting pioneer of a progressive view of nature that considers the welfare of human and non-human culture as inseparably related – means that White emerges today as something of a local hero. In a fascinating introduction to the *Natural History*, nature writer Richard Mabey considers that 'parish' is the crucial idea behind White's unparalleled description of local ecology:

> 'Parish' is a very laden concept. It has to do not just with geography and ecclesiastical administration, but with history and a system of loyalties. For most of us, it is the indefinable territory to which we feel we belong, which we have the measure of. Its boundaries are more the limits of our intimate allegiances than lines on a map. These allegiances have always embraced wild life as well as human ...[32]

Mabey coins the term 'parochial ecology' to capture White's settled attention to Selborne – 'the landscape of the pastoral dream made flesh'. But there is no 'illusory' nostalgia to this affirmation: for Mabey, it became a guiding theme for his pioneering environmental work, as expressed in his books *The Common Ground* and *Second Nature*. As he writes in the former: 'The idea of parish ... must underlie ... a conservation policy which takes any account of human feelings.'[33] Highlighting another priest-naturalist, John Stevens Henslow, rector of Hincham in Suffolk, Mabey argues that, for the man who taught Charles Darwin and encouraged his voyage on the *Beagle*, 'it was in his parish that his most important work was done ... he was not just Hincham's rector but its *curator*'.[34]

Leaving aside the enviable freedom of the single-parish incumbent in this era to attend to broader interests, the essence of Mabey's tribute to Henslow is profoundly significant. While it is not his concern to explore the theological implications of being the 'curator' of a locality, the resonances with the pastoral 'cure' still retained by the parish priest are, nevertheless, clear, and it may be contended with some justification that truly parochial ministry is pastoral on both counts – formed by an ecology of care for a particular place, its people and the relation of both to God.

One of the riches of the parochial tradition is thus what Oliver O'Donovan describes as the 'reciprocal relation between nature and culture ... mediating a possibility for human life in community'.[35] By virtue of its territorial stability, the parish is uniquely placed to offer such mediation: a fact that has long been recognized in the pioneering work of Common Ground, the environmental charity that Richard Mabey founded in 1982 with Sue Clifford and Angela King. This saw particular expression in the Parish Maps project which, for ten years from 1986, encouraged local neighbourhoods to depict in imaginative ways the territory to which they especially identified. Accepting the ways in which this scheme was 'tugged away from the city' by the inescapably rural overtones of the term 'parish', David Crouch and David Matless observed how it 'connects settlement and surrounding land ... to a long English cultural tradition of presenting place, especially rural place, in reverential, ritual, sacred terms'.[36]

While the imaginative affiliation of 'landscape' with rural rather than urban topography became a conditioning factor on what was produced (and by whom), Common Ground chose the parochial concept, because, as Sue Clifford plainly acknowledges: 'The ecclesiastical parish has been the measure of English landscape since Anglo-Saxon times.' 'Parish', Clifford argued, offered what no other English term could: an equivalent to the German *heimat* – a way of describing 'the intersection of culture and nature' and 'deeply felt ties of familiarity, identification and belonging'.[37] Digging more deeply into the affective connotations of 'landscape', however, the charity also offered 'parish' as their definition of English particularity expressly because of its rich notes of *personal* association and attachment – the 'place of responses' as Mabey calls it.

Parish thus becomes an imaginative bridge between 'real' space-time community and the less tangible echoes that sound out a place of personal settlement and wellbeing. In a further assessment of Gilbert White's parochial ecology, David Elliston Allen, in his landmark *History of the Naturalist in Britain*, described Selborne as 'that secret, private parish inside each one of us'.[38] Notwithstanding its need for broader cultural application (the 'each one of us' in Allen's statement being limited to those to whom the word 'parish' carries such emotional significance), the image of parish as a secret place of belonging is deeply suggestive. Because, in the English context, such notions are harnessed to the pastoral idyll,[39] they must reconnect with a more hopeful destiny, so that parochialism is prevented from becoming merely a vain quest for unattainable place or a stagnant cipher for lost homeland.

Land's end: relocating nostalgia

Nostalgia is the constant, if unreliable, companion of parish studies. Perhaps this is because both nostalgic (and its correlate, utopian) ideas are offspring of a shared Christian 'parent narrative'. As the geographer Yi-Fu Tuan comments, tellingly, 'Most utopias can be placed somewhere between the Garden of Eden and the New Jerusalem ... the road connecting the two is history.'[40] The 'utopian paradigm', according to Tuan, is 'the man-nature-God relation' which, if so, makes the question of whether Eden or New Jerusalem can be 'reached' in space-time an essentially theological one.[41] For W. H. Auden, these twin poles held powerful symbolic and ethical significance: 'Eden is a past world in which the contradictions of the present world have not yet arisen; New Jerusalem is a future world in which they have at last been resolved.'[42] Considering this potency in pastoral poetry, Laurence Lerner argued that, while both are 'ways of refusing history' because they are 'placed outside of ordinary time',[43] Eden and New Jerusalem have, nevertheless, substantial practical influence: 'The one structures our experience with sadness, the other with fierce hope. One speaks of an elegy, the other a call to action. In Christian mouths this call has often had a note of sharp paradox.'[44]

These visionary forms of place are not confined to poetic reverie: as Mannheim advanced in his landmark study *Ideology and Utopia*, they directly influence political life at both national and local levels.[45] 'New Jerusalem' thinking was, to take one pertinent example, an acknowledged – though not unproblematic – concept behind the shift (considered in Chapter 4) from local to national settlement at the creation of the welfare state in the 1940s.[46] Cultural epistemology – the way in which particular societies 'know what they know' – is mediated by transcendent ideas, such as the medieval worldview of heaven and hell.[47] In Western culture, Mannheim argues, these have taken the form of either ideologies (ideas that may be integrated with the existing order) or utopias (visions of society unattainable without a revolutionary overturning of the *status quo*). Interestingly, Mannheim cites the Christian notion of brotherly love as one such utopian idea: if society were *actually* to operate accordingly, he ventures, the social system would have to be completely 'broken up' and reformed.[48]

The parish, as with other ecclesiological forms, has a singular place in this typology, in that it is both ideological – rooted in the existing order – *and* utopian, aspiring to an eternal, 'unreachable' form of community: that is, the kingdom of heaven. In utopian thought, imagination is the bridge that links the idealized landscape (future and past) to the present and inspires particular kinds of action according to the nature of the place being imagined.[49] Central to this potential is their utility as images of desire: as places we yearn to reach. The longing for home – the literal meaning of 'nostalgia' – thus holds a unique capacity to influence local and, indeed, global practice. French sociologist Danièle Hervieu-Léger, in her influential study *Religion as a Chain of Memory*, has argued that, following the decline of an explicitly Christian sense of eschatological belonging, European culture has experienced a 'dislocation' that lacks the 'imaginative and social energy' necessary to realize a common utopian vision.[50]

When a society loses such forward momentum, the desire for idealized place tends to roll backwards, making nostalgia the inevitable counterpart to utopian thought; an equal and opposite magnetism drawing Western societies back to Eden or Arcadia. This gravitation has generally been perceived to be a negative – or, at best, unprofitable – consequence of cultural change. In his 1966 essay 'The Idea of Nostalgia', the literary critic Jean Starobinski charted in detail the progress of nostalgia as a cultural condition, from its coining in 1688 as a word to describe the physical and mental effects of homesickness experienced by soldiers fighting in the European Religious Wars to its replacement by the more recognizable affective form in use today. The latter he defines, pejoratively, as 'useless yearning for a world or way of life from which one has been irrevocably severed'.[51] Yet Starobinski's thesis that the nostalgic 'return' has no beneficial effect for civilized societies unattached to the 'village' ideal ('it is not the uprooting which causes trouble', he claims)[52] now appears both dated and flawed. More recently, Svetlana Boym has contended that nostalgia is actually of profound significance in contemporary politics, being both a product and producer of social space – a geographical phenomenon:

> What is crucial is that nostalgia was not merely an expression of local longing, but the result of a new understanding of time and space that made the division into 'local' and 'universal' possible. The nostalgic creature has internalized this division, but instead of aspiring for the universal and the progressive he looks backwards and yearns for the particular.[53]

While taking forward with great élan its contemporary understanding and impact, the impression created by Boym is still of nostalgia as an effect, a *by-product* of modernity, which does not quite escape the 'useless' connotations ascribed to it by Starobinski. The assumed narrative of nostalgia is that its redundancy – and therefore its ripeness for parody and dismissal – arises from the impossibility of return. Because it attempts to recreate a fictional past, nostalgia is commonly portrayed as deliberately ignorant: a denial of history. *And did those feet in ancient time? No, therefore* (the assumption often goes) – *end of story*.[54] I would argue that, especially in its contemporary form, parochial nostalgia – the desire for homeland, or the longing to belong – manifests itself far more dynamically as a highly significant component in place-formation. Postmodern nostalgia is not concerned so much with the – clearly impossible – *restoration* of an imagined former place, but selects elements of the idealized 'nostalgic' home (one of which is a sense of 'parish') to integrate with the present, in much the same way that enthusiasts for vintage lifestyle renew and adapt earlier forms and designs. Vintage, one might say, does not 'actually' wish to live in, for example, the 1950s, or simply to reflect upon it, but rather desires to employ aspects of a certain period or place in the contemporary situation, performing what Akiko Busch has described as 'the graceful coexistence of technology and nostalgia'.[55]

There is, in sum, rather less 'yearning' and far more 'aspiring' involved in contemporary nostalgia, indicating a demonstrably productive utilization of the past. What might be termed *generative nostalgia* is thus deeply consumerized and creative, and clearly extends beyond lifestyle to operate as an engine for migration, aspiration and the creation of home. Experience suggests that – albeit more for some social groups than others – the parish church remains a resonant feature of the ideal social landscape and, as such, continues to be a significant 'producer' of social space.[56] Nostalgia may yet be a symptom of spiritual or social sickness, but its toying with time is by no means without purpose. Indeed, as demonstrated above, such imaginative geographies (past and future-orientated) have successively proved to be engines of resistance to versions of the present 'problematic' place.

All of which does not mean that the parish is immune to the dysfunctional type of nostalgia often hovering over the political debate about 'Englishness' and social inclusion. It is, without question, associated with an eschatology of doom that, in its most hopeless form, evokes the bleak sentiments uttered in 1955 by W. G. Hoskins at the close of his otherwise brilliant work

The Making of the English Landscape: 'Barbaric England of the scientists, the military men and the politicians: let us turn away and contemplate the past before all is lost to the vandals.'[57]

As Tuan asserted, the danger of 'geopiety' (his term for the spiritual attachment to place) is a 'passion for preservation' – a movement into which the parochial is all too easily conscripted and thereby fossilized. The resultant worship of 'heritage'[58] can find the parish church uneasily presented as, in effect, a redoubt against invasion: a contemporary, politicized version of its (deliberately nostalgic) depiction in Cavalcanti's wartime propaganda film *Went the Day Well?* Such cornered parochialism is arguably the consequence of two forces: an inadequately dynamic understanding of space – whereby 'land' and 'place' are conceived statically, with time as the dynamic force threatening to bear them away – and the failure, in so far as the Anglican Church is responsible, to make explicit connection between Christology and locality, with the result that the parish is inadequately defended against such notions. The danger – heightened in the current climate – is that debate about place becomes unhelpfully bipolar, whereby attachment to territory falls victim to easy caricature as reactionary, exclusive and politically right wing, while liberal geographical discourse can appear detached and curiously *placeless*. The Church of England's response must not be to dispense with the territorial principle for being locked into anachronistic perceptions of landscape, but to find the means whereby heritage becomes a key to unlock, not barricade, the future.

This cannot be realized without prosecuting a genuinely evangelical appreciation of place that relocates nostalgia in a Christian eschatology of belonging – a task sublimely evoked by Simone Weil: 'Every human being has at his roots here below a certain terrestrial poetry, a reflection of the heavenly glory, the link, of which he is more or less vaguely conscious, with his universal country.'[59] Given that a misplaced attitude towards nature implies, in some way, a misplaced attitude towards God,[60] the redemption of Weil's 'terrestrial poetry' is likewise an essentially theological quest. Bonhoeffer's versatile concept of Christ as the 'centre' – both of human community and between God and nature – was found to be particularly helpful in describing the orientation of parochial theology, in which the world 'unwittingly' (Karl Barth's term is the equivalent of Weil's 'vague awareness') participates. In this scheme, the Church's role is to articulate and relocate that 'longing for home' of which the world is tacitly aware. Returning to doctrine, then, the reconciliation of the earthly and heavenly places at the cross, revealed in the scriptural events of resurrection and ascension, may be understood as confirming the new trajectory of human place towards its end in Christ.[61] The bestowal upon the Church of the Holy Spirit subsequently confirms the Church's local vocation, to the extent that, as Torrance puts it: 'The church on earth, in the continuing space-time of this world, is the place where God and man are appointed to meet.'[62]

Christian eschatology, therefore, both expresses and resolves the impossibility, humanly speaking, either of returning to Eden or reaching the New Jerusalem. 'In this eschatological reserve and deep teleological ambiguity', Torrance writes, 'the church lives and works.'[63] The point to impress here is that this dynamic eschatological 'situation' is geographical as much as historical – moreover, that space as well as time is radically 'open' to the Holy Spirit's anticipation of heaven. The vocation of the Anglican parish is, therefore, to give spatio-temporal expression to the 'new place' in the midst of the old – a task that, crucially, involves the demotion of past and present places from their claim to ultimacy, which is the very root of territorial idolatry.

Bonhoeffer's categories of 'ultimate' and 'penultimate', outlined in his *Ethics*, are extremely helpful in articulating this Christology of place. Pivotal here is Christ's 'taking our place' at the cross – which he interprets both as God's solidarity with, and judgement upon, 'the ways and things before the last'. While this echoes the Barthian 'no' to natural revelation and may appear as the opposite of Weil's confession of humanity's innate 'terrestrial poetry', one has to question whether it is not simply the negative form of which the other is the positive affirmation – in other words, the yearning cry for the soul's 'secret parish' only finds its answering, homecoming call in Christ, God made place for us.[64]

For Bonhoeffer, acknowledgement of the present place's 'penultimacy' typically produces two responses in Christian theology: one based solely on the cross, emphasizing the ultimate's active judgement of the penultimate (expressed in its most extreme form in the view that 'the world is ripe for burning'), or the other, based solely on the incarnation – a 'compromise' with the world that sees the ultimate as 'totally on the far side of the everyday', effectively sustaining the status quo. When, however, incarnation and atonement are taken in one movement, there is 'neither a destruction nor a sanctioning of the penultimate'.[65] In other words, earthly place ('parish' for our purposes) gains its particular glory and purpose in relation to the ultimate, eternal place. Heaven stoops to conquer earth in the person of Christ, who calls the world forward in the power of the Holy Spirit to its consummation in the new place, which is the kingdom of God. This 'heavenly priority', in Bonhoeffer's view, enables natural life to be liberated from its bondage to decay: 'It is only from Christ Himself that it receives its validation. Christ Himself entered into the natural life, and it is only through the incarnation of Christ that the natural life becomes the penultimate which is directed towards the ultimate.'[66]

Translating this dynamic, the parish, as a local ecology, becomes *free* to the extent that it is in Christ, through whom the parochial vocation to natural life is realized. There is clearly an unresolved tension here between the world's *de facto* reconciliation to God – the sense that it is already 'in Christ' through his saving work – and its evident continuing fallenness. As was considered in Chapter 2, a lively apprehension of the work of the Holy Spirit is required in order to ground this, so that the destined home – unlike Utopia – may truly be anticipated in the present locale. Nevertheless, Bonhoeffer's ordering of 'ultimate' and 'penultimate' gives liberating perspective to the parochial vocation and chimes with C. S. Lewis's briefer (although broader in scope) reflection in his essay *First and Second Things*, written in 1942. Only by relegating 'second things' to their appropriate place in the light of 'first things', writes Lewis, can the former retain their glory and true situation – noting the paradox that:

'You can't get second things by putting them first; you can get second things only by putting first things first.'[67] This automatically begs the question (Lewis concludes) as to 'which things come first?' – although the inference is clear when applied to place-theology. The only escape from the fatal desire to possess the land, as the biblical narrative attests, is to relinquish it, to 'give up one's place' for God and neighbour in order to receive it afresh in the kingdom. This is an eminently hopeful calling, offering both resolution of nostalgia and release from the idolatry of homeland, to which the parochial tradition is chronically prone. While it does not satiate the 'longing for home' – indeed, *separation* is the inevitable corollary of our eschatological situation – it does settle and solve this in the conviction that where we belong, finally, is in Christ.[68]

Conclusion

> I went out into the churchyard where the green stones nodded together, and I took up a handful of earth and felt it crumble and run through my fingers. 'Well', smiled the vicar, as he walked towards me between the yew trees, 'that, I am afraid, is all we have'. 'You have England', I said.[69]

This, the closing sentence from H. V. Morton's extraordinarily popular interwar travelogue *In Search of England*, conveys perfectly the connections and contradictions at the heart of the word 'parish': its evocation, like no other term in English, of the spiritual bond between nation and nature, as well as its susceptibility – by dint of age and sheer symbolic potency – to detachment from reality. From the Anglo-Saxon stone crosses that, in many cases, predated the building of a local church, the Anglican parish has had a stake in the soil. Ironically, however, part of the cost of this stakehold in English life has been a weakened cruciform vision of the land that has frequently lost the critical stance towards culture vital in a Christian worldview. By way of redress, this final chapter has described five aspects of its 'natural' vocation:

1 The link, established very early on, between parish and 'soil', through both the former's alliance with the ownership and tenure of land, and the accompanying 'Christianization' of the landscape.

2 Second, the indisputable place of the parish (especially the parish church) in imagined landscapes of England, creating a powerful and often problematic association with pastoral belonging.

3 Because of the above, that parish has come to denote (among other things) an ecology of care that bonds local society to the natural environment.

4 Fourth, that the 'longing to belong' often associated with parochialism is both a central motive in place-formation and, it is argued, a symptom of spiritual 'homelessness'.

5 Lastly, that so far as the Church is concerned the above must be located within a Christian eschatology of belonging: not in order to divert attention away from the land, but in order that present place is freed from its claim to ultimacy.

The constant challenge is that 'parish' is such a wayward metaphor – chronically prone to the kind of idealism that all too easily clouds a realistic assessment of its worth.[70] Nevertheless, that same quality also signals the soul of the parochial idea: the search for an earthly approximation of the heavenly home. So perhaps the answer is to have a proper confidence in these transient plots: after all, to be confident in the local is to be confident in the validity of human experience in God's purposes. Qualifying his bold claim that 'all great civilizations are parochial', the poet Patrick Kavanagh offers this more cautionary advice, fitting for all who are keen to see its renewal:

Advising people not to be ashamed of having the courage of their remote parish, is not free from many dangers. There is always that element of bravado which takes pleasure in the notion that the potato-patch is the ultimate. To be parochial [one] needs the right kind of sensitive courage and the right kind of sensitive humility.[71]

Notes

1 From his 1958 essay 'Culture is Ordinary'.

2 Cited in W. E. Tate, *The Parish Chest*, Cambridge: CUP, 1969, p. 10.

3 See F. M. Stenton, *Anglo-Saxon England*, Oxford: OUP, 1947, p. 148; and Dorothy Whitelock, *The Beginnings of English Society*, Harmondsworth: Penguin, 1965, p. 166.

4 Anthea Jones, *A Thousand Years of the English Parish*, Moreton-in-Marsh: Windrush Press, 2000, p. 15.

5 N. J. G. Pounds, *A History of the English Parish*, Cambridge: CUP, 1962, p. 31.

6 John Godfrey, *Anglo-Saxon England*, Cambridge: CUP, 1962, p. 329.

7 Alan Everitt, *Landscape and Community in England*, London: Continuum, 1985, pp. 4–6. Everitt notes the consequent higher level of nonconformity in religion in Kent and the more evident alliance of squire and parson in Northamptonshire.

8 Keith Thomas, *Religion and the Decline of Magic*, Harmondsworth: Penguin, 1973, p. 65. Nicola Whyte concludes that parochial perambulations had 'a major impact on landscape history' in the Norfolk villages that are the focus of her study (in *Inhabiting the Landscape*, Oxford: Windgather Press, 2009, p. 165).

9 Whyte, *Inhabiting the Landscape*, p. 186. See 'Mapping the Imagination', in Rachel Hewitt, *Map of a Nation: A Biography of the Ordnance Survey*, London: Granta, 2010, ch. 8.

10 Maurice Beresford notes the 1559 Parliamentary Act, whereby 'the clergy shall once a year at the time accustomed walk about their parishes with the Curate and other substantial men of the parish' (in *History on the Ground*, London: Methuen, 1971, p. 29). Fletcher suggests that practical rather than theological underpinnings were now stressed (in 'The Parish Boundary: A Social Phenomenon in Hanoverian England', *Rural History*, 14.2 (2003), p. 184).

11 Nicola Whyte, 'Landscape, Memory and Custom: Parish Identities c. 1550–1700', *Social History*, 32.2 (2007), pp. 178f; Whyte, *Inhabiting the Landscape*, ch. 3.

12 For the liturgical aspects of parish perambulations, see Beresford, *History on the Ground*, p. 29.

13 Alexandra Walsham uses this phrase to describe the transformation of the English landscape following its conversion to Christianity (in *The Reformation of Landscape*, Oxford: OUP, 2012, pp. 26ff).

14 Sam Turner, *Making a Christian Landscape: How Christianity Shaped the Countryside in Early Medieval Cornwall, Devon and Wessex*, Exeter: University of Exeter Press, 2006, p. 169. Likewise, Nicola Whyte writes that the 'lived environment' of the medieval period 'formed the

material context for beliefs extending far beyond the precincts of the church and graveyard' (in *Inhabiting the Landscape*, p. 20).

15 Turner, *Making a Christian Landscape*, p. 189.

16 Walsham, *Reformation of the Landscape*, p. 47.

17 Nicola Whyte affirms that landscape operates as a continual palimpsest of successive worldviews (in *Inhabiting the Landscape*, p. 8).

18 Whyte, *Inhabiting the Landscape*, p. 393. Beaver affirms the ongoing effect of parishes on topography after the Reformation, describing how, in the Vale of Gloucester, 'language, ritual and cultural distinctions imposed an order on the landscape itself' (in *Parish Communities in the Vale of Gloucester, 1590–1690*, Harvard: Harvard University Press, 1998, p. 44).

19 In Brian Short (ed.), *The English Rural Community: Image and Analysis*, Cambridge: CUP, 1992, ch. 8.

20 Quoted in Lowerson, in Short (ed.), *Rural Community*, p. 160. David Lowenthal has observed that, 'Like the archetypal sacred garden the English landscape is not natural but created, suffused with human as well as divine purpose' (in 'British National Identity and the English Landscape', *Rural History*, 2.2 (1991), p. 215).

21 Arthur Mee, *The Enchanted Land*, 2nd edn, London: Hodder & Stoughton, 1951, p. 49.

22 Doreen Massey, Landscape/Space/Politics: An Essay: https://thefutureoflandscape.wordpress.com/landscapespacepolitics-an-essay/

23 See K. D. M. Snell and Paul S. Ell, *Rival Jerusalems: The Geography of Victorian Religion*, Cambridge: CUP, 2009, Part I; B. I. Coleman, *The Church of England in the Mid-Nineteenth Century: A Social Geography*, London: The Historical Association, 1980, pp. 38–9; Anthony Russell, *The Country Parish*, London: SPCK, 1986, pp. 11ff.

24 Mingay observes that the agrarian depression of the late nineteenth century 'marked the end of parochial paternalism, the passing of traditional society …' (in G. E. Mingay, *Rural Life in Victorian England*, London: Heinemann, 1977, p. 51). The landed assets of the Church of England, which remain the material basis of its security, have recently come under scrutiny in The Centre for Theology and Community's report *Our Common Heritage*: http://www.theology-centre.org.uk/wp-content/uploads/2013/04/OCH-Final-Final.pdf

25 Coleman, *Church of England*, p. 15.

26 Laurence Lerner, *The Uses of Nostalgia*, London: Chatto & Windus, 1972, p. 18.

27 Peter Bishop, *An Archetypal Constable: National Identity and the Geography of Nostalgia*, London: Athlone Press, 1995, p. 57; compare Lerner, *Nostalgia*, p. 41. Likewise, Fred Inglis writes: 'Faced with any landscape-painting, we look in it for a home which we can persuade ourselves we have always known' (in Simon Pugh (ed.), *Reading Landscape*,

Manchester: MUP, 1990, p. 208). Writing of the palimpsest nature of urban landscapes, Patrick Keiller describes how 'we look in landscape for our own place of belonging' (in *The View from the Train: Cities and Other Landscapes*, London: Verso, 2013, pp. 23ff).

28 See Raymond Williams, *The Country and the City*, London: Chatto & Windus, 1973, chs 3 and 8; Ronald Blythe notes the persistent myth that 'real values' are to be found in a rural parish (in *Akenfield*, Harmondsworth: Penguin, 1969, p. 16).

29 See N. J. G. Pounds, *A History of the English Parish*, Cambridge: CUP, 2000, p. 113. Pounds notes that urban parishes came later than rural ones; see also Godfrey, *The Church in Anglo-Saxon England*, p. 311. P. J. Taylor, quoted by David Storey, *Territories: The Claiming of Space*, Harlow: Pearson, 2001, p. 86.

30 As geographer David Harvey has considered, in *The Condition of Postmodernity*, Oxford: Blackwell, 1990, ch. 17. This is affirmed by David Lowenthal: 'in the face of massive change we cling to the remaining familiar vestiges' (in *The Past is a Foreign Country*, Cambridge: CUP, 1985, p. 399).

31 Charles Lancaster in *Seeing England: Antiquaries, Travellers & Naturalists*, Stroud: Nonsuch, 2008, p. 269.

32 In Gilbert White, *The Natural History of Selborne*, ed. Richard Mabey, Harmondsworth: Penguin, 1977, p. xvii.

33 Richard Mabey, *The Common Ground: A Place for Nature in Britain's Future?*, London: Hutchinson, 1980, p. 36.

34 Mabey, *The Common Ground*, p. 37 (my italics).

35 Oliver O'Donovan, 'The Loss of a Sense of Place', *Irish Theological Quarterly*, 55.1 (1989), p. 47.

36 David Crouch and David Matless, 'Refiguring Geography: Parish Maps of Common Ground', *Transactions of the Institute of British Geographers*, 21.1 (1996), pp. 238–9. Hoskins, noting the ecological and antiquarian tradition of Anglican parsons, describes the parish as 'the smallest field' of English history (in *Local History in England*, London: Longman, 1984, pp. 26–29).

37 Sue Clifford and Angela King (eds), *From Place to PLACE*, London: Common Ground, 1996, pp. 3–7.

38 David Elliston Allen, *History of the Naturalist in Britain*, Harmondsworth: Penguin, 1978, p. 51. Also cited in Richard Mabey (ed.), in his Introduction to Gilbert White's *History of Selborne*, p. xvii.

39 'Nowhere else is landscape so freighted as legacy', observes David Lowenthal in 'British National Identity and the English Landscape', *Rural History*, 2.2 (1991), p. 213.

40 Yi-Fu Tuan, *Space and Place: The Perspective of Experience*, Minneapolis: University of Minnesota Press, 1977, p. 199. W. H. Auden, by contrast, sees both as the 'refusal of history'.

41 A question that More leaves unresolved in *Utopia*, as Tuan affirms (see *Space and Place*, p. 199).

42 W. H. Auden, quoted in Lerner, *Nostalgia*, p. 66. Elliston Allen tellingly describes Gilbert White's *Natural History of Selborne* as 'the journal of Adam in paradise ... the testament of static man' (in *The Naturalist in Britain*, p. 50).

43 Lerner, *Nostalgia*, p. 72.

44 Lerner, *Nostalgia*, p. 65.

45 A point reinforced by Richard Bauckham's perceptive analysis of the Revelation to St John in relation to first-century geopolitics (in 'The New Jerusalem as Place', in *The Theology of the Book of Revelation*, Cambridge: CUP, 1993, pp. 132ff).

46 Derek Fraser explores the social effect of 'New Jerusalem' thinking in *The Evolution of the Welfare State*, Basingstoke: Palgrave Macmillan, 2003, ch. 9.

47 See Charles Taylor on 'Modern Social Imaginaries' (in *A Secular Age*, London: Harvard University Press, 2007, ch. 4).

48 Karl Mannheim, *Ideology and Utopia*, London: Routledge, 1960, pp. 125ff.

49 A. L. Morton has demonstrated how a peculiarly English vision of 'Utopia' has enabled a radical social critique at different stages of the nation's history (in *The English Utopia*, London: Lawrence & Wishart, 1978).

50 Danièle Hervieu-Léger, *Religion as a Chain of Memory*, Cambridge: Polity, 2000, pp. 90–2. According to Peter Bishop, nostalgia posits two different times, a problematical present and a past that is the object of yearning (in *An Archetypal Constable*, London: Athlone, 1995, pp. 56–7).

51 Jean Starobinski, 'The Idea of Nostalgia', *Diogenes*, 14.54 (June 1966), p. 101.

52 Starobinski, 'The Idea of Nostalgia', p. 103.

53 Svetlana Boym, in *The Future of Nostalgia*, New York: Basic Books, 2001, ch. 1, p. 11.

54 Blake's *Jerusalem* is, of course, a reflection – albeit somewhat cracked – upon incarnation. To dismiss its lyrics as factually incorrect is to miss the point, for it holds in balance perfectly the twin poles of nostalgia and utopia: conservatives love it for the former; socialists for the latter.

55 Akiko Busch, *Geography of Home*, New York: Princeton Architectural Press, 1999, p. 26.

56 In this sense, 'parish' accords with David Lowenthal's concept of 'creative anachronism' (in *The Past is a Foreign Country*, ch. 7).

57 W. G. Hoskins, *The Making of the English Landscape*, Harmondsworth: Penguin, 1970, p. 291. This astonishing statement is examined in David Matless, *Landscape and Englishness*, London: Reaktion, 1998, pp. 276ff.

58 Tuan, *Space and Place*, p. 197. Patrick Wright's *On Living in an Old Country*, Oxford: OUP, 2009, is still the most devastating critique of the heritage 'cult'.

59 Simone Weil, *Waiting on God*, London: Fontana, 1950, p. 134.

60 As T. S. Eliot writes, in *The Idea of a Christian Society*, London: Faber & Faber, 1939, p. 62. See also William Temple, *Nature, Man, and God*, London: Macmillan, 1949, pp. 473ff.

61 Torrance stresses that it is the *eschatos* not the *eschaton* that is primary: not the end of all things, but the end of all things *in Christ* (in *Space, Time and Resurrection*, Edinburgh: Handsel Press, 1976, p. 151).

62 Torrance, *Resurrection*, p. 129.

63 Torrance, *Resurrection*, p. 156.

64 Thus William Temple: 'The distinction between Natural and Revealed Religion is ... concerned ... solely with determining the method of examination' (in *Nature, Man and God*, London: Macmillan, 1949, p. 7). See also Robert J. Palma, *Karl Barth's Theology of Culture: The Freedom of Culture for the Praise of God*, Pennsylvania: Pickwick Publications, 1983.

65 Dietrich Bonhoeffer, *Ethics*, London: SCM Press, 1964, p. 133.

66 Bonhoeffer, *Ethics*, p. 145. Bonhoeffer contests that, while 'nature' may not be *reconciled* to God in the same manner as humanity, it is *redeemed*. It is worth noting that Bonhoeffer's usage of 'nature' is somewhat specialized, meaning 'fallen' creation in its limited capacity for renewal. See also Bonhoeffer's *Christology*, London: Fontana, 1971, p. 67.

67 C. S. Lewis, *First and Second Things*, Glasgow: Fount, 1985, p. 22. In this spirit, Madeleine Bunting writes: 'belonging [to the land] is first of all about commitment rather than possession' (in *The Plot*, London: Granta, 2009, p. 275).

68 John Godfrey concludes that 'the *paroikia* is ... an idea which presupposes a community of care and interest ... looking forward as sojourners to the perfect society and worship of heaven' (in *The English Parish 600–1300*, London: SPCK, 1969, p. 82). See also Frederick Buechner, *The Longing for Home*, New York: HarperCollins, 1996, p. 2. Augustine writes, 'only in you do I find a gathering place for my scattered parts' (in *Confessions*, Harmondsworth: Penguin, 1961, p. 249); also, *City of God*, p. 429 on 'longing' to become citizens of heaven.

69 H. V. Morton, *In Search of England*, Harmondsworth: Penguin, 1960, p. 277.

70 It may always have been so. Ian Archer's aforementioned research into Elizabethan London enjoyably describes how 'parish records are soaked in the rhetoric of neighbourly unity ... in doggerel of embarrassing awfulness' (in *Pursuit of Stability*, Cambridge: CUP, 2003, p. 84).

71 Patrick Kavanagh, *A Poet's Country, Selected Prose*, Dublin, Lilliput Press, 2003, p. 237.

Conclusion: A Kind of Belonging

The parish is the primary embodiment of Anglican social space. It is not by any means the only communal form in the Church of England: other geographical arrangements of mission and ministry (diocesan, religious, educational, for example) are likewise 'producers' of space, but none approaches the symbolic and practical influence of the parish system, over an exceptionally long timespan. This book has pondered that legacy, while also seeking to underpin it with some sorely needed geographical and Christological foundations – an enterprise whose findings it may now be helpful to outline:

1 Parish (like all descriptions of place) is part idea, part way of life: formed in the creative interplay of ontology, revelation, tradition and vocation. In this cycle of place-formation, the reality or 'being' of a locale is first apprehended before it is filtered and conditioned according to cultural tradition, then acted out in practice: each successive action reproducing and 'deepening' the place first perceived.

2 The Church's understanding of who Jesus is and what he signifies is at the heart of parochial praxis, wittingly or otherwise. While the secularity of the parish – an inevitable preoccupation with the everyday 'stuff' of communal life – has often dictated its structure, Christology is the plumb line for assessing its significance in theological terms. Applying the doctrinal theme that describes Christ 'taking our place' in redeeming action is offered as one way of interpreting Christian salvation in explicitly local terms.

3 Contemporary human geography provides indispensable

tools for understanding the English parish, emphasizing the dynamism of place and its openness to various kinds of social and ethical production. In this light, the parish emerges as a particular form of theological space, grounded in the practice of neighbourhood.

4 The resulting 'vocation' of the parish has featured, historically, three intersecting dimensions: the first being *national*, such that parochial identity has ever been understood in symbiotic relation with its national counterpart, creating a unique compound of sacred and secular society.

5 This call to 'common ground' presents the parish as the enduring archetype of English *neighbourhood*, whose territorial boundaries have left a monumental, if mixed, cultural legacy: both enabling and, at times, disabling the formation of Christian community.

6 Lastly, the Anglican parish is inseparable from the physical or *natural* landscape, in both imagination and practice. Being thereby prone to functioning as an idol of pastoral nostalgia, this connection must equally be rooted in a Christian worldview that points to 'land's end'. Thus, while the parish easily becomes an eschatological cul-de-sac, it can also reorientate us towards the New Jerusalem.

Central to this threefold vocation in the context being considered here is the parish's relationship to the Church's 'of England' status. In an Anglican perspective, I have argued that places are 'of England' not by starting with the nation, but primarily by being 'of' (rather than merely 'in') their immediate locality. England, in other words, is what you end up with, not begin with. This, I suggest, is the grain of Anglican localism and a partial check on the more imperious and damaging aspects of national loyalty. The correspondence of parochial and national vocations is thus implied by an integration of sacred and secular life, whereby the Church contributes towards the formation of civil society – most especially through the formation of neighbourhood. This second dimension of parochial community forms local settlement through its commitment to localities small enough for people to know and be known – an allegiance at once geographical (committed to being 'nearby' in spatial terms) and historical (committed to remaining 'with' over time). Crucially, also, it expresses the essential unity of human culture and natural ecology, which in Christian theology find their common ground and destiny in Christ. The Church's narrative does not portray human 'belonging' – either here or hereafter – as detached from the natural world: rather, relocates it in a vision of resurrected creation.

As such, the parish has encapsulated an approach to Christian faith that emphasizes narrative 'belonging' as much as individual conviction. The loss of a deep, cultural sense of Christian identity – one of the buttresses of belief in any location – is of course one of the prime reasons why faith is perceived as being so implausible for many at the present time. It is doubtful whether more people were individually persuaded of the Christian gospel in the past than they are today: there were fewer options; men and women – then as now – deferred to the powerful and prevailing worldview; and Christianity was bound up with a certain kind of accepted behaviour, especially in relation to local charity and national allegiance. Whether as a substitute for 'personal faith' or as the companion to an array of alternative beliefs (various shades of paganism, for example), this corporate 'owning' of the Christian story meant people belonged to it, and it to them, in a way that has all but evaporated from memory.

Given this dislocation, it is hardly surprising that the English may 'miss' parish in much the same way as they may 'miss' God.[1] But while the Anglican Church can capitalize on a unique endowment, it cannot live in retrospect alone, embracing as it does a view of history that looks back principally in order to reconceive the future. Christ, after all, is portrayed as the second Adam, who recapitulates the human story in order to change its ending. The only prescription for cultural amnesia therefore is *anamnesia* – the kind of hopeful remembrance at the core of the Christian gospel. How, though, to recapitulate the English parish? It is a commonplace to observe that, in the contemporary scene, parish 'works' better in some communities than in others.

History relates fairly emphatically that it always did. In numerous settings, both rural and urban, there is mounting pressure to reconceive parochial organization – not least because the places we inhabit have often changed out of all recognition. Though local belonging may be valued as much as ever – may even be 'parochial' in a loose sense – for very many people, in the Church and without, the ecclesiastical parish is altogether an irrelevance. It has not been the purpose here to address in depth the varied and importunate questions now before the parish system but, clearly, this study anticipates such an engagement. It will be worthwhile, then, to conclude by viewing the terrain ahead from the standpoint reached.

With this perspective, three principal challenges present themselves, of which the most acute is the ongoing viability of parochial organization and its extraordinary legacy of built heritage. Increasingly, the conversation surrounding the future of the parish homes in on the sheer material unsustainability of this burden, in terms of the Church's deployment of resources, ministerial and financial. Interestingly, this crisis is impelling parishes to reconnect their buildings with the sense of shared space being described – in usage and, more and more, in ownership. If parish is characterized by the interpenetration of sacred and secular, then the explicitly 'sacred' space of church buildings must be radically opened to the secular (as was once the norm), in much the same way as it might be hoped 'secular' space would be open to the sacred. Church bookings policies speak volumes about where we believe 'God is' and it is surely no bad thing if the current situation forces us to grapple with that vital question. Just as it challenges parishes to reappraise their built heritage, the resourcing crisis likewise occasions the recovery of the priestlike task of parish ministry. The threefold parochial vocation essayed here is inherently priestly, in the sense that it is concerned with manifesting the reconciliation of God to the world in Christ, and – through the Church's liturgical life and local mission – 'offering' one to the other. While not the prime focus here, the calling of the Anglican congregation in most situations is thus to be a parish priesthood, the realization of which presents particular challenges to both low and high church traditions.[2]

Given that this crossroads for Anglican ministry makes inevitable the further restructuring of localities in many areas – especially the rural communities typically (though not always accurately) perceived to be the parochial heartlands – it is imperative that strategic decision-making by dioceses and by the church commissioners is not only theologically literate, but also *geographically* so.[3] However their reconfiguration takes place, parishes must remain the Church's basic expression of locality: no other term can compete with either their symbolic resonance or radical potential. This status as the primary level of neighbourhood retained, the burden of governance and co-ordination of ministry, mission and resources may increasingly be removed from it – most likely to a revitalized and empowered deanery, as John Tiller envisaged.[4] Vital to such a co-operative process, however, is the question of how parochial boundaries may be reconceived, especially in areas where, to paraphrase the Psalmist, the lines have not fallen in pleasant places. If the parish is to survive, these must be adjusted in ways that allow narrative continuity to meet contemporary purpose – and be recognized (not least by their clergy) to be permeable and open to a measure of social negotiation, as they were before the introduction of modern mapping. This means, in short, that the parish system needs to become a little less *systematic* – and, by learning from its pre-modern origins, recover an earlier approach to social structures based on local agreement and practice. As Bishop Edward Stillingfleet pointed out, over 300 years ago:

> The settling parochial rights or bounds of parishes depends upon ancient and immemorial custom. For they were not limited by any Act of Parliament, nor set forth by special commissioners, *but as the circumstances of times and places and persons did happen to make them greater or lesser* ... [Therefore] care is taken by Annual Perambulations to preserve those bounds of parishes, which have been long settled by custom.[5]

What 'good fences' might look like has been a perennial challenge for the parish, especially at times of accelerating social change. In fact, at every critical point in its history, parochial organization has adapted and accommodated new forms of community (the guild system, for example), proving to be far more dynamic than is usually assumed. The old accusation that its boundaries acted as a kind of prophylactic for mission and evangelism – especially church-planting – was barely sustainable a generation ago and is even less so now.[6] That said, where they are dysfunctional, it must be possible for boundaries to be reviewed more readily: to find contemporary equivalents to the 'annual perambulation' that they may perform as a 'dotted line' defining relations without as much as within.

The second, related challenge concerns the movement within the Church to accommodate new types of local ministry that (it is often argued) offer a more contemporary response to the missionary challenges faced by the Church of England. 'Fresh Expressions' and 'Mission-Shaped Church' initiatives over the last 20 years have led to the now familiar espousal of a 'mixed economy' that allows both for parochial and pioneering forms of ministry.[7] While seeking to redress the unhelpfully adversarial tone of this debate, this can, at the local level, appear as mere passive accommodation and demands positive, visionary analysis in spatial terms. If social space, like skin, is constantly renewing itself, then it is essential that the Church's spatial praxis is intelligible in the contemporary situation – enabling the recognition of 'Christ in our place' wherever that place happens to be.

Nevertheless, the local church is always called both to reflect and transform culture, which raises the vital question: is it more authentically Christian to be rooted rather than mobile in spatial terms? Or, by extension, can the privileged position afforded to the parish be defended by appeal to anything more than antiquity? After all, so the argument runs, the parish emerged in an agrarian era when culture had to be settled on the soil for communities to survive: it did not need to before that period, any more than it does now. The Church's local form is simply its cultural dress, which must be changed if it doesn't fit the times.

Persuasive though it may be, this proposition founders by not realizing the theological potency of both history and geography. Having established that spatial praxis is not ethically or theologically neutral, it must follow that some forms of locality will be more authentically 'Christian' (or indeed 'Anglican') than others. For this reason, I would want to respond to the above questions with a qualified 'yes', affirming the wisdom in Wendell Berry's assertion that: 'If it is to cohere, a community must remember its history and obligations; it is therefore irreconcilably opposed to "mobility" as a social norm.'[8]

Mobility is, as Bergmann attested in his study of the theme, a political, religious and economic issue.[9] What, in Chapter 3, was referred to as 'local monogamy' can be especially countercultural in the many contexts where the poor are far less mobile than the rich: the latter being one of the essential geographical insights of the last 50 years.[10] As nomadic peoples are only too aware, all human culture is married to the land and we cannot divorce ourselves from it for long without very significant consequences. Social wellbeing in every sphere is inseparably linked to that of the earth: neither ecologically nor theologically can we presume to live 'above' physical place. In this respect, parochialism is playing an increasing role in framing resilient local practices, as Transition Towns and other related movements bear witness.[11] Settlement, then, is a spiritual issue – and for Christian neighbourhood to extend further than a kind of social first aid, it has to 'take place' in shared space over time. Every Good Samaritan lives somewhere.

My qualifications to this affirmation of 'rootedness' over 'mobility' are twofold, the first being that, according to the Book of Deuteronomy, our Father was a wandering Aramean and the spiritual descendants of Abraham are reckoned to be a pilgrim people, on their way to a better place. A biblical perspective thus prevents any Christian community from becoming *too* settled, and this truth must constantly be recalled in order to discomfort easy parochialism. The second is that faithfulness to place is no less dynamic than mobility, geographically speaking. It is vital that, in pursuing a new vision for local ministry, the easy caricature of the parish as somehow spatially 'static', while more networked arrangements are by definition 'fluid' is, to put it bluntly, geographically unsustainable. That *all* forms of place are (and always were) characterized by flow and interrelation is perhaps the prime contribution of current spatial theory and this must be understood and applied in order to reinvigorate the territorial principle.

This is required – to address the third contemporary challenge to the parish system – because of what might be called the 'end of entitlement' for the Church of England.

Whatever evolving form its established status takes, there can be little doubt that the long recession of the Church's worldly power is likely to continue, which affords an opportunity for parishes to develop a more radical local praxis, especially in a period of accelerating devolution and localism. Certainly, with ecological and political debate increasingly homing in on less centralized, more communitarian solutions, any moves towards abandoning the parochial idea would appear fatally short-sighted. As the 'New Parish' and related movements gaining momentum among North American churches clearly indicate,[13] this approach has such social capital at the present time that, if the parish no longer existed, it might need to be reinvented.

Loss of power usually equates to loss of place. Undoubtedly, the proprietorial style in which Anglicans have, for all the reasons discussed, 'possessed the land' is liable to a kind of territorial arrogance that is unsupportable unless the legacy can be reframed as a contribution towards the common good. A humbler role for the parish may thus find the seeds of renewal in its classical origins as the society beside the boundaries, the *paroikia*. That the Church employed and adapted a term essentially denoting those who do not belong to describe a new kind of community is as enticing a piece of ecclesiological paradox as one is likely to encounter – brimming with potential for imaginative reinterpretation. The usual translation of *paroikos* and its variants into English scriptures as 'stranger' has served to keep this exegetical jewel surprisingly well hidden. Nevertheless, the image with which we began: of Christ as parishioner, without a city wall – the alien and accidental neighbour – offers a key to restoring the parish as place of radical settlement and welcome.

Stillingfleet, writing in 1702, explained the great advantage and edifying power of the parochial system to be its capacity for making 'a broken, divided people' become 'one body within certain bounds'.[14] It does this only by drawing near those who were once far off – and by seeing neighbourhood as something offered especially by and to the outsider. It is not a little ironic that 'parochial' has come to epitomize insularity and self-containment when its original meaning is far closer to our contemporary definitions of interloper or refugee: but this, at least, is an irony we can work with to great benefit.

What kind of place is the parish? As a fusion of territory and tradition it represents, in closing, a kind of belonging – a school for belonging, even – whose rich theological significance the vagaries of time, place and politics do not diminish, but rather ground in truly incarnate form. The practice, not merely the principle, of neighbourhood is where its threefold vocation coheres and is most clearly displayed: where theoretical conceptions of English life are teased out from the constraining tangle of human affairs. This is not to downplay the idealism that shapes community: rather, it is to conclude that localized practice is the test of all descriptions of place, translating and tethering them to the particular situation. If the Christian claim is that, as Jacob affirmed, God is in 'this place' – and, moreover, that the same God was in Christ reconciling this place to himself – then the Anglican parish, for all its archaism and compromise, may have proved the point.

Notes

1 See Dennis O'Driscoll's affecting poem 'Missing God' (in *Exemplary Damages*, London: Anvil Press, 2002).

2 In short, for evangelicals to view 'the priesthood of all believers' as a genuine ecclesial vocation and not mere shorthand for their misgivings about the priesthood of the ordained ministry; and for Anglo-Catholics

to hold priestly ordination a little less preciously and to be willing to consider a radical extension of orders to include those lay members who, in many places, already perform and enable an effective priestly function.

3 The Church of England's recent electoral 'manifesto' was a refreshing shift in this direction, placing neighbourhood and belonging at the heart of the Anglican vocation. See *Who Is My Neighbour?*, London: CHP, 2015.

4 In *A Strategy for the Church's Ministry*, London: CIO, 1983.

5 Edward Stillingfleet, *Ecclesiastical Cases Relating to the Duties and Rights of Parochial Clergy etc.*, 2nd edn, London: Henry Mortlock, 1702, pp. 243–4.

6 Perhaps the most amusing articulation of this stance was David Pytches and Brian Skinner's designation of the parish system as the 'condom of the Church of England' (in *New Wineskins*, Guildford: Eagle, 1991, p. 20). Stillingfleet, tellingly, recognizes similar arguments at play in the seventeenth century (see Stillingfleet, *Ecclesiastical Cases*, pp. 87–8).

7 See *Mission-Shaped Church*, p. xi.

8 Wendell Berry, *The Way of Ignorance*, Washington: Shoemaker & Hoard, 2005, p. 79.

9 See Sigurd Bergmann, Thomas Hoff and Tore Sager, *Spaces of Mobility: The Planning, Ethics, Engineering and Religion of Human Motion*, London: Equinox, 2008, ch. 1.

10 Doreen Massey notes the 'cartography of power' behind current patterns of global migration and mobility (in *For Space*, London: Sage, 2005, p. 85).

11 For example, see Rob Hopkins, *The Transition Handbook: From Oil Dependency to Local Resilience*, Totnes: Green Books, 2008. In urban south London, for example, the parish church has played a pioneering role in advancing this movement.

12 See Charles Taylor, *A Secular Age*, London: Belknap Press, 2007, pp. 14ff.

13 Paul Sparks, Tim Soerens and Dwight J. Friesen, *The New Parish: How Neighborhood Churches are Transforming Mission, Discipleship and Community*, Illinois: IVP, 2014; and Jay Pathak and Dave Runyon, *The Art of Neighboring*, Grand Rapids: Baker Books, 2012.

14 Stillingfleet, *Ecclesiastical Cases*, p. 95, thus evoking Psalm 68: 'He is the God that maketh men to be of one mind within an house.'

Bibliography

Agnew, John, Livingstone, David N. and Rogers, Alasdair (eds), *Human Geography* (Oxford, Blackwell, 1996).

Ahern, Geoffrey and Davie, Grace, *Inner City God* (London, Hodder & Stoughton, 1987).

Allen, David Elliston, *The Naturalist in Britain* (Harmondsworth, Penguin, 1976).

Allen, John and Massey, Doreen (eds), *Geographical Worlds* (Oxford, Oxford University Press, 1995).

Ambler, R. W., *Churches, Chapels and Parish Communities of Lincolnshire, 1660–1900* (Lincoln, History of Lincolnshire Committee, 2000).

Anderson, Benedict, *Imagined Communities* (London, Verso, 2007).

Archbishops' Commission on Rural Areas, *Faith in the Countryside* (Worthing, Church Publishing, 1990).

Archer, Ian W., *The Pursuit of Stability: Social Relations in Elizabethan London* (Cambridge, Cambridge University Press, 2003).

Aristotle, *The Nichomachean Ethics* (Oxford, Oxford University Press, 1980).

Aristotle, *Physics* (Oxford, Oxford University Press, 1996).

Athanasius, Saint, *On the Incarnation* (London, Mowbray, 1982).

Audi, Robert, *Epistemology* (Abingdon, Routledge, 2003).

Aughey, Arthur and Berberich, Christine (eds), *These Englands* (Manchester, Manchester University Press, 2011).

Augustine, Saint, *City of God* (Harmondsworth, Penguin, 1972).

Bachelard, Gaston, *The Poetics of Space* (Boston, Beacon Press, 1994).

Baker, A. E. William, *Temple and His Message* (Harmondsworth, Penguin, 1946).

Barth, J. R., *Coleridge and Christian Doctrine* (New York, Fordham University Press, 1987).

Barth, Karl, *The Doctrine of Creation, Part 2, Church Dogmatics III.ii* (Edinburgh, T&T Clark, 1960).

Barth, Karl, *The Doctrine of Creation, Part 2, Church Dogmatics III.iii* (Edinburgh, T&T Clark, 1960).

Barth, Karl, *The Humanity of God* (London, Fontana, 1967).

Barth, Karl (eds G. W. Bromiley and T. F. Torrance), *The Doctrine of Reconciliation, Church Dogmatics IV.i* (Edinburgh, T&T Clark, 1960).

Bauckham, Richard, *The Theology of the Book of Revelation* (Cambridge, Cambridge University Press, 1993).

Baxter, Christina (ed.), *Stepping Stones* (London, Hodder & Stoughton, 1987).

Bede, *A History of the English Church and People* (Harmondsworth, Penguin, 1955).

Beresford, Maurice, *History on the Ground* (London, Methuen, 1971).

Berger, John, *Ways of Seeing* (Harmondsworth, Penguin, 1972).

Berger, Peter (ed.), *The Desecularization of the World* (Grand Rapids, Eerdmans, 1999).

Berger, Peter and Luckmann, Thomas, *The Social Construction of Reality* (Harmondsworth, Penguin, 1967).

Berry, Wendell, *What Are People For?* (London, Random, 1990).

Bethge, Eberhard, *Dietrich Bonhoeffer, A Biography* (London, Collins, 1977).

Bettenson, H. (ed.), *Documents of the Christian Church* (Oxford, Oxford University Press, 1956).

Bettenson, H. (ed.), *The Early Christian Fathers* (Oxford, Oxford University Press, 1956).

Bishop, Peter, *An Archetypal Constable: National Identity and the Geography of Nostalgia* (London, Athlone, 1995).

Blair, Peter Hunter, *Anglo-Saxon England* (Cambridge, Cambridge University Press, 1977).

Bonhoeffer, Dietrich, *Creation and Fall* (New York, Macmillan, 1959).

Bonhoeffer, Dietrich, *Act and Being* (London, Collins, 1962).

Bonhoeffer, Dietrich, *Sanctorum Communio* (London, Collins, 1963).

Bonhoeffer, Dietrich, *Ethics* (London, SCM Press, 1964).

Bonhoeffer, Dietrich, *Letters & Papers from Prison* (London, SCM Press, 1967).

Bonhoeffer, Dietrich, *Christology* (London, Fontana, 1971).

Bosworth, Gary and Somerville, Peter (eds), *Interpreting Rurality* (Abingdon, Routledge, 2014).

Boulton, Jeremy, *Neighbourhood and Society: A London Suburb in the Seventeenth Century* (Cambridge, Cambridge University Press, 2005).

Bourdieu, Pierre, *Outline of a Theory of Practice* (Cambridge, Cambridge University Press, 1977).

Boym, Svetlana, *The Future of Nostalgia* (New York, Basic Books, 2001).

Brown, Callum, *The Death of Christian Britain* (London, Routledge, 2001).

Brown, David, *God and Enchantment of Place: Reclaiming Human Experience* (Oxford, Oxford University Press, 2004).

Brown, David and Loades, Ann (eds), *The Sense of the Sacramental* (London, SPCK, 1995).

Brown, Malcolm, *Faith in Suburbia: Completing the Contextual Trilogy* (Edinburgh, Contact Pastoral Trust, 2005).

Bruce, Steve, *Religion in Modern Britain* (Oxford, Oxford University Press, 1995).

Bruce, Steve, *God is Dead: Secularization in the West* (Oxford, Blackwell, 2002).

Bruce, Steve and Voas, David, 'The Resilience of the Nation State: Religion and Polities in the Modern Era', *Sociology*, 38.5 (2004).

Brueggemann, Walter, *The Land* (London, SPCK, 1978).

Buechner, Frederick, *The Longing for Home* (New York, HarperCollins, 1996).

Busch, Akiko, *Geography of Home* (New York, Princeton Architectural Press, 1999).

Canter, David, *The Psychology of Place* (London, Architectural Press, 1977).

Cavanaugh, William, *Theopolitical Imagination: Discovering the Liturgy as a Political Act in an Age of Global Consumerism* (Edinburgh, T&T Clark, 2002).

Chadwick, Owen, *The Victorian Church Part II* (2nd edn, London, A&C Black, 1972).

Chamberlin, Russell, *The Idea of England* (London, Thames & Hudson, 1986).

Chaplin, Jonathan, 'Can Nations be "Christian"?', *Theology* CXII.870 (2009).

Chorley, Richard J. (ed.), *Directions in Human Geography* (London, Methuen, 1973).

Clark, David, 'The Sociological Study of the Parish', *The Expository Times*, 82 (1971).

Clark, Kenneth, *Landscape into Art* (Penguin, Harmondsworth, 1956).

Clifford, Sue and King, Angela (eds), *From Place to PLACE* (London, Common Ground, 1996).

Clifford, Sue and King, Angela (eds), *England in Particular* (London, Hodder & Stoughton, 2006).

Coleman, B. I. (ed.), *The Idea of the City in Nineteenth-Century Britain* (London, Routledge & Kegan Paul, 1973).

Coleman, B. I., *The Church of England in the Mid-Nineteenth Century: A Social Geography* (London, The Historical Association, 1980).

Coleman, Simon and Collins, Peter (eds), *Religion, Identity and Change* (Aldershot, Ashgate, 2004).

Coleridge, Samuel Taylor, *Biographia Literaria, or Biographical Sketches of my Literary Life and Opinions* (London, J. M. Dent, 1960).

Coleridge, Samuel Taylor, *On the Constitution of Church and State* (London, J. M. Dent, 1972).

Colls, Robert, *Identity of England* (Oxford, Oxford University Press, 2002).

Congar, Yves, *The Meaning of Tradition* (New York, Hawthorn Books, 1964).

Cosgrove, Denis, *Social Formation and the Symbolic Landscape* (Wisconsin, University of Wisconsin Press, 1998).

Coverley, Merlin, *Psychogeography* (London, Pocket Essentials, 2010).

Cox, Jeffrey, 'Secularization and Social History', *Theology*, 78.90 (1975).

Cox, Jeffrey, *English Churches in a Secular Society: Lambeth, 1870–1930* (Oxford, Oxford University Press, 1982).

Cray, Graham (ed.), *Mission-Shaped Church* (London, CHP, 2004).

Croft, Steven, *The Future of the Parish System* (London, CHP, 2006).

Crouch, David and Matless, David, 'Refiguring Geography: Parish Maps of Common Ground', *Transactions of the Institute of British Geographers*, 21.1 (1996).

Darby, H. C. (ed.), *A New Historical Geography of England* (Cambridge, Cambridge University Press, 1973).

Davie, Grace, *Religion in Britain since 1945: Believing Without Belonging* (Oxford, Blackwell, 1994).

Davies, W. D., *The Gospel and the Land: Early Christianity and Jewish Territorial Doctrine* (Berkeley, University of California Press, 1974).

Davison, Andrew and Milbank, Alison, *For the Parish: A Critique of Fresh Expressions* (London, SCM Press, 2010).

De Certeau, Michel, *The Practice of Everyday Life* (Los Angeles, University of California Press, 1984).

Descartes, Rene, *Discourse on Method* (Harmondsworth, Penguin, 1960).

De Chardin, Teilhard, *Hymn of the Universe* (New York, Harper & Row, 1961).

De Gruchy, John (ed.), *Cambridge Companion to Dietrich Bonhoeffer* (Cambridge, Cambridge University Press, 1999).

Day, Abby, 'Believing in Belonging: An Ethnography of Young People's Constructions of Belief', *Culture and Religion*, 10.3 (2009).

Dickens, A. G., *The English Reformation* (London, Fontana, 1964).

Dormor, D., McDonald, J. and Caddick, J. (eds), *Anglicanism: The Answer to Modernity* (London, Continuum, 2003).

Douglas, Mary, *Purity and Danger* (London, Routledge, 2002).

Ecclestone, Giles (ed.), *The Parish Church?* (Oxford, Mowbray, 1988).

Edwards, David, *Christian England*, vol. 2 (London, Collins, 1983).

Eliot, T. S., *The Idea of a Christian Society* (London, Faber & Faber, 1939).

Elliston Allen, David, *The Naturalist in Britain* (Harmondsworth, Penguin, 1978).

Erdozain, Dominic, *Christianity Without the Mumbo-Jumbo: The Making of a Secular Outlook in Modern Britain*, address to KLICE conference, 2009.

Eriksen, Thomas Hylland, *Small Places, Large Issues: An Introduction to Social and Cultural Anthropology* (London, Pluto Press, 1995).

Everitt, Alan, *Landscape and Community in England* (London, Continuum, 1985).

Farmer, D. H., *The Age of Bede* (Harmondsworth, Penguin, 1983).

Fletcher, David, 'The Parish Boundary: A Social Phenomenon in Hanoverian England', *Rural History* 14.2 (2003).

Forsyth, P. T., *The Person and Place of Jesus Christ* (London, Hodder & Stoughton, 1909).

Foucault, Michel, *Power/Knowledge: Selected Interviews and Other Writings, 1972–1977* (New York, Pantheon, 1980).

Francis, Leslie J., *Church Watch: Christianity in the Countryside* (London, SPCK, 1996).

Fraser, Derek, *The New Poor Law* (London, Macmillan, 1976).

Fraser, Derek, *The Evolution of the British Welfare State* (Basingstoke, Palgrave Macmillan, 2003).

French, Katherine, *The Parish in English Life, 1400–1640* (Manchester, Manchester University Press, 1997).

French, Katherine, *The People of the Parish: Community Life in a Late Medieval Diocese* (Pennsylvania, University of Pennsylvania Press, 2000).

Gadamer, Hans-Georg, *Truth and Method* (London, Continuum, 1989).

Garmonsway, G. N. (ed.), *The Anglo-Saxon Chronicle* (London, J. M. Dent, 1972).

Garnett, Jane, Grimley, Matthew and Harris, Alana (eds), *Redefining Christian Britain: Post-1945 Perspective* (London, SCM Press, 2007).

Gay, John, *Geography of Religion in England* (London, Duckworth, 1971).

Giddens, Anthony, *The Constitution of Society* (Oxford, Blackwell, 1984).

Godfrey, John, *The Church in Anglo-Saxon England* (Cambridge, Cambridge University Press, 1962).

Godfrey, John, *The English Parish, 600–1300* (London, SPCK, 1969).

Goffman, Erving, *The Presentation of the Self in Everyday Life* (Harmondsworth, Penguin, 1969).

Goffman, Erving, *Relations in Public* (Harmondsworth, Penguin, 1971).

Gorringe, Timothy, *A Theology of the Built Environment* (Cambridge, Cambridge University Press, 2002).

Gray, Donald, *Earth and Altar* (Norwich, Canterbury Press, 1986).

Green, S. J. D., *The Passing of Protestant England: Secularization and Social Change, c. 1920–1960* (Cambridge, Cambridge University Press, 2010).

Greenfeld, Liah, *Nationalism: Five Roads to Modernity* (Harvard, Harvard University Press, 1992).

Greening Lamborn, E. A., *The Parish Church* (Oxford, Oxford University Press, 1929).

Gregory, Derek and Walford, Rex (eds), *Horizons in Human Geography* (London, Macmillan, 1989).

Gregory, Derek and Urry, John, *Social Relations and Spatial Structures* (London, Macmillan, 1985).

Gregor Smith, R. (ed.), *World Come of Age* (London, Collins, 1967).

Griffiths, Paul, Fox, Adam and Hindle, Steve (eds), *The Experience of Authority in Early Modern England* (London, Macmillan, 1996).

Grimley, Matthew, *Citizenship, Community and the Church of England: Liberal Anglican Theories of the State between the Wars* (Oxford, Clarendon Press, 2004).

Guest, Mathew, Tusting, Karen and Woodhead, Linda (eds), *Congregational Studies in the UK: Christianity in a Post-Christian Context* (Aldershot, Ashgate, 2006).

Gunton, Colin, *Yesterday and Today: A Study of Continuities in Christology* (London, DLT, 1983).

Gunton, Colin, *Christ and Creation* (Carlisle, Paternoster Press, 1992).

Gunton, Colin, *The One, the Three and the Many* (Cambridge, Cambridge University Press, 1993).

Gunton, Colin, *The Promise of Trinitarian Theology* (Edinburgh, T&T Clark, 1997).

Gunton, Colin (ed.), *Trinity, Time and Church: A Response to the Theology of Robert W. Jenson* (Grand Rapids, Eerdmans, 2000).

Gupta, Akhil and Ferguson, James (eds), *Culture, Power, Place: Explorations in Critical Anthropology* (Durham, Duke University Press, 1997).

Hammond, Peter C., *The Parson and the Victorian Parish* (London, Hodder & Stoughton, 1977).

Hale, A. J., *The Origins of the Parish and Hundred of Tandridge* (Godstone, Waterprint, 1996).

Halvorson, Michael J. and Spierling, Karen E. (eds), *Defining Community in Early Modern Europe* (Aldershot, Ashgate, 2008).

Hamlyn, D. W., *The Theory of Knowledge* (London, Macmillan, 1971).

Hammersley, Martyn and Atkinson, Paul, *Ethnography: Principles in Practice* (London, Routledge, 2007).

Hart, Trevor and Thimell, Daniel (eds), *Christ in Our Place* (Exeter, Paternoster Press, 1989).

Hartridge, R. A. R., *A History of Vicarages in the Middle Ages* (Cambridge, Cambridge University Press, 1930).

Harvey, David, *The Condition of Postmodernity* (Oxford, Blackwell, 1990).

Hastings, Adrian, *A History of English Christianity* (London, SCM Press, 1991).

Hastings, Adrian, *The Construction of Nationhood: Ethnicity, Religion and Nationalism* (Cambridge, Cambridge University Press, 1997).

Hauerwas, Stanley, *A Community of Character: Towards a Constructive Christian Social Ethic* (London, University of Notre Dame Press, 1981).

Hauerwas, Stanley, *The Peaceable Kingdom: A Primer in Christian Ethics* (Notre Dame, University of Notre Dame Press, 1983).

Hauerwas, Stanley, *In Good Company: The Church as Polis* (Notre Dame, University of Notre Dame Press, 1995).

Hauerwas, Stanley, *War and the American Difference* (Grand Rapids, Baker Academic, 2011).

Hauerwas, Stanley and Wells, Samuel (eds), *Blackwell Companion to Christian Ethics* (Oxford, Blackwell, 2004).

Healy, Nicholas, *Church, World and the Christian Life: Practical-Prophetic Ecclesiology* (Cambridge, Cambridge University Press, 2000).

Hebert, A. G., *Liturgy and Society* (London, Faber & Faber, 1961).

Hensley Henson, Herbert, *The Church of England* (Cambridge, Cambridge University Press, 1939).

Herbert, David, *Religion and Civil Society* (Aldershot, Ashgate, 2003).

Hervieu-Léger, Danièle, *Religion as a Chain of Memory* (Cambridge, Polity, 2000).

Hirsch, Eric (ed.), *The Anthropology of Landscape: Perspectives on Place and Space* (Oxford, Oxford University Press, 1995).

Hooker, Richard, *Of the Laws of Ecclesiastical Polity* (London, J. M. Dent, 1954).

Hoskins, W. G., *The Making of the English Landscape* (Harmondsworth, Penguin, 1970).

Hoskins, W. G., *Local History in England* (London, Longman, 1984).

Hubbard, Phil and Kitchin, Rob (eds), *Key Thinkers on Place and Space* (London, Sage, 2011).

Hunt, Tristram, *Building Jerusalem: The Rise and Fall of the Victorian City* (London, Phoenix, 2005).

Huxley, Aldous, *The Doors of Perception and Heaven and Hell* (Harmondsworth: Penguin, 1959).

Inge, John, *A Christian Theology of Place* (Aldershot, Ashgate, 2003).

Inge, John, 'Theological Reflections on the Place of the Sacred in Society', *Ecclesiastical Law Journal*, 7.35 (2004).

Iremonger, F. A., *William Temple, Archbishop of Canterbury: His Life and Letters* (Oxford, Oxford University Press, 1948).

Jammer, Max, *Concepts of Space: The History of Theories of Space in Physics* (Cambridge, Harvard University Press, 1969).

Jenkins, Timothy, *Religion in English Everyday Life: An Ethnographic Approach* (Oxford, Berghahn, 1999).

Jenkins, Timothy, *An Experiment in Providence: How Faith Engages with the World* (London, SPCK, 2006).

Jenson, Matt, 'Real Presence: Contemporaneity in Bonhoeffer's Christology', *Scottish Journal of Theology*, 58.2 (2005).

Jones, Anthea, *A Thousand Years of the English Parish* (Moreton-in-Marsh, Windrush Press, 2000).

Kant, Immanuel, *Critique of Pure Reason* (London, J. M. Dent, 1934).

Kavanagh, Patrick, *A Poet's Country, Selected Prose* (Dublin, Lilliput, 2003).

Keiller, Patrick, *The View from the Train: Cities and Other Landscapes* (London, Verso, 2013).

Kent, Joan R., 'State Formation and Parish Government', *The Historical Journal*, 38.2 (1995).

Kent, John, *William Temple: Church, State and Society in Modern Britain, 1880–1950* (Cambridge, Cambridge University Press, 1992).

Keynes, Simon and Lapidge, Michael (eds), *Alfred the Great* (Harmondsworth, Penguin, 1983).

Kong, Lily, 'Mapping "New" Geographies of Religion: Politics and Poetics in Modernity', *Progress in Human Geography*, 25.211 (2001).

Kumin, Beat, *The Communal Age in Western Europe, c 1100–1800* (New York, Palgrave Macmillan, 2013).

Lakoff, George and Johnson, Mark, *Metaphors We Live By* (London, University of Chicago Press, 1980).

Lefebvre, Henri, *The Production of Space* (Oxford, Blackwell, 1991).

Lefebvre, Henri, *Rhythmanalysis* (London, Bloomsbury, 2013).

Lerner, Laurence, *The Uses of Nostalgia* (London, Chatto & Windus, 1972).

Lewis, C. S., *The Discarded Image* (Cambridge, Cambridge University Press, 1964).

Lewis, C. S., *First and Second Things* (London, Fount, 1985).

Lovibond, Sabina, *Realism and Imagination in Ethics* (Minneapolis, University of Minnesota Press, 1983).

Lowenthal, David, *The Past is a Foreign Country* (Cambridge, Cambridge University Press, 1985).

Lowenthal, David, 'British National Identity and the English Landscape', *Rural History*, 2.2 (1991).

Lowenthal, David and Bowden, Martyn J. (eds), *Geographies of the Mind: Essays in Historical Geosophy* (Oxford, Oxford University Press, 1975).

Mabey, Richard, *The Common Ground: A Place for Nature in Britain's Future?* (London, Hutchinson, 1980).

Mabey, Richard, *Gilbert White* (London, Profile, 2006).

Mabey, Richard (ed.), *Second Nature* (London, Jonathan Cape, 1984).

Macfarlane, Robert, *The Old Ways* (London, Hamish Hamilton, 2012).

Machin, G. I. T., *Politics and the Churches, 1832–1868* (Oxford, Oxford University Press, 1977).

MacIntyre, Alasdair, *Is Patriotism a Virtue? The Lindley Lecture for 1984* (University of Kansas, 1984).

Macmurray, John, *The Clue to History* (London, SCM Press, 1938).

Macmurray, John, *The Self as Agent* (London, Faber, 1991).

Macmurray, John, *Selected Philosophical Writings* (Exeter, Imprint Academic, 2004).

Mannheim, Karl, *Ideology and Utopia* (London, Routledge, 1960).

Massey, Doreen, *Geography Matters!* (Cambridge, Cambridge University Press, 1984).

Massey, Doreen, 'Landscape/Space/Politics: an essay' https://thefutureof landscape.wordpress.com/landscapespacepolitics-an-essay/

Massey, Doreen (ed.), *A Place in the World? Places, Cultures and Globalization* (Oxford, Oxford University Press, 1995).

Massey, Doreen, *For Space* (London, Sage, 2005).

Martin, David, *A Sociology of English Religion* (London, Heinemann, 1967).

Marty, Martin E. (ed.), *The Place of Bonhoeffer* (London, SCM Press, 1963).

Matless, David, *Landscape and Englishness* (London, Reaktion, 1998).

Maurice, F. D., *Theological Essays* (London, James Clarke & Co., 1956).

Maurice, F. D., *The Kingdom of Christ* (London, SCM Press, 1958).

McLean, David, 'The Changing Legal Framework of Establishment', *Ecclesiastical Law Journal*, 7.34 (2004).

McLeod, Hugh, *Religion and Society in England 1850–1914* (Basingstoke, Palgrave Macmillan, 1996).

Mee, Arthur, *Enchanted Land* (London, Hodder & Stoughton, 1951).

Mitchell, J. B., *Historical Geography* (London, English Universities Press, 1954).

Morris, Jeremy, *Religion and Urban Change: Croydon, 1840–1914* (Woodbridge, Boydell Press, 1992).

Morris, Jeremy, 'The Strange Death of Christian Britain: Another Look at the Secularization Debate', *The Historical Journal*, 46.4 (2003).
Morton, A. L., *The English Utopia* (London, Lawrence & Wishart, 1978).
Morton, H. V., *In Search of England* (Harmondsworth, Penguin, 1960).

Newman, John Henry, *An Essay on the Development of Christian Doctrine* (Harmondsworth, Penguin, 1974).
Nicholls, David, *Church and State in Britain since 1820* (London, Routledge & Kegan Paul, 1967).
Norman, E. R., *Church and Society in England 1770–1970* (Oxford, Clarendon Press, 1976).

O'Donovan, Oliver, *On the Thirty-Nine Articles* (Exeter, Paternoster Press, 1986).
O'Donovan, Oliver, 'The Loss of a Sense of Place', *Irish Theological Quarterly*, 55.1 (1989).
O'Donovan, Oliver, *Resurrection and Moral Order: An Outline for Evangelical Ethics* (Leicester, Apollos, 1994).
O'Donovan, Oliver, *The Common Objects of Love: Moral Reflection and the Shaping of Community* (Grand Rapids, Eerdmans, 2002).
Oliver, John, *The Church and Social Order: Social Thought in the Church of England, 1918–1939* (London, Mowbray, 1968).

Palma, Robert J., *Karl Barth's Theology of Culture* (Pennsylvania, Pickwick, 1983).
Pelikan, Jaroslav, *The Vindication of Tradition* (New Haven, Yale University Press, 1984).
Perry, P. J., *A Geography of 19th-Century Britain* (London, Batsford, 1975).
Phillips, John A., *The Form of Christ in the World: A Study of Bonhoeffer's Christology* (London, Collins, 1967).
Plant, Stephen, *Plato Timaeus and Critias* (Harmondsworth, Penguin, 1977).
Plant, Stephen, *Dietrich Bonhoeffer* (London and New York, Continuum, 2004).
Polanyi, Michael, *Personal Knowledge* (New York, Harper & Row, 1962).
Popper, Karl, *The Poverty of Historicism* (London, Routledge, 1961).
Pounds, N. J. G., *A History of the English Parish* (Cambridge, Cambridge University Press, 2000).
Powicke, Maurice, *The Reformation in England* (Oxford, Oxford University Press, 1941).
Preston, Ronald, 'William Temple as a Social Theologian', *Theology*, 84.334 (1981).

Prochaska, Frank, *Christianity and Social Service in Modern Britain* (Oxford, Oxford University Press, 2006).

Pugh, Simon (ed.), *Reading Landscape: Country-City-Capital* (Manchester, Manchester University Press, 1990).

Reader, John, *Local Theology: Church and Community in Dialogue* (London, SPCK, 1994).

Reader, John, *Reconstructing Practical Theology* (Aldershot, Ashgate, 2008).

Reader, John and Baker, Christopher R., *Entering the New Theological Space* (Aldershot, Ashgate, 2009).

Richards, I. A. (ed.), *The Portable Coleridge* (Harmondsworth, Penguin, 1977).

Rowell, Geoffrey (ed.), *The English Religious Tradition and the Genius of Anglicanism* (Wantage, IKON, 1992).

Russell, Anthony, *The Country Parish* (London, SPCK, 1986).

Russell, Bertrand, *The ABC of Relativity* (London, George Allen & Unwin, 1977).

Sack, Robert, *Human Territoriality: Its Theory and History* (Cambridge, Cambridge University Press, 1986).

Sack, Robert, 'The Power of Place and Space', *Geographical Review*, 83.3 (1993).

Schama, Simon, *Landscape and Memory* (London, Fontana, 1995).

Schreiter, Robert, *Constructing Local Theologies* (New York, Orbis, 1985).

Scruton, Roger, *Kant* (Oxford, Oxford University Press, 1982).

Scruton, Roger, *England and the Need for Nations* (London, Civitas, 2006).

Sedgwick, Peter (ed.), *God in the City* (London, Mowbray, 1995).

Shepard, Alexandra and Withington, Phil (eds), *Communities in Early Modern England* (Manchester, Manchester University Press, 2000).

Sherley-Price, Leo (trans.), *Bede: A History of the English Church and People* (Harmondsworth, Penguin, 1955).

Short, Brian (ed.), *The English Rural Community: Image and Analysis* (Cambridge, Cambridge University Press, 1992).

Sibley, David, *Geographies of Exclusion* (London, Routledge, 1995).

Smart, Ninian *et al.* (eds), *Nineteenth Century Religious Thought in the West* (Cambridge, Cambridge University Press, 1985).

Smith, Alan G. R., *The Emergence of a Nation State: The Commonwealth of England 1529–1660* (London, Longman, 1984).

Snell, K. D. M., 'Gravestones, Belonging and Local Attachment in England', *Past & Present*, 179 (2003).

Snell, K. D. M., *Parish and Belonging: Community, Identity and Welfare in England and Wales 1700–1950* (Cambridge, Cambridge University Press, 2006).

Snell, K. D. M. and Ell, Paul S., *Rival Jerusalems: The Geography of Victorian Religion* (Cambridge, Cambridge University Press, 2009).

Soja, Edward W., *Postmodern Geographies* (London, Verso, 2011).

Spencer, Nick, *Parochial Vision: The Future of the English Parish* (Carlisle, Paternoster Press, 2004).

Spencer, Stephen, 'William Temple's Christianity and Social Order: After Fifty Years', *Theology*, 95.32 (1992).

Stapleton, Julia, *Christianity, Patriotism and Nationhood* (Maryland: Lexington, 2009).

Stapleton, Julia, 'The Voice of Chesterton in the Conversation of England', *The Chesterton Review*, XXXV. 3 and 4 (2009).

Starobinski, Jean, 'The Idea of Nostalgia', *Diogenes*, 14.54 (June 1966).

Stenton, F. M., *Anglo-Saxon England* (Oxford, Oxford University Press, 1947).

Stevenson, John, *British Society 1914–45* (Harmondsworth, Penguin, 1984).

Storey, David, *Territories: The Claiming of Space* (Harlow, Pearson, 2001).

Tate, W. E., *The Parish Chest* (Cambridge, Cambridge University Press, 1969).

Taylor, Charles, *A Secular Age* (London, Belknap Press, 2007).

Temple, F. S. (ed.), *William Temple: Some Lambeth Letters* (Oxford, Oxford University Press, 1963).

Temple, William, *Christianity and Social Order* (Harmondsworth, Penguin, 1942).

Temple, William, *Nature, Man and God* (London, Macmillan, 1949).

Thomas, Keith, *Religion and the Decline of Magic* (Harmondsworth, Penguin, 1973).

Thomas, Keith, *Man and the Natural World* (Harmondsworth, Penguin, 1984).

Thompson, P. D., *Parish and Parish Church* (Edinburgh, Thomas Nelson, 1948).

Thrift, Nigel, *Spatial Formations* (London, Sage, 1996).

Tiller, John, *A Strategy for the Church's Ministry* (London, CIO, 1983).

Torrance, T. F., *Space, Time and Incarnation* (Oxford, Oxford University Press, 1969).

Torrance, T. F., *Space, Time and Resurrection* (Edinburgh, Handsel Press, 1976).

Torrance, T. F. (ed.), *Belief in Science and in Christian Life* (Edinburgh, Handsel Press, 1980).

Torrance, T. F., *Divine and Contingent Order* (Oxford, Oxford University Press, 1981).

Torrance, T. F., *Transformation and Convergence in the Frame of Knowledge* (Belfast, Christian Journals Limited, 1984).

Torry, Malcolm (ed.), *The Parish: People, Place and Ministry: A Theological and Practical Exploration* (Norwich, Canterbury Press, 2004).

Toulmin, Stephen, *Cosmopolis: The Hidden Agenda of Modernity* (Chicago, University of Chicago Press, 1990).

Toulmin Smith, Joshua, *The Parish* (London, H. Sweet, 1857).

Tournier, Paul, *A Place for You* (London, SCM Press, 1968).

Tuan, Yi-Fu, *Space and Place: The Perspective of Experience* (Minneapolis, University of Minnesota Press, 1977).

Turner, Sam, *Making a Christian Landscape: How Christianity Shaped the Countryside in Early Medieval Cornwall, Devon and Wessex* (Exeter, University of Exeter Press, 2006).

Vitek, William and Jackson, Wes, *Rooted in the Land* (Newhaven, Yale University Press, 1996).

Voas, David and Crockett, Alasdair, 'Religion in Britain: Neither Believing nor Belonging', *Sociology*, 39.1 (2005).

Walford, Rex, *The Growth of 'New London' in Suburban Middlesex and the Response of the Church of England* (Lampeter, Edwin Mellen Press, 2007).

Wallace, Catherine M., 'Coleridge's Biographia Literaria and the Evidence for Christianity', in Anderson, Norman and Weiss, Margene (eds), *Interspace and the Inward Sphere: Essays on the Romantic and Victorian Self* (Illinois, Western Illinois University Press, 1978).

Walsham, Alexandra, *The Reformation of the Landscape* (Oxford, Oxford University Press, 2012).

Warwick, Alan R., *The Phoenix Suburb: A South London Social History* (London, Blue Boar Press, 1982).

Webb, Sidney and Beatrice, *English Local Government: The Parish and the County* (London, Frank Cass & Co., 1963).

Webb, Sidney and Beatrice, *The Development of English Local Government 1689–1835* (London, Oxford University Press, 1963).

Weil, Simone, *Waiting on God* (London, Fontana, 1950).

Weil, Simone, *The Need for Roots* (London, Routledge & Kegan Paul, 1978).

Wells, Samuel, 'How Common Worship Forms Local Character', *Studies in Christian Ethics*, 15.1 (2002).

Wells, Samuel, *Transforming Fate into Destiny: The Theological Ethics of Stanley Hauerwas* (Carlisle, Paternoster Press, 1998).

Wells, Samuel, *God's Companions: Reimagining Christian Ethics* (Oxford, Blackwell, 2006).

Wells, Samuel and Coakley, Sarah (eds), *Praying for England: Priestly Presence in Contemporary Culture* (London, Continuum, 2008).

Welsby, Paul A., *A History of the Church of England, 1945–80* (Oxford, Oxford University Press, 1984).

White, Gilbert, *The Natural History of Selborne*, ed. by Richard Mabey (Harmondsworth, Penguin, 1977).

Whitelock, Dorothy, *The Beginnings of English Society* (Harmondsworth, Penguin, 1965).

Whyte, Nicola, 'Landscape, Memory and Custom: Parish Identities, c. 1550–1700', *Social History*, 32.2 (2007).

Whyte, Nicola, *Inhabiting the Landscape: Place, Custom and Memory 1500–1800* (Oxford, Windgather Press, 2009).

Wilberforce, Henry William, *The Parochial System: An Appeal to English Churchmen* (Memphis, General, 2012).

Willey, Basil, *Samuel Taylor Coleridge* (London, Chatto & Windus, 1972).

Williams, Raymond, *The Country and the City* (London, Chatto & Windus, 1973).

Williams, Rowan, 'Convictions, Loyalties and the Secular State', *Political Theology*, 6.2 (2005).

Williams, S. C., *Religious Belief and Popular Culture in Southwark c. 1880–1939* (Oxford, Clarendon Press, 1999).

Wilson, Bryan, *Religion in Secular Society* (Harmondsworth, Penguin, 1969).

Winchester, Angus, *Discovering Parish Boundaries* (Princes Risborough, Shire, 2000).

Winter, Michael and Short, Christopher, 'Believing and Belonging: Religion in Rural England', *The British Journal of Sociology*, 44.4 (1993).

Worrall, B. G., *The Making of the Modern Church: Christianity in England Since 1800* (London, SPCK, 1993).

Wright, Luke Savin Herrick, *Samuel Taylor Coleridge and the Anglican Church* (Notre Dame, University of Notre Dame Press, 2010).

Wright, Patrick, *On Living in an Old Country* (Oxford, Oxford University Press, 2009).

Wright, Patrick, *The Village That Died for England: The Strange Story of Tyneham* (London, Vintage, 1995).

Wright, Susan (ed.), *Parish, Church and People: Local Studies in Lay Religion 1350–1750* (London, Hutchinson, 1988).

Wrightson, Keith, *English Society 1580–1680* (London, Routledge, 1982).

Wynn, Mark, *Faith and Place: An Essay in Embodied Epistemology* (Oxford, Oxford University Press, 2009).